WOMEN AND CREATIVITY

Psychoanalysis & Women Series
Series Editor: Frances Thomson-Salo

WOMEN AND CREATIVITY
A Psychoanalytic Glimpse
Through Art, Literature, and
Social Structure

Edited by

*Laura Tognoli Pasquali
and Frances Thomson-Salo*

A volume in the Psychoanalysis & Women Series
for the Committee on Women and Psychoanalysis
of the International Psychoanalytical Association

KARNAC

First published in 2014 by
Karnac Books Ltd
118 Finchley Road
London NW3 5HT

British Library Cataloguing in Publication Data

A C.I.P. for this book is available from the British Library

ISBN-13: 978-1-78220-145-8

Typeset by V Publishing Solutions Pvt Ltd., Chennai, India

www.karnacbooks.com

CONTENTS

ACKNOWLEDGEMENTS

We dedicate this book to the memory of Alcira Mariam Alizade. She was a most generous and tireless promoter of COWAP's activities. Her intelligence, passion, and vitality were invested in theoretical and clinical studies of sexuality and gender, where her contribution was most valued. Her original thinking, writing, and editorship of the Karnac Women and Psychoanalysis book series, made her a significant person for contemporary psychoanalysis. Mariam Alizade was very creative, with many ideas that were yet to come.

* * *

We wish to thank the authors who contributed so generously to this book.

Lastly we thank the International Psychoanalytical Association for their ongoing commitment to the work of the Committee on Women and Psychoanalysis.

* * *

Permissions

The Cunningham Dax Collection for permission to reproduce *Vinegar Woman* by Joan Rodriqez. The Cunningham Dax Collection, amassed over a seventy year period, consists of over 15,000 artworks including works on paper, photography, paintings, sculptural work, journals, digital media and video created by people with an experience of mental illness and/or psychological trauma. The Cunningham Dax Collection is part of the Dax Centre. The Dax Centre promotes mental health and wellbeing by fostering a greater understanding of the mind, mental illness, and trauma through art and creativity. For more information on the Cunningham Dax Collection and The Dax Centre, visit: www. daxcentre.org.

The three Maternity Centre photos in Chapter Eleven are taken by one of the chapter authors, Sandra Morano and we thank all those in the photographs for permission to print the pictures.

ABOUT THE EDITORS AND CONTRIBUTORS

Mariam Alizade (1.7.1943–6.3.2013), a psychiatrist and training analyst of the Argentine Psychoanalytic Association, was Chair of the IPA Committee on Women and Psychoanalysis (2001–2005) and former COWAP Latin American co-chair (1998–2001). She authored *Feminine Sensuality* (Karnac, 1992); *Near Death: Clinical psychoanalytical studies* (Amorrortu, 1995); *Time for Women* (Letra Viva, Buenos Aires, 1996); *The Lone Woman* (Lumen, 1999) and *Positivity in Psychoanalysis* (Lumen, 2002). In the Karnac Women and Psychoanalysis book series she was the editor of *The Embodied Female, Studies on Femininity and Masculine Scenarios* and of the collected papers of the COWAP Latin American Intergenerational Dialogues (Lumen).

Barbie Antonis has been a consultant adult psychotherapist for the past twenty years at Parkside Clinic in west London. A fellow of the British Psychoanalytic Society, she teaches candidates at the British Society (seminars on infant observation and the Contribution of Independent Women Psychoanalysts), and is a member of the fellowship committee and in private practice as a psychoanalyst. An integral part of her experience as a psychoanalyst is the love of jazz, which she also sings with London-based Blues groups and jazz trios.

Marina Arutyunyan, PhD, is a psychologist, psychoanalyst, and training analyst of the Moscow Psychoanalytic Society. She was involved for many years in gender and socialisation studies in the framework of the Russian Academy of Science.

Nicoletta Livi Bacci has since the seventies been active in social work, gender issues and the feminist movement. In 1979 she was a co-founder of the "Libreria delle donne" di Firenze (Florence women's bookstore), a specialised outlet for women's literature, and a seminal group for discussion of, and advocacy for women's rights. In the early nineties, in association with a group of independent women she was a founder and later president for seventeen years of "Artemisia", a nonprofit association against domestic violence towards women and children. In 1995 it opened the first aid centre in Tuscany providing free legal, psychological, and social counselling to abused women and children. Later two secret shelters were also opened.

Anna Barlocco is a psychoanalyst of the Italian Psychoanalytical Society. As a psychiatrist she has practiced both in therapeutic communities for patients with psychotic and severe personality disorders and in the mental health services of Savona e Albenga, and has been a consultant psychiatrist for the Ministero di Grazia e Giustizia in Savona Prison. At present she practices privately as a psychoanalyst and is working in the Emergency Psychiatric Ward of San Paolo Hospital in Savona where she also treats prenatal and postpartum disorders. She has been on the editorial committee of *Il Vaso di Pandora, Dialoghi in Psichiatria e Scienze Umane* and co-edited *Il corpo e la parola* (1995, Astrolabio). She is the author of several papers and presentations at psychiatric conferences.

Jhuma Basak, PhD in psychology, is a member and training analyst of the Indian Psychoanalytical Society (Kolkata), a member of the Japan Psychoanalytical Association (Tokyo) and of the International Psychoanalytical Association. Currently she is an associate professor of NSHM Knowledge Campus Kolkata in the Institute of Media and Design. She has a private practice as a psychoanalyst and a consultant at the Crystal Clinic, Kolkata (working with adolescents and adults). She has read papers at the forty-second, forty-third, forty-sixth and forty-seventh IPA Congresses, and her publications have been translated into French, Italian, German, Spanish, and Hungarian. She holds a deep interest in cultural psychoanalysis.

Cecile Bassen, MD, is a training and consulting analyst of the Seattle Psychoanalytic Society and Institute and the Northwestern Psychoanalytic Society, and clinical faculty of the Department of Psychiatry and Behavioral Sciences at the University of Washington. She has a longstanding interest in the psychology of gender, and is North American co-chair of the IPA Committee on Women and Psychoanalysis (COWAP). She sees adults and adolescents in psychoanalysis and psychotherapy in her private practice in Seattle.

Irma Brenman Pick came to London from South Africa in 1955 and trained first at the Tavistock Clinic as a child psychotherapist, then at the British Institute of Psychoanalysis as an adult and child analyst. She is now a distinguished fellow and training analyst in the British Society, and a past President of the Society. Her published papers include "On adolescence", "Working through in the countertransference", and "Concern: spurious and real"—all in the *International Journal of Psychoanalysis*. Together with her late husband Eric Brenman, she has taught extensively abroad.

Tonia Cancrini, philosopher, full member and training analyst of the Italian Psychoanalytical Society (SPI) and a specialist in the psychoanalysis of children and adolescents, was former secretary of the Children-Adolescents Committee and member of the SPI National Executive Committee as secretary of the National Training Institute. She was a professor of Philosophical Hermeneutics at the Faculty of Literature and Philosophy of the University of Tor Vergata. Her particular interests are mental and emotional development with particular attention to the primitive levels of the mother–son relationship, and pain and affects in psychoanalytic technique, with particular reference to transference/countertransference. Cancrini has published widely including the following books: *Syneidesis. Il Tema Semantico Della "Con-scientia" Nella Grecia Antica* (Edizioni dell'Ateneo, 1970); *Psicoanalisi, Uomo e Società* (Editori Riuniti, 1981); *Un Tempo per il Dolore. Eros, Dolore e Colpa* (Bollati Boringhieri, 2002) and *Una Ferita All'origine* (Borla, 2012).

Luisa Cerqua is a member of the Italian Psychoanalytical Society (SPI) and a specialist in child and adolescent analysis.

Maria Pia Conte was born in Genova and studied medicine at Genoa University and psychiatry in Siena. She took part in the student movement from 1968 and the feminist movement from 1973. She followed an infant observation course at Milan University, organised according to the Tavistock model and trained as a psychoanalyst, becoming a member of the SPI in 1999. She has worked in the Italian public health service from 1976 to 1997 working mainly with children with language problems and deafness, and in private practice from 1993. From 2009 she has worked on a voluntary basis in a centre for abused women.

Jones De Luca is a psychologist and psychotherapist, and is currently the honorary secretary of the Società Psicoanalitica Italiana (SPI). De Luca has supervised programmes for the educational services, parent counselling services, and cross-disciplinary teams in the Italian national health service. She has participated in projects supervised by the Italian National Research Council, and taught students in psychiatry and professional education, at the University of Udine, and in psychotherapy at the University of Padua. She has participated in initiatives of the Centri di Psicoanalisi including through individual contributions on aggressive fantasies in mothers, fertility, bipolar disorders, and ethics. She was the chief-editor of the SPI's website SPIweb. She has published several works in *Consultatorio Familiare*, as well as other articles, film reviews, and book reviews.

Nadia Fusini teaches comparative literature and English literature at SUM—Istituto di Scienze Umane, Florence. She previously held the chair of Shakespearean Criticism at Sapienza University of Rome. She has translated and written extensively on Virginia Woolf, Shakespeare, John Keats, Samuel Beckett, Mary Shelley, and many others; her translation of Woolf's *The Waves* won the Mondello Literary Prize in 1995. Her most recent books include *Di Vita si Muore. Lo Spettacolo Delle Passioni nel Teatro di Shakespeare* (Mondadori, 2010); *La Figlia del Sole. Vita Ardente di Katherine Mansfield* (Mondadori, 2012), and *Hannah e le Altre* (Einaudi, 2013).

Maria Adelaide Lupinacci is a medical doctor, a specialist in the psychoanalysis of children and adolescents, and a training psychoanalyst of the Italian Psychoanalytic Society (SPI) and a member of the International Psychoanalytic Association. She has been chair of the Child and Adolescent Committee of the Training Institute of the SPI. She is particularly interested in exploring early states of mind as precursors in development and in pathology and has published in journals and in books about mental pain, the early Oedipus complex, transference and countertransference, guilt, and space and time in mental life. She lives and works in Rome in full-time private psychoanalytic practice.

Ingrid Moeslein-Teising is a psychoanalyst of the German Psychoanalytic Association (DPV/IPA), group analyst (DAGG), a doctor in psychosomatic medicine working in private practice and a head physician in an inpatient psychosomatic clinic in Bad Hersfeld. She teaches at the Alexander-Mitscherlich Institute, Kassel. Her scientific interests, publications, and presentations focus on the woman in psychoanalysis. She has contributed to workshops on COWAP topics in DPV conferences, to European COWAP conferences and to the 2007 IPA Congress Berlin. In 2009 she became a member of the IPA Committee on Women and Psychoanalysis. With Frances Thomson-Salo edited *The Female Body— Inside and Outside.*

Sandra Morano graduated in medicine and specialised in obstetrics and gynaecology. From 1980 she worked in health centres as a consultant treating gynaecological pathologies of pregnancy, from which her interest in protecting maternity and childbirth stems. In 1992 she entered analysis, and promoted the first educational programme in Italy for mothers, midwives, and obstetricians. She is professor in Obstetrics and Gynaecology at Genoa University and consultant obstetrician at the IRCCS Azienda Ospedaliera Universitaria S. Martino IST University Hospital of Genoa. In 2000 she created the first Alternative Birth Centre in Italy, to promote continuity of women-centred care and reduce caesarian section rates. She currently teaches obstetrics and gynaecology at the Medical School and Midwifery School of Genoa University and at the Nursing School in Gaslini Hospital in Genoa.

Maria Teresa Palladino is a psychoanalyst in private practice in Torino, a full member and child and adolescent analyst of the Italian Psychoanalytic Society, and the International Psychoanalytic Association. She teaches at Turin University on the Master of Health Psychology. She has been involved in COWAP activities for more than ten years and is currently an Italian COWAP representative. Her main fields of interest are the mother–daughter relationship and eating disorders. She presented "Separation in Mother–Daughter Relationships" at the 2003 Sorrento COWAP conference and has written on gender identity problems (see "Antiche dilemmi e nuove declinazioni del femminile", in *Figure del Femminile*, edited by Malia Giuffrida, Rome, 2009).

Ester Palerm Mari, MD and clinical psychologist, is a member of the Spanish Psychoanalytical Society (SEP), a component society of the International Psychoanalytical Association. Dr Palerm served on the board of directors of the SEP from 2008 to 2012. She was part of the staff of the Psychosomatic Unit at the Hospital de St. Pau i la Santa Creu in Barcelona and has a private practice in Barcelona where she works as a psychoanalyst and psychotherapist for children, adolescents, and adults. She has written papers on a number of themes such as pregnancy, delivery, and the postpartum period. She is a member of the IPA Committee on Women and Psychoanalysis.

Anna Maria Risso is a medical doctor and a full member of the Italian Psychoanalytical Society and is a former professor of clinical psychology at the University of Genoa. She has been very active in teaching in the medical school and in the psychiatric department, and was asked to teach obstetricians, paediatric doctors and nurses, and the school of medical oncology. She has presented numerous papers in major Italian journals of psychiatry and psychoanalytic psychotherapy about group functioning and primitive mental functioning. She has been a lecturer, chair, and discussant at major national and international conferences and is the president of the Genoa Psychoanalytical Centre.

Jordi Sala is a training analyst of the Spanish Psychoanalytical Society, working in private practice and also in a public mental health service for children and adolescents in Barcelona, Spain. He is a former general editor of the European Psychoanalytical Federation Bulletin (2004–2008), and is editor of the *Catalan Review of Psychoanalysis* and editor of *Focal Psychoanalytic Psychotherapy with Children* (2009).

Gertraud Schlesinger-Kipp is a psychologist, psychoanalyst, and a training analyst of the German Psychoanalytic Association (DPV), where she also served as president. She is a consultant to and former member of the Committee on Women and Psychoanalysis and a past

European representative on the board of the IPA. She has a particular interest in psychological aspects of ageing and on the impact of World War II on German children, and is the author of a book and several papers on these subjects.

Christiane S. Schrader is a psychologist, psychoanalyst, supervisor, and a member of the Frankfurt Psychoanalytic Institute, of the German Psychoanalytic Association (DPV) and the IPA. After ten years of working in a psychosomatic clinic she established her private practice. She has a particular interest in the psychology of ageing and is training psychoanalysts and psychotherapists in the treatment of elderly patients. She has published on trauma, female development, partnership, and ageing.

Almuth Sellschopp, Prof. Dr phil., trained in medical psychology, and was a professor of the psychosomatic faculty of the University Clinic Munich (retired), a training and supervising analyst of the DPV/IPA, and a member of the Curatory Breuninger Foundation for Health and Medicine. She worked on female leadership issues with a research publication in press. She carried out scientific work on alexithymia and psycho-oncology, was a member of many government projects to improve the care of cancer patients and was a counsellor for German Cancer Aid and won the German Cancer Aid Prize. She was a member of the organising team of the DPV/IPA Summer University.

Juan-Eduardo Tesone is a physician, psychiatrist, and psychoanalyst, a full member of the Société Psychanalytique de Paris, member with training functions of the Argentine Psychoanalytic Association, an associate professor of the School of Psychology of Paris Ouest-Nanterre, professor of the D.U.E.F.O. of the Medical School of La Pitié-Salpêtrière, University of Paris VI, a full professor of the Doctorate program in psychoanalysis of the School of Psychology of Salvador University, Buenos Aires, and professor of the Masters Programme in Interdisciplinary Studies on Subjectivity at the School of Philosophy of the University of Buenos Aires. He is the author of more than one hundred articles in Spanish, French, English, Italian, German, Portuguese, Croatian, and Turkish, co-author of several books and the author of *In the Traces of our Name: The Influence of Given Names in Life* (Karnac, 2011).

Frances Thomson-Salo trained with the British Psychoanalytical Society, and is past president of the Australian Society, overall chair of the IPA Committee of Women and Psychoanalysis, editorial Board member of the *International Journal of Psychoanalysis*, an honorary principal fellow of the Department of Psychiatry, University of Melbourne, and affiliate researcher of the Murdoch Children's Research Institute.

Laura Tognoli Pasquali, a medical doctor, trained in the British Psychoanalytical Society with the Kleinian group and in 1976 qualified as an analyst. Now she is a training analyst and lives in Italy in a small village by the sea where she can cultivate a lifelong interest: growing flowers and plants. Taking care of fragile young shoots, finding the best milieu for growing and strengthening their roots, helps thinking, reflecting, and dreaming about the basic needs and desires of human beings. Colours, shapes, and scents of a flourishing garden strike the mind with the mystery of beauty which has the power to organise the conflicts of emotions in meaningful patterns and promote α function and symbol formation. Taking care of plants has widened her love for teaching and her attention to clinical work. She has seen many women and men on her couch and thought deeply about their life experiences; as a result she was pleased to accept to become a member of the Committee on Women and Psychoanalysis.

Maria Grazia Vassallo Torrigiani is a psychoanalyst member of Italian Psychoanalytic Society. Her main research interests are psychoanalytic clinic work, femininity, image and art. She has published papers in a number of journals, in books (in *The Body Image in Psychoanalysis and Art*, edited by E. Blum, H. Blum & A. Pazzagli, 2007), and presented at many national and international conferences. She has organised several conferences in Pisa on themes relevant to the relation between psychoanalysis and cinema, visual art, music, and religion, often in cooperation with the three Universities in Pisa. She published articles and videos in SPIweb, the Italian Psychoanalytic Society's website, coordinates many online publishing projects and is a member of the IPA Website Editorial Board.

INTRODUCTION

Laura Tognoli Pasquali and Frances Thomson-Salo

This book was conceived a year ago in Genoa where many psychoanalysts gathered at a conference to share their thoughts and reflections on women and creativity. The germinal idea slowly grew to becoming a fact, a realisation and has now reached its final shape in a collection of papers written by women and men from different backgrounds, countries, and personal experiences but, we think, linked by the strong desire to understand something more of the mystery of life and its reproduction and therefore of creativity.

We want to make clear that we do not think creativity belongs to women as much as we do not believe it is a prerogative of men. Creativity belongs to a couple: its roots are strongly planted in the fertile encounter between two human beings able to produce a new subject, something never seen before. And when we say a couple we obviously have in mind man and woman but we think at the same time of mother and baby, of father and mother, teacher and pupil ... all potentially creative couples who accompany us throughout life, firstly filling our bodies with their presence and then becoming part of ourselves, inner experiences able to promote all kinds of creative links: a shape and a thought, a word and an idea, an experience and an emotion, a colour and an image.

But, if creativity belongs to a couple why are we pleased to present a book on women's creativity? We are pleased because it is not infrequent, particularly in some countries, to find an attitude of dismissive amusement if one talks of women's creativity. "What has creativity got to do with women?" was the comment of a "smiling friend" when told that a conference on women's creativity was being organised. Perhaps it is only a joke but certainly it is evocative of a culture that has robbed women of their richness.

Even psychoanalysis has, for a long time, refused to recognise the value and the specificity of mental and biological creativity in women. It is deeply hurting when, as can often happen, creativity and generativity are confused and devalued while generativity is treated only as a concrete fact without any symbolic meaning, without recognising its specific value in promoting the development of female psychology.

Mother is the "holding mother", the object of the baby, not a subject with her attributes, needs, and desires. Rivers of words have run in psychoanalytic literature to describe the role of vagina in female sexuality and almost nothing has been written to describe the womb, the creative internal chamber that every baby girl, with a mixture of fear and wonder, knows very well that she owns inside herself: the chamber where life starts, the chamber which links the "to be" and the "not to be", the other and this world. We cannot speak about woman's creativity while ignoring the presence of the womb, this inside presence the unconscious phantasy of which inevitably forges a woman's development and, we believe, that of the man, too.

The psychoanalytic psychology of women needs to be reviewed, to be viewed specifically as linked to gender and at the same time followed in its vicissitudes through the constantly changing dynamic encounter between man and woman within the couple, how each of them is affected and shaped by the other in his or her growth throughout maturity. And how both of them are unconsciously moulded and forged by the psychic nature of the social tissue in which they sink their roots. We should reflect on how envy and gratitude, love and hate, are strong passions active in moulding not only the relationship between the partners but also the course of their thinking.

It is important to follow the projections inside the couple and try to understand how these projections are taken in to become part of the personality. This is particularly important for women as their internal space often operates as a suitable container for whatever enters inside: guilt, fragility, fear … Furthermore, we do not forget that it is Eve, not Adam, who is the first to bear the guilt for the original sin.

If we can think together we may be able to produce a new view of women's and men's development based not so much on sexuality but on the exchange between human beings, on their reciprocal phantasies of being men and women, on their growing together and on their forging each other to become what they are. These are some of the reasons why woman's creativity needs to be specifically addressed and ideas shared in study groups, psychoanalytic congresses, papers, and books.

The authors do not in their individual chapters define creativity in great detail in Kleinian or Winnicottian terms—whether the unconscious movement from defence to reparation, or searching inside oneself for a lonely reparation, trying on one's own to repair the self, or looking for another who is able to provide the containment which was originally felt to be missing. Nor do they explore whether the creative act is about a repair of internal parental couple or totally different, but trust that in their explorations a sense of how they are using it will arise, that something will emerge from their exploration of different aspects of creativity and that the readers will find their own creative links. The four parts address aspects of how creativity is viewed in psychoanalytic theory and worked with in the consulting room, with particular reference to human generativity and the life cycle, within the arts in the broadest sense and its workings in society and culture in the widest sense.

* * *

In Part I, Creativity in psychoanalytic theory, we see analysts in their consulting rooms or sitting at the desk trying to convey firstly to themselves, and then to others, the thinking and the emotions that patients have entrusted to them. Psychoanalysis is in itself a very creative work because it helps thinking to come alive. As did Socrates long ago, psychoanalysts assist in the search for answers to the problems of life, not through formal science but within one's personal thoughts and emotions. The psychoanalyst helps the birth of a thinking freed from the resistances provoked by misconceptions and from the omnipotent conviction of already knowing everything.

First, Irma Brenman Pick's chapter, "Creativity and authenticity", focuses on what she terms emotional creativity rather than artistic creativity, and she considers this, in relation to woman as mother, and also woman as psychoanalyst. Maternal creative function Brenman Pick thinks of as part of the analyst's creative function and may be present in a female or male analyst. She is especially interested in the authenticity of the creative maternal function which in life, as well as in analysis, needs to come together with an internal father to protect and value the knowledge of what is authentically provided, whilst bearing the more depressive guilt about one's own inauthenticities. In this way creative capacity in the analyst includes the capacity to bear loss. Her chapter, with its clinical material, foreshadows the clinical discussions of Part II. Jordi Sala's discussion takes up a number of points from this chapter, and in particular whether anything truly creative can ever be born out of inauthenticity. In the chapter "Listening, technique, and all that jazz", Barbie Antonis suggests that the jazz groove and idiom has a close parallel to the clinical technique of the British Independent psychoanalysts. This analogy may encourage a particular kind of listening and this, in the context of the training experience of psychoanalytic infant observation, can facilitate the development in the candidate of a creative authenticity, a gradual finding of one's own voice, in psychoanalytic identity.

In "William, did you say, '*Much Ado about Nothing*'?", Juan Eduardo Tesone suggests that for creativity to emerge, in men or in women, it is helpful for their psychic agencies and repression to be porous enough, for the dialogue between their life and death drives to be free of fear, for their multiple identifications, both feminine and masculine or indeterminate to refract freely, and for working through the traumatic to find a livable and fertile solution in creative work. Ingrid Moeslein-Teising discusses this paper, powerfully illustrating her points about the female core, gender tension, creativity, and woman as an artist with extracts from Shakespeare's *Macbeth*.

Reflecting in her chapter "Female elements and functions in creativity", Maria Adelaide Lupinacci asks herself if there is such a thing as a specificity of female creativity. She puts forward the idea that, as both the feminine and the masculine elements contribute in varying degrees to creativity, ultimately creativity belongs to the couple or better to a "convivial" relationship of the female/male dyad. She then explores how feminine elements of creativity, along with masculine ones, are necessary for a personality to be rich and complete. In "Women and creativity" Maria Pia Conte outlines how women not only struggle to identify with the baby inside, dependent and full of needs, but also with the mother outside, a living being who is expected to have enough space to mate, to introject, and to allow transformation while remaining one's own self. The gradual acknowledgement of all these functions and needs structures women's minds and opens up new levels of symbolisation, working through and creativity.

* * *

Part II, Creativity in psychoanalytic practice throughout the life cycle, witnesses the difficulties, the hopes, the desires, the fears portrayed through the analysis of women during their life cycle from childhood to old age. In the middle of this part we sojurn in the labour room as a very important place in a woman's experience. Part II starts with a clinical paper, "When creativity restarts, distorted, and adaptive forms" in which Frances Thomson-Salo explores an idea that when creativity has been stifled for a long time it may first start again in a distorted form that in analysis should not be disparaged, and there needs not to be initially a focus on too heavily interpreting the negative transference. This is illustrated with vignettes from child, adolescent, and adult patients, describing creativity with female patients or sometimes co-created as a female analyst with a male patient. With "A little girl's analysis", Luisa Cerqua and Tonia Cancrini invite us to witness the working together of the analyst and her supervisor in treating a clumsy, lonely girl. Through their creative alliance, which reminds one of a parental couple, the supervisor helps the analyst to tolerate and contain the girl's strong, frightening primitive anxieties and in so doing allows the analyst to free her reverie and to promote the girl's growth.

"A psychoanalyst in the labour room: the birth of emotions" by Laura Tognoli Pasquali is not a clinical paper even though it is centred around a dream. The analyst moves from her consulting to the labour room where she is invited to be present at the beginning of life, a very emotional situation where the pressure of emotions is so strong and frightening that it needs to be denied. She thinks difficult feelings need obstetric attention to be helped at birth and if this is done in the place where life starts, the labour room can become the meeting point between the mind and the body, a place where medicine can delve into areas that physiology cannot control, and enter the realm of the mind which is feelings, conflicts, fears, anxieties belonging to a real human being made of body and mind. With the next paper, "Generativity and creativity: Dialogue between an obstetrician and a pychoanalyst", Sandra Morano and Anna Maria Risso invite us again into the labour room to witness the pain but also the joy of procreation. In their vivacious dialogue we can see how childbirth can become a creative experience not dissimilar from other means of creativity if the mother-to-be is left free to find her own way physically and emotionally to give birth to her child in the presence of safe and understanding assistance.

Anna Barlocco explores creativity in the analytic couple. She thinks that one of the most important therapeutic factors of analysis is a couple's experience of true closeness, and only in this intimate climate can creativity be promoted. In her paper, "Dreaming about pregnancy when it is not there" she shows how dreaming with her two patients, a man and a woman, about pregnancy and what was preventing it, living together their frightening anguish and excessive hopes, promoted an analytic nearness which gave the analyst access into the most creative area of their personality.

In the following chapter, "A particular kind of sterility" by Jones de Luca, the analyst's creativity is more surmised than evident in the writing and describes how a female patient in analytic therapy is enabled to become pregnant and bear a child. According to De Luca the patient's sterility was generated by obsessive and violent symptoms arising as a horde of wild thoughts preventing fertilisation. The analyst's capacity to survive the strong projections and to contain them, maintaining a basically strong positive and safe maternal transference, enabled the patient very quickly to become pregnant and move into motherhood as a good enough mother. Creativity is again in the foreground in Ester Palerm Mari's very vivid discussion of this case, when she says how important and creative the integration of containment with working through is in analysis, and how countertransference helps in retaining a creative view, joining together the analyst's and the patient's contribution as well as the relationship they create in each session.

Then Christiane Schrader, in "'With you I can bleat my heart out'— Older women in psychoanalytic practice", comments on aspects of ageing in today's women and explores the role of creativity in their capacity to resist and cope with ageing. Many older women patients today belong to the generation described with a hint of irony by Margarete Mitscherlich-Nielsen (1995) as "peaceable". She depicted women eager to keep the peace, having grown up in a patriarchal society, intimidated, inhibited in their self-assertion and aggression, and often with massive repercussions on their creativity. Mitscherlich's psychodynamic findings are the starting point of a case study of a sixty-nine-year-old patient who in therapy emerged out of a restrictive peaceable position.

* * *

Art communicates one's personal experience of oneself and of the world in symbolic forms through a great variety of means and materials. These different ways are explored in Part III, creativity in the arts and literature. Maria Grazia Vassallo Torrigiani in her chapter, "Using contents from a sewing box: some aspects of the artwork of Sonia Delaunay and Louise Bourgeois", turns her attention to particular aspects of the artistic production: to weaving, sewing, embroidery always considered female activities *par excellence*. They involve the domestic virtue of caring for the body, and satisfying its needs for protection, warmth, comfort, and wellbeing, an artistic language originating in the female-maternal regions of the mind, and representing a kind of symbolic extension of the female-maternal function.

It is a film that inspires Maria Teresa Palladino. In her "Commentary on *Brodeuses*" she illustrates the deep psychic work necessary in order to accept an initially unwanted pregnancy. Following the vicissitudes of Claire, the adolescent protagonist of the film, the author highlights the difficulties that young girls sometimes face in confronting their creativity, and how this is connected with the troubles they experienced in the relationships with their mothers. The possibility for a woman to think of herself as a mother comes at the end of a growth path, which the film represents as an identification with a "foster" mother. This new identification is only made possible by a separation of the daughter from her mother.

Nadia Fusini's "The voice of the mother in *To the Lighthouse*" is a reading of Virginia Woolf's marvellous novel focused on the mother's presence, on her inescapable, insurmountable, insuperable, unforgettable body.

* * *

In Part IV, Living creatively in society, a theme emerges of women's apparent masochism, and the violence that may then be more easily inflicted on them, with some possibilities to emerge creatively from this. We need to be aware of the cultural context within which a number of the papers on the psychoanalytic view of femininity and female creativity were written and its related effects. When the experience of analysts from different cultures is collated, not only patients but analysts as well can be seen to be plunged into the same culture, undergoing the strong pressure of the social community to which they belong, and the powerful group mentality can be seen in their writings.

Cecile Bassen in "Happily ever after: Depictions of coming of age in fairy tales" explores how the widespread and enduring popularity of fairy tales suggests that they speak deeply to something in all of us of children's psychological conflicts and important developmental issues. Their universality suggests that they not only reflect cultural beliefs but also perpetuate them, exerting a powerful magnetic pull on unconscious perceptions and beliefs—influencing children as they construct and revise conscious and unconscious beliefs, and resonating unconsciously in adults. She explores how two well-known fairy tales, Cinderella and Snow White, reinforce problematic gender stereotypes with their emphasis on beauty, the virtues of passive endurance and selflessness, and the love of a powerful man as the solution to powerlessness. Her focus on the inhibition of assertion and aggression and the reinforcement of passivity in women leads on to the following two papers.

The theme of the obstacle to women's creativity posed by masochism continues in the chapter, "Cultural altruism", where Jhuma Basak considers aspects of this in the cultures in India and Japan. She examines the sociocultural and psychological construct of self-sacrifice through a psychoanalytic perspective, which leads to possible masochism in women in these Eastern societies. In her clinical vignette a woman's depressive guilt can be seen to be a hindrance to creative explorations, impacting on women's emotional wellbeing in those societies. In "Horses and other animals: some background obstacles to female creativity in Russia", Marina Aruntunyan explores how some aspects of Russian history and culture maintained a mix of contradictory attitudes and representations, which despite all conscious efforts at integration often result in representational splitting at societal and individual levels. She suggests that this contributes in many women to a masochistic character structure which presents obstacles to their freely using their capacity for creativity. After a sketch of the broader historical picture in Russia, Aruntunyan illustrates her points with vignettes from four women patients, with some dream material.

In "Is healing possible for women survivors of domestic violence?" Nicoletta Livi Bacci describes how women abused by their intimate partners suffer injury at all levels. She follows the process of healing and empowerment that battered women, and battered mothers, who managed to leave an abusive partner, can undertake inside women's shelters in Italy. The impact of these injuries is often so strong that only with the help of shelter professionals can women learn how to redirect the strength that they drew on to cope with the difficult situation of beginning a new life. In the chapter commemorating Margarete Mitscherlich, "No peaceable woman: Creativity in feminist political psychoanalysis", four analysts, Ingrid Moeslein-Teising, Gertraud Schlesinger-Kipp, Christiane Schrader and Almuth Sellschopp, elaborate the reference in Schrader's chapter to Margarete Mitscherlich-Nielsen and expand on the theoretical contribution and work of this creative woman psychoanalyst, who was very important in the history of psychoanalysis in Germany.

Last, a chapter written sequentially by two analysts, on the same topic, is intended to evoke in the analytic group reflection on the question "Should we as psychoanalysts apologise to women?" Maria Pia Conte and Laura Tognoli Pasquali with different styles and words express the same sadness and hope: sadness because psychoanalysis has for a long time not recognised the value and the specificity of mental and biological creativity in women, and the hope of one day seeing psychoanalysts fully acknowledge the debt to women's functions and mind, and apologise for having colluded with aggression, denial, and male narcissism at the expense of women, and men, too.

The hope in this book is that from the voices speaking with passion new ideas will arise in the readers' journey.

PART I

CREATIVITY IN PSYCHOANALYTIC THEORY

CHAPTER ONE

Creativity and authenticity

Irma Brenman Pick

I have chosen, in this chapter, not to address artistic creativity, rather to focus on what I think of as emotional creativity; I shall consider this, in relation to woman as mother, and also woman as psychoanalyst. The maternal creative function I think of as a part of the analyst's creative function; this capacity may be present in female or male analysts. Furthermore, I am especially interested in the authenticity (or not) of the (creative) maternal function and of analytic function.

Authenticity is based on some acceptance of external reality and some acceptance of oneself as one really is. I say "some" acceptance advisedly, for I believe this always to be partial. Whilst on the one hand we value authenticity, there is also a question of how much authenticity we want, or in fact, can bear? We might think about how much "creativity" goes into creating inauthenticity, and to what extent inauthenticity is valued.

Indeed, in Western culture those in what we might call "maternal" roles—nurses, teachers, carers generally—are paid at devalued rates. It appears there is a consensus that they are not "worth" more. Meanwhile, those involved in creating "inauthenticity" seem instead to be massively overvalued! Janine Chasseguet-Smirgel wrote in 1984: "I happen to live in a country in a town and at a time where false values aesthetic and intellectual as well as ethical seem to be gratified with admiration and success at the expense of true values" (Chasseguet-Smirgel, 1984, p. 66).

Montaigne retold classical stories such as that of Lycas who went about his daily life, and successfully held down a job, while believing that everything he saw was taking place on a stage, as a theatrical performance. When a doctor cured him of this delusion, Lycas became so miserable that he sued the doctor for robbing him this pleasure in life.

I think that from very early on there is a conflictual struggle between creativity in the service of authenticity and creative inauthenticity. If we think about it biblically, in the beginning, God created heaven and earth. He needed no one to help him, the universe was entirely of his making. This then applied to his son too. In Christianity no couple is required. God created all life and goodness, even his own son, as a gesture of his greatness, and for this God is worshipped.

It seems that we go about our daily lives enthralled by such idealisations. We might think about how this arises. In the beginning of life the infant hallucinates the breast. Like God, he is happy in the belief that he is master of the universe, with omnipotent power over his objects. This "heaven" is shattered when he is exposed to the reality of hunger and need; then instead, all hell breaks loose. Yet this Majesty the Baby attracts worship too (or, alternatively, may attract abuse when, perhaps, he shatters the parents' un-worked through infantile need to be idealised and worshipped too). The facts of life are not always welcome; neither for baby nor parent. We seem to need to create phantasies or beliefs that obscure our awareness of our dependence on others. We may more easily accept dependence on deities rather than on ordinary fallible human objects.

Bion (1962) has described the complexities around the earliest negotiations of dependence. He focuses on the way in which the mother takes in the baby's emotional experience. If she is able to feel and also give meaning to that experience she transforms it into something digestible for the baby. This ordinary task of transforming the baby's raw communication is a fundamentally creative act, akin, in my view, to the sexual act itself.

If the mother has taken inside of herself what Dana Birksted-Breen has called "penis as link", she together with this internalised penis/father creatively transforms the baby's projections. This union or internal mating offers mother space to think about her infant's experience.

We might say that unconsciously there is an internal union between the mother's mind that takes in the projections (vagina) and the father's mind (penis) that supports thinking creatively about what is taking place, and has a structuring function.

This establishes the creative relationship between mother and baby. In optimal circumstances the baby internalises, and then identifies with such a mother. Gradually the baby reciprocates by being able to take in, or internally "create", a sense of how she and eventually they, mother and father too, feel.

So, there is more than one link in the task of emotional creativity. There is the link between a mother who takes in how her baby feels and a baby who has an experience of such a mother. Crucially there is the link with the internal penis/father who, from the start, unites with mother's maternal capacity.

In the development of the infant, alongside a (shall we say healthy) identification with the mother, there is always some more spurious "take over" of her function. For example, watching a small girl push a doll in her buggy it is not difficult to recognise both aspects of identification. That is, both a real internalisation of the maternal function, as well as a little girl in a delusional state of mind, in which she *is* "the mother", walking out with father and "their" baby.

In Freud's writings on early development he, of course, posited a period of phallic monism whereby only one sexual organ is known in childhood; in contrast, Melanie Klein (1980) in "The effect of early anxiety-situations on the sexual development of the boy", we know, opposed this notion, since for her there is always an unconscious knowledge of the vagina and the womb.

How has this unconscious knowledge of the female organs been come by, and if it is there, why is it so frequently repudiated? Why does phallic defensiveness have such a hold on both male and female psyche. Indeed there has been a long and rich discussion of these issues in psychoanalytic and feminist literature.

In my opinion, the unconscious knowledge of mother's (hidden) interiority, may be based on, or at least reinforced by, the experience of a mouth taking in sustenance from the breast. This, of course, goes alongside the experience of a mother taking in how the baby feels. I believe this constitutes the foundation or prototype for the knowledge of a vagina that takes in and links with a penis, and a womb that holds and nurtures the foetus.

If there is this unconscious knowledge of the female sexual organs, why does the sexual development of the girl continue so frequently to be seen as the girl born only in "lack" (of penis)? Might it be that the baby's "lack" is projected into the mother, and there is then a collusive consensus to support the inauthentic proposition that the "lack" remains lodged in her?

This creative function of the mother, so profoundly important for the emotional development of the child, that upon which the infant most depends, may be that which is most susceptible to envious attack. When Klein spoke of the envy of the breast, it is not only the breast as need-satisfying object, provider of milk for survival, which is envied. Perhaps, even more significantly, the focus of envy may be that very quality of the mother/breast which takes in how the baby feels. After all, "anyone" can shove a bottle into the mouth of a baby. Indeed it was initially posited that (for the first eighteen months) the infant did not make a relationship with the mother. Bottle or breast was seen only as a need-satisfying object. As if maternal care and feeding could be reduced to this. Crudely put—all the difference between a personally meaningful intercourse and a "fuck" from an impersonal phallus.

We may ponder then about what is the first creative act for the infant? Is this based on the infant taking in from the mother not only the milk she provides, but also the experience of her understanding of the infant, her taking the infant in? Or is it based in that which goes alongside this—the experience of the "creation" of a hallucinatory breast. Does competition arise between the infant's (omnipotently) created hallucination, an implant, and the real breast? May the "false" breast be given more value than the real breast?

Furthermore, what if the mother's own identity is based on falseness? Does the infant then take over and identify with that false self mother/appropriated breast and/or in so doing, attack the mother's real qualities? My interest in this chapter lies in considering what happens when authentic maternal function is replaced by a masquerade. In Joan Riviere's (1929) seminal paper, "Womanliness as masquerade", she writes about defensive femininity, arising out of the girl being, emotionally, in possession of father's penis, having castrated him, and appropriated and stolen him from mother. Riviere reports patients' dreams of people putting on masks, and describes a fraudulent femininity— a mask of womanliness to avert anxiety and the retribution which the girl child fears from both men and women. Riviere traces the roots of this development to frustration during sucking or weaning. There is then an exacerbation of the desire to bite off the nipple and to destroy, penetrate, and disembowel the mother of her contents (which crucially includes father's penis).

Clinical illustrations of inauthenticity and authenticity

I hope now to illustrate these themes with two clinical examples, the first briefly, the second at more length.

Miss X

Miss X, a young woman from another country arrives for a first consultation, in pouring rain, some thirty-five mintues late. Immaculately turned out, she appears "cool as a cucumber", politely apologetic.

She tells me she is not happy with the way her life is; she has just turned forty. Born abroad the family came to the UK when she was a few months old; later a younger brother was born, and only when she was about five years old did she discover that there was a sister who had been left behind five years earlier.

I remark on the fact that she is so polite about being late; although she has come a long way for an appointment which I think must be important for her, she is cool, as if she has not left a child part of herself behind, or, at any rate, we should not notice that. She is apparently not a bit distressed about what (in this case the thirty-five minutes) she has lost, just as she shows no apparent upset in the way she is telling me about these distressing events. It seems as though she has no feelings at all.

She responds by saying: "Well, yes, that was the problem I went into therapy for but I had thought I was cured. I don't have feelings; I do not know how I feel, I have no feelings at all." With these words she bursts into tears, needs tissues, and shows herself terribly embarrassed to be crying. I comment: as though she should not have feelings. There would, she believes, be no sympathy for her upset; only excruciating shame. What gradually emerges is the contempt she feels for a mother who could not speak English, who would became angry if the children were upset in any way; in short, a mother who could not cope. Whilst she, the patient, appears to have appropriated the persona of one who copes perfectly with life.

Here we have a picture of a mother depicted as having no interior life, and a young woman with all the trappings of femininity but evidently without an interior life either. The creative endeavour appears to have been dedicated to the production of inauthenticity, a false self as provider breast, a mask. Of course it is very painful to become aware that at age forty, she has lost her real "child" self and is losing the capacity to have her own child.

Mrs Z

I would like now to describe, at more length, a patient with the implants I mentioned at the start of this paper. She hails from a country where "la bella figura" (presenting a beautiful appearance) is all. She is a young married woman with a young daughter. She herself appears to have, I believe, a mother who masquerades in the way that Riviere has described. At the moment that this young woman entered analysis, with a rather desperate wish to train as an analyst, her mother (also in a helping profession), "supported" her by suggesting and paying for the patient, to have breast implants. It did seem that from the outset a competition was set up between false breast (implants) and a potentially more real "breast"/analysis.

I will present now a series of Mrs Z's dreams. These took place over several months.

The first is a dream in which:

> She is on a bus which would not stop; finally they near big shop fronts. (Are these the false/breast implants, a front, or a representation of what the "real" analyst may offer?)

She speaks of reading Melanie Klein and of her difficulties understanding what she is reading even as she imagines herself teaching Klein in the University. As though she would not need to understand—only *be* the teacher.

Like the bus, she talks on non-stop—about the nice tea party she had provided for her husband's birthday; mother was there speaking about a famous woman who has invited them all to tea; mother says that this woman's husband has just died so they should all go to the tea; the patient's husband does not want to participate in this. Mother is a real socialite, says the patient. She continues with her associations—that later she and mother went shopping for clothes. She was so busy shopping that she forgot to collect her child from the nursery school.

I was interested in how much time she spends on clothing herself (the false breasts) in the clothes of being a particular kind of mother/ analyst. She makes a "nice" tea, prepares to visit the bereaved; she does all that she believes is expected of a good ("socialite") woman. She wants to teach Klein even though she does not understand her, just as she would like to be in the psychoanalytic training, with the big and famous. In the sessions she offers the analyst dreams and a multitude of associations, as though she is in possession of the big, manic (shop) fronts. She believes that that is what is wanted by the mother/analyst, and that neither will notice that, in this process, there is a bereaved/ bereft person, and a forgotten child—the widowed woman, and the child who is not collected from school (not unlike the abandoned sister in the account of the patient I mentioned earlier).

There is, nevertheless, an unconscious knowledge of a bereaved person; some recognition that the false socialite self/mother masks an underlying depression. I would also add that mother and she are both bereft, as if a capacity for real experience of life has been lost. She tries, perhaps in a manic way, to repair this depressed mother by providing missing "big fronts" so that, in a sense, she offers mother implants. Yet, sadly they are fronts—cover ups rather than "the real thing". But there is also someone, the patient's husband, and now the analyst, and I would suggest, even some part of the patient, projected into both husband and analyst, who does not wish to participate in this cover up. I think this comes from a search for a more genuine way of relating, a mind seeking another mind that will understand her real feelings. I think there is also hatred of this "socialite" mother who is experienced as needy and demanding of care and repair.

We have here then a complicated picture; I believe the patient feels that she has appropriated the implants/false breasts. She believes that she, in robbing the mother of the breasts, has caused mother's depression. At the same time I think that she feels enraged to be made to feel responsible for mother's depression and for being expected to visit/ cure the mother when in fact she herself feels so deprived of real care.

Winnicott (1948/1974) has written vividly about children of depressed mothers who feel that they have to repair or "mother" their mothers. I would add that the urge to repair the mother is compounded by the hatred felt toward this mother who in her depression is unable to take in how the infant really feels. So at some level the child believes that it is her hatred which has damaged mother. There is then a feeling of guilt for the hateful attacks, whilst at the same time rage at having to feel guilty when she feels this very mother to have been guilty of depriving her.

Later she dreams that:

> She and her mother live in neighbouring houses; they are looking into the backs of the gardens; mother says we should buy more garden—it would be nice if we put the two houses together.

She speaks of wanting to train as an analyst as though she would like their (her and her mother/analyst's) houses to be joined together in this way. She refers to other dreams which have been wonderful—like Hollywood movies. She describes her present home; she wants to create a nice bright family space; she wants a big table where she and her little girl can "engage in creative play"—this said in a way that sounds quite phoney.

The patient brings rich dreams which are frequently imaginative and accurate, but it is as if she and her analyst do not need to really take their meaning seriously—they are just "creative play". Similarly, she has a "wonderful" idea of training as an analyst—for her a Hollywood (hollow-wood) solution. Her picture is one of getting in by the back-door, joining up with a "false self" mother/analyst, creating a setting for so-called creative play. Does she believe that the analyst too got in by the backdoor, created such a setting for "play" with patients, a more successful false self than the patient? I shall return to this question.

At the same time, as I have already suggested, this young woman is capable of doing genuine work with a real analyst, who is also appreciated by her. She has also chosen a down-to-earth husband who does not want to participate in this charade of "having tea with the bereaved". Yet she appears entranced by the inauthentic solution and while she values the analysis, like Lycas she often wants to sue the analyst who is experienced as interfering with this love affair.

So the real work is repeatedly devalued in comparison with the Hollywood solution. In fact the patient sets up a competition between her analyst's and her mother's ways of life, similarly between her husband and her mother and, of course, between herself and her analyst. We could say that the analysis began with a competition between analysis and implants! In fact, I believe that this patient is bound to a picture of the analyst as false, just like her mother's "implants"; she wants to maintain that all achievement comes via the backdoor.

The following day the patient finds herself in a situation with a number of very deprived people; she is struck by how deprived they are. When she thinks about this deprivation she thinks about her own child who is quite disturbed; she is also perhaps coming closer to a deprived part of herself. That night she has a dream in which:

> she is tired after a long journey, a really long journey, she says, in the countryside; she thinks of a friend with a disturbed child; she is impressed with the way the parents are facing up to the disturbance. The child's teachers are trying to minimise the difficulties but she thinks this is not helpful.

But no sooner does the analyst feel some hope in relation to this insight, than the patient has another dream:

> about a mother, from her little girl's nursery school, whose husband has died. In the dream the patient is feeding this mother choc ices. The ices melt; someone suggests re-freezing them, and the patient says—let's just get some more.

So, after a long journey (in the analysis) there is recognition of disturbance, and a realisation that minimising these difficulties is not helpful. Insight has been achieved. No sooner is this acknowledged, however, than the analyst becomes someone "whose husband has died", who is bereft of her own strength, and instead is being flattered—fed choc ices by the patient. Any genuine appreciation is quickly twisted into flattery—into that which the patient is providing to make the analyst happy. The analyst is not to notice that in this process she has been robbed of her potency. Faced with loss, the loss of her omnipotence, the patient reverts to being the provider of choc ices—even as she melts, she freezes again! Let's get some more (of this frozen stuff). Yet is there also a more "authentic" picture of her real mother who the patient believes would feel bereft if her daughter no longer minimised the difficulties and became more separate from her?

And a final dream:

> Peter, recently separated from his wife, visits her (the patient); she fancies Peter. She is not wearing much. He comes behind her and

puts his hands on her breasts. She freezes, thinking that he will discover that her breasts are not real.

In the previous dream, the patient offered choc ices to the bereaved woman, something of no real substance. Here, there is a dream about a man having to deal with separation/loss. Does he look to her breasts as a comfort, or does he excite himself with a devaluing of his loss—sexualisation as a defence? In any case she fears he will discover that she cannot offer real breast function, only the false implants. Is the analyst sufficiently robust to tolerate an enquiry into whether she too is scantily equipped and wanting to be reassured or flattered; whether she too is trying to get in by the backdoor? Are the analytic breasts authentic, or does the analyst, also, fear being "found out".

I think that there is a great anxiety in the patient that her inauthenticity will be discovered and that the solution of false implants will end in a total collapse, an absolute deflation or crash. The implants in my view represent for her inflation born out of manic omnipotence. The omnipotence steals everything including the patient's more authentic qualities. There is then a fear of a ferocious, vengeful superego which will strip her of everything, leave her with nothing. Eric Brenman termed this an "asset stripping" superego.

So that which is authentic has little hope of survival. This is often played out in the analyst as well. I will conclude with some thoughts about corresponding issues of authenticity and inauthenticity in the analyst. When analysis is based on idealisation, the analyst's fear of being "found out" may be considerable. For even at best we are part authentic and part inauthentic. Faced with anxiety we may all return to a place where we fear that we will be discovered to have appropriated that which is not ours. We may then freeze, or offer "choc ices", reassurance, or phallic magnificence and intellectualisation, or become an asset stripping superego to patient or self. All of these will impede a more creative enquiry into what is false and what is authentic, or rather how much is false and how much authentic.

For when we are confronted with the inauthenticity of the patient, this may touch on our own; we need to be able to work this through internally in order to be equipped to engage in a creatively authentic way for the patient. I refer here to my paper, "Working through in the countertransference". Of course some "successful" analyses may take place as a theatrical performance, in the way that Lycas lived his life.

I believe that the capacity to do creative analytic work is based in the bringing together of emotion and thought, mother and father, male and female, and good and bad parts of the self. Thus, for example, we may actually feel flattered, want to "get off" on this, and have to come together with an internal father to provide help in bearing to know about this. The father's role here might be seen as supporting the mother to bear her imperfection, and yet have the robustness to protect and value the knowledge of what is authentically provided, whilst bearing the more depressive guilt about her own inauthenticities. In this way creative capacity in the analyst includes the capacity to bear loss, not least the loss of the illusion of perfection!

References

Bion, W. R. (1962). *Learning From Experience*. London: Tavistock.

Birksted-Breen, D. (1996). Phallus, penis and mental space. *International Journal of Psychoanalysis, 77*: 649–657.

Brenman Pick, I. (1985). Working through in the countertransference. *International Journal of Psychoanalysis, 66*: 157–166.

Chasseguet-Smirgel, J. (1984). *Creativity and Perversion*. New York: W. W. Norton.

Klein, M. (1980). The effect of early anxiety-situations on the sexual development of the boy. In: *Psychoanalysis of Children* (pp. 240–278). London: Hogarth.

Riviere, J. (1929). Womanliness as masquerade. *International Journal of Psychoanalysis, 10*: 303–313.

Winnicott, D. W. (1948). Reparation in respect of mother's organised defence against depression. In: *Collected papers: Through Paediatrics to Psychoanalysis*. The International Psycho-Analytical Library, *100*: 1–325. London: Hogarth. Also in the Institute of Psycho-Analysis (pp. 91–96). (1975).

CHAPTER TWO

Discussion of "Creativity and authenticity" by Irma Brenman Pick

Jordi Sala

I wish to thank Irma Brenman Pick for her dense and thought-provoking work, which deserves to be read and reread slowly and thoughtfully. I shall limit my comments to a few aspects.

A main thesis of Brenman Pick's is that the maternal creative function must form part of the analytic function, and she is interested in exploring the authenticity/inauthenticity of both functions. From the start of the chapter she links authenticity to some kind of acceptance of internal and external reality. She immediately goes on to ask: "how much 'creativity' goes into creating inauthenticity?" (Brenman Pick, this volume), and asserts later that "there is a conflictual struggle between creativity in the service of authenticity and creative inauthenticity" (Brenman Pick, this volume).

Here, however, I wonder whether it is possible to make use of certain creative capacities in the service of a spurious, inauthentic result. I agree that this creative capacity is never entirely pure, as it is born within and out of a mixture of feelings. But I find it difficult to understand that nothing truly creative can ever be born out of inauthenticity.

I consider authenticity to be an essentially intrapsychic matter. We could describe it as a quality of the mental state corresponding to the recognition of one's own psychic reality along with the assumption of one's responsibility with regard to this reality. Therefore, among the necessary ingredients of authenticity we could name sincerity, honesty, the desire to understand the truth of one's emotional state and insight. I shall come back to this point later.

Irma Brenman Pick seems to suggest that an example of inauthentic creativity is that of an omnipotent god who needs no contribution of any kind from anyone else in order to manifest himself. For such a god, no partner is required. Furthermore, the same might apply to the creature within each of us which believes itself to be in possession of the breast. Strictly speaking, we know that we do not need to understand the activity inspired by such a phantasy as a genuinely creative activity, but rather as a hallucinatory one.

Brenman Pick writes that she cannot conceive of the maternal functions as an omnipotent act carried out by a mother who, in possession of all creativity, is sufficient unto herself. She understands these functions as an activity that transforms the communications of the baby, which is possible due to the fact that in the mind of the mother there is also the presence of an "other". As she puts it:

> There is more than one link in the task of emotional creativity. There is the link between a mother who takes in how her baby feels and a baby who has an experience of such mother. And crucially there is the link with the internal penis/father who, from the start, bonds with mother's maternal capacity. (Brenman Pick, this volume).

I would like to add one thing here: the "other" (penis-as-link, father) binds but also separates this mother/baby unity in relation to the fusional tendencies of both, which might serve as instruments of idealisation.

Similarly, the analyst needs a "third" party, the presence of an "other", if he is going to be creative in his endeavours not to allow himself to be trapped within the omnipotent idealisations with which the patient, at certain moments, tries to fuse. In his receptive and interpretative function the analyst tries to work within a triangular mental space in which the patient's communications are received and processed creatively (a space created by communications with the patient, the receptive function of the analyst and the reflexive function concerning countertransference). For this reason the analysis of countertransference is so crucially important ("… this walking the tightrope between experiencing disturbance and responding with interpretation that does not convey disturbing anxiety", Brenman Pick, 1985, p. 157). We could say that the "third" participant is the analyst's thinking about the feelings that the patient arouses within him. Needless to say, this activity on the part of the analyst in the session is only possible where there is authenticity, an indispensable ingredient in our analytic activity in which one is willing to engage with the patient's communications and with the impact that these communications continuously have on us. As Brenman Pick (1985) writes, this is a very important matter: the patient explores and becomes aware of to what extent the analyst avoids the issues that disturb him most, or whether, on the contrary, they are courageous enough to face them head-on.

If I follow her conception correctly, there must be a process of identification rather than of appropriation of the creative qualities of the mother for authentic creativity to be present. In her 1995 paper "Concern: spurious or real" she was already pointing out that the manic appropriation of the breast and its functions cannot be viewed in amorous terms ("side by side with the partial achievement of the depressive position there is an early (manic) 'take over' of the breast, in which the infant 'becomes' the breast and shows behaviour which is in part a fake of a very concerned mother …", Brenman Pick, 1995, p. 257). Such appropriation is rather a manifestation of hate, a confused "identification" in which no one knows who is who and who is hurting whom. My view is that in appropriation what is missing (denied) is the third party, the one who binds and separates. In that paper Brenman Pick spoke of a means of facing such situations which we could describe as *triangular*. The patient has to be held with both hands, she says: with one hand to receive their feelings of vulnerability and anxiety, and with the other to show, firmly, how they feel both triumphant and dangerous, and at the same time in a state of desperation, precisely because of these feelings and because of the risk of their falsehood being found out ("they fear too that when the idealisation of a false object is uncovered they will be stripped of their good object", Brenman Pick, 1995, p. 269).

Now I will move on to the clinical illustrations of the magnificent way in which Brenman Pick illustrates these aspects. I will comment only on Mrs Z's case.

In the case of Mrs Z, Brenman Pick offers us a collection of five dreams, all of them brief. I believe that she has no doubt with regard to the elaborative function of dreams and to their contribution to the analytic task in that dreams speak about the mental state of the patient but also about the state of his/her relationship with the analyst. What does this sequence of dreams, taken as sequence, suggest to us?

Let me remind you of something obvious: a real creative maternal relationship implies a mother with a receptive mental state and a small child who is in need of her. In the same way, a creative analytic relationship implies, among other things, the presence of a receptive analyst and a patient in a state of need. In the material presented to us we see, on the one hand, the patient collaborating with the analyst in the production and narration of dreams and associations.

But, let us consider where the *need* is located in this dream sequence. In the first one we learn from the patient's associations, that both the *depressed mother and dependent child* are ignored and forsaken. In the second dream, it is *the mother/analyst who needs* to bond with her daughter/patient, who, for her part appears to be living in a euphoric mental state. In the third dream, in the wake of the images of deprivation that the patient saw on her way to the session, we have a *disturbed creature who reminds her of her own daughter and of deprived aspects of her own self*. In this dream there are parents who face a difficulty, and teachers who try to downplay it. But that is not all: the patient appears to be impressed by this parental function and, besides, denounces the futility of downplaying difficulties. At this point we see that Mrs Z is very close to insight. In the fourth dream, it is not the patient, but once again *a mother in need who is grieving*, who has lost her husband, a mother who is offered a false remedy which brings no real consolation. From Brenman Pick's point of view, there must be something painful about this approach to insight when in the next dream the *lack is once again located in the mother/analyst*.

In fact, insight involves painful acknowledgement. Nevertheless, I believe that despite her defensive manoeuvres, the patient, in her fourth dream, shows that she is closer to understanding what false remedies (melting choc ice) really are, and that the insight has not entirely been lost. In my view, this process could be continuing in the fifth and last dream with the *fear of her falsehood being discovered*, which is now presenting as an appropriation of false breasts which can have no real maternal function.

To sum up, I would say that Brenman Pick, through her way of understanding and working with dreams, has presented the struggle that the patient is undergoing between authenticity and inauthenticity, between, on the one hand, her search for real contact with a depressed object and her need, and, on the other, all the avoidance manoeuvres that she sets in motion, through the "creation" of an inauthentic "as if" self. In the context provided, we gain a strong impression of the creative effort that has gone into the analyst/patient dynamic, an effort that is supported by the analyst's analysis of the transference and countertransference. I think that Brenman Pick will agree with me when I say that insight, the engagement with and acknowledgement of one's own psychic reality is the result of an authentic creative process: within the patient, two parts that have been split off are brought into contact with each other, owing to the work done by both analyst and patient in cooperation with each other. This concrete creative act of insight reveals not only that there had been some kind of destructive mental activity under way, but that there is a task of healing and repair to be engaged with. Without the assumption of this need for reparation insight does not amount to much.

To conclude, and in the hope that I have not diverged too far from the line of argument that Brenman Pick presents in her paper, I would like to raise a few questions:

a. At the end of the chapter Brenman Pick writes that: "the father's role here might be seen as supporting the mother to bear her imperfection, and yet have the robustness to protect and value the knowledge of what is authentically provided ..." What role is assigned to the father as a real figure?
b. Brenman Pick writes that "the creative endeavour appears to have been dedicated to the production of inauthenticity" (Brenman Pick, this volume). How can this be accounted for and can what is not authentic necessarily be destructive?
c. Brenman Pick also states that Western culture devalues what we might call "maternal" roles. Could this devaluation have unconscious roots in the intolerance towards the privileged creative function that a mother has in giving structure to the mind of the baby? We live in a society that is bent on stimulating mania and omnipotence. Could it not be that we might emerge from the current crisis with a positive revaluation of the creative functions of the mother, of what is genuine and authentic and which will enable us better to accept our limitations?

Let me finish with a sentence of Brenman Pick's (this volume) with which I wholeheartedly agree: "I believe that the capacity to do creative work is based in the bringing together of emotion and thought, mother and father, male and female, and good and bad parts of the self."

References

Brenman Pick, I. (1985). Working through in the countertransference. *International Journal of Psychoanalysis, 66*: 157–166.
Brenman Pick, I. (1995). Concern, spurious or real. *International Journal of Psychoanalysis, 76*: 257–270.

CHAPTER THREE

Listening, technique, and all that jazz

Barbie Antonis

Feeling the groove

A year or so back I had a curious experience: The room was still. Everyone seemed very absorbed. It looked as though all attention was on the speaker. The talk continued. I felt free to attend and to drift so that concentration was wonderfully focused and free floating at the same time. When he spoke, the words carried immediate resonance. In fact they were "music to my ears" but why was this so disturbing as well? Why? I felt excited, also mystified and alert, alive. The experience almost bordered on the uncanny. The voice was that of a professor and head of Department of Jazz, Simon Purcell … I knew that … yet the words seemed to be those of a colleague, Michael Parsons, psychoanalyst of the British Psychoanalytical Society speaking about an entirely different subject, an independent theory of clinical technique (Parsons, 2009). Was I imagining things? What was I imagining? I remained poised in this state of unknowing until I realised the very surprising and then even delightful concordance/coincidence of these two internal experiences. They had come together. They were different and similar both at once.

What Simon Purcell was saying was something like this: There is great value, importance, in suspending premature judgement; in the listening you will be able to appreciate the gaps, the silences, the pauses, the groove is what you can feel and become attuned to. Allow for the complexity of the voices from the different instruments, their different tones, and naturally there is the impact of tempo. Sometimes it is the voice and lyrics that carry the strong power of the music. These are some elements that are relevant to the jazz idiom. He added:

> You'll gain much from not rushing to know the piece. You really have to let yourself be with it, so that for a moment or more you're not sure if it's *in* you or outside. But between the inside and the outside there's the emotion and you feel it in the body. (Purcell, personal communication)

Since this experience I have tried to understand what was at work in my internal linkage, my helpful confusion with its personally important resonances. Perhaps this was an instance, with some variation, of what Ogden (1998) calls the "oversound" when voices—here a jazz pianist and educator, and my own imagined creation (of Michael Parsons), arrived and joined, at the same time, offering a "third position"—that of "the music to my ears"—which concerned the overlap of independent psychoanalytic technique with jazz.

Intro(duction) to the melody

I use the above account to open questions which are pertinent to this book's theme: creativity, authenticity, imagination, play. What is it to say that someone or something is authentic? A dictionary definition will do up to a point. Would truth or genuineness do? Would we all agree about the test for authenticity? Is this a quality that as psychoanalysts we think we would know in others? As the field of creativity is so vast I will be necessarily selective and aim to speak to my own response to the title, "Women and creativity", to consider an aspect of imagination, which is particular and personal to me.

It struck me, in wondering where to begin in writing, that my dilemma and uncertainty mirror the nature of my topic. If we think of an instrument vibrating, several strings at once, this may help to express how important it is to tolerate and hold the tension between thoughts and ideas, without necessarily resolving it prematurely. I want to describe this as the experience of *becoming aware of listening and attention*: what to attend to, what to listen to, how to speak authentically or even what to speak to and with what voice.

"Individuality of voice"

My enquiry here is about the development of one's identity as a psychoanalyst and how this, the analyst's authentic voice, becomes her own and is facilitated. One might say this differently as "finding one's own voice as a psychoanalyst". The questions that interest me are to do with what fosters the imagination and creativity in this identity, and as a corollary, should training organisations be alert to what might suppress or interfere with this potential and therefore inhibit the expression of authenticity, and dull creativity? (Antonis, 2002, 2004). My colleague, Christopher Bollas (2007) holds that these qualities, authenticity, imagination, and creativity are intrinsic to the personality; an innate "personal idiom" of the individual, not susceptible to nurturing or facilitation beyond infancy and childhood. This is not my position but it is clearly a question open to speculation and debate.

Just as each of us has a distinctive voice and characteristic tone that is recognisibly our own, it is important to ask what promotes its expression? As Ogden (1998) reminds us "individuality of voice is not a given; it is an *achievement*. Uniqueness of voice might be thought of as an individual shape created in the medium of the use of language" (Ogden, 1998, p. 444, italics added).

As a singer my aim might be to develop my personal instrument—my voice—through training, to convey individuality; a personal style over and above the basic capacities of accurate pitch, musicality, emotional expression and communication and, of course knowing the song in its original form. After all, it is taken as given that jazz vocalists always listen to the original written melody and lyrics before playing with any improvisations of their own. This is to "make the song their own". The alternative would be mere imitation, clone-like and devoid of any personal creativity.

In music as in psychoanalytic experience, joy and sorrow exist simultaneously and therefore can allow us to feel a sense of harmony. Even when music is linear there are always opposing elements that co-exist, occasionally even in conflict with each other. Music accepts "comments" from one voice to the other at all times and tolerates subversive accompaniments as a necessary antipode to leading voices. So conflict, denial and commitment can co-exist at all times in music.

In his writings on art, creativity, and music, Anton Ehrenzweig, friend and colleague of the psychoanalyst, Marion Milner, draws on a term expressed by the artist, Paul Klee. This refers to the kind of unconscious multidimensional scanning, also named *"polyphonic"*, which exists both in the visual arts and also in music. This "full emptiness" of unconscious scanning occurs in many examples of creative work. Ehrenzweig says:

> Polyphonic hearing [also] overcomes the conscious division between figure and ground. In music the figure is represented by the melody standing out against an indistinct ground of the harmonic accompaniment. Musicians are loath to call the polyphonic strands of a well-constructed harmonic progression a mere accompaniment. Often the accompanying voices form *parallel* melodic phrases expressive in themselves. (Ehrenzweig, 1967, p. 25, italics added)

And Itamar Levi, psychoanalyst and artist, acknowledging a debt to Ehrenzweig, writes:

> Analytic listening, although dependent on passively letting go, is also actively searching for moments of intense emotions, or of suppressed ones, for messages sent from the body, for the pulse of life, transmitted in the realm of sound. (Levi, 2003, p. 2)

It may be helpful if I now present the ideas I have formulated.

"Polyphonic listening"

The hypothesis I want to explore is this: By encouraging/giving permission for polyphonic listening (Ehrenzweig/Levi) the analyst/ candidate can become aware of her listening to herself in a *new* way, and in relation to how the patient hears her and what the patient communicates. Secondly, in the facilitation of this way of listening the candidate/analyst can begin to *trust* her own voice and listen in a more open and creative way.

In drawing out this descriptive formulation in the process of psychoanalytic work I am referring to the capacities and experience not just of listening and attention, but *hearing, voicing, imagining, discovering, uncovering, learning.* And *becoming.* My sources in scanning the territory of development, learning, listening and voicing come from a psycho-analytic perspective, infused with a love of singing jazz.

Towards the end of their personal and thoughtful account of the process of analytic development, "On becoming a psychoanalyst", Gabbard and Ogden write:

> … maturation as an analyst involves increasingly allowing our-selves to be caught up in the moment (in the unconscious of the analysis) and carried by the music of the session. Analysis is not an experience that can be mapped out and planned. Events happen between two people in a room together, and the meaning of those events are discussed and understood. Analysts learn more about who they are by participating in the "dance" of the moment. The extent to which the analysis is "alive" may depend on the analyst's *willingness and ability to improvise, and to be improvised by*, the uncon-scious of the analytic relationship. (Gabbard & Ogden, 2009, p. 323, italics added)

I find the phrases "caught up in the moment", "carried by the music", "participating in the dance" and "ability to improvise and to be impro-vised by" especially resonant. Yes, my "ear" was "caught" and my vocalist's sense of key, tone and phrasing aroused. But *where* is the music and how is it to be perceived, and felt and recorded?

The "sonorous bath"

The "realm of sound" (Levi, 2003, p. x) sounds boundaryless. Indeed, Lecourt (1990) describes the musical envelope, which she names the "sonorous bath", as having certain principal qualities including the absence of boundaries in space, the lack of concereteness and omnipres-ent simultaneity. Sonic experience, while pervasive and affecting, has dimensions which are difficult to "pin down", almost elusive. The new-born's first cry starts up the relationship between internal and external that characterises all sonic vocal productions. As Lecourt recognises, the mother's voice, identified very early in development (even before birth), qualities of vocalisation and the pattern of sonorous exchanges, come to *organise* relational spaces in a differentiated, zoned, sonorous "bath".

An emphasis on both emotionality and fullness is also expressed in Meltzer's (1986) concept of the "theatre of the mouth", used to describe the "baby's lalling or babbling", as he plays with the effects of placing the tongue in the mouth, to recreate some of the pleasures of the relationship with the breast while producing sounds. The lalling, suggests Urwin (2002), provides both continuity of emotional experience rather than discontinuity and the substitutability which symbol formation requires, here across modalities, through touch to taste to sound in space.

Background accompaniment

In our 2008 paper for the second edition of *Female Experience*, (Raphael-Leff & Perelberg), Elizabeth Wolf and I looked at the writing of some women psychoanalysts of the independent tradition and found innovations in their contributions that brought developments in technique and to the understanding of the emergence of a sense of self and identity. Independent clinical technique is as much at the centre of my concern as is the related issue of the analyst's authentic voice and I am interested in how these might articulate with and creatively influence each other.

Ella Sharpe, Marion Milner, and Enid Balint all furthered the understanding of the development of a *creative* sense of self and *authentic* aliveness.

Drawing on her love of literature, especially teaching Shakespeare, Ella Sharpe (1875–1947) brought to her psychoanalytic training and subsequent teaching and supervising of candidates in the British Society during the 1930s until her death in 1947 a deep awareness of the qualities of poetic diction, metaphor, and meter. She seemed to underline the value of listening for sounds, pauses, and volume in her guidelines to students. Writing on the clinical technique of psychoanalysis, her attention was so often directed to the importance of the patient's *"tempo"* and curiosity. She is credited with the idea that *the unknown is implicit in the known*. Finally, Sharpe was not just interested in dreams and their interpretation but also with the experience of dreaming and its impact on the dreamer (Whelan, 2000).

To dream, to remember, to become alive to previously disavowed unbearable experience form themes in Enid Balint's 1987 paper. She stresses the critical importance of a mother's role "to recognise her infant, make him feel he belongs … so that he can find a place in which to exist in this world" (Mitchell & Parsons, 1993, p. 97) This mother would then be "truly present" and provide the context for the emergence of the child's "imaginative perception" of reality which forms the very source of creative life. Enid Balint was also explicit about matters of clinical technique, writing both of her awareness of each analyst having "a special identity of one's own" and the importance to foster the patient's retrieval of infantile perceptions by being "quiet and not intrusive, but also absolutely there … what matters is for the analyst simply to go on breathing" (Mitchell & Parsons, 1993, p. 102)—being observant, attuned and alive to the different levels of listening that the analytic process creates.

I mentioned Marion Milner earlier, briefly, when referring to Ehrenzweig and polyphonic listening. Milner, a psychoanalyst with unusual artistic sensitivity as acknowledged by so many contemporary psychoanalysts (Bollas, 2007; Caldwell, 2007; Cohen, 2010; Kennedy, 2007; Parsons, 2000, 2005, 2009) was a creative artist in her own right. She contributed significantly to the understanding of artistic creativity and opened ways of seeing and discovering analytic creativity too. Milner wrote about her own curiosity and imaginative process as an ongoing active "scanning" oscillating between the "diffused wide stare" which she said made "the world seem most intensely real and significant" (Milner, 1956, p. 195) and the more surface, narrow form of attention. What Milner made so clear in her clinical technique was the importance of her availability to the patient "to discover his own way of using her" (Parsons, 2009, p. 232).

What seems striking to me is the parallel between Milner's creative awareness of this developmental necessity, the basis for an infant's discovery "of the malleable boundaries between what is and what is not itself" (Cohen, 2010) and the process of finding an analytically authentic voice, suggesting useful implications for analytic teaching and training. There is also evident resonance with Gabbard and Ogden's (2009) notion of "being improvised" by and within the analytic encounter. I suggest these links could be further elaborated and described as "playing *with* the object" and "playing *the* object".

The "analytic third"

The symphony of psychoanalytic song offered by Ogden provides further accompaniment for this excursion through the verse with its "melody" and towards the "bridge"—a jazz concept I shall explain later. His many papers speak so appositely and closely to this theme of listening, voicing, and the emergence of reverie, an experience he describes as "being at the frontier of dreaming" (Ogden, 2001, p. 7). He draws on the musical dynamics of acoustic experience, opening the reader to the possibility and relevance of the sonic dimension in the psychoanalytic process and beyond. Blake's (2010) concept of the primacy of the ear is intimately approached. Ogden writes that:

> in an analytic setting, analyst and analysand together generate conditions in which each speaks with a voice arising from the unconscious conjunction of the two individuals. The voice of the analyst and the voice of the analysand under these circumstances are not the same voice, but the two voices are spoken, to a significant degree, from a common area of jointly (but asymmetrically) constructed unconscious experience. I have spoken of this intersubjective experience generated by the unconscious interplay of analyst and analysand as the analytic third. (Ogden, 1998, p. 444)

What I hear from Ogden is how he privileges the unconscious communication between analyst and analysand and articulates the generation, within the intersubjective matrix, of the analytic third, a creation that is new, ushering in the potential for the creative in both analyst and analysand. This develops on the basis of a keen attention to deep listening, listening that involves "listening to listening" (Faimberg, 1995, p. 667). It is this quality of listening, which is not just a given but requires development over time, that seems to me to be one of the significant features of psychoanalytic technique in the independent tradition which can potentiate the creativity within the psychoanalytic process.

Improvisation and dialogue in jazz

There is a small literature in which the link between jazz and psychoanalysis is discussed. These papers, of an applied psychoanalytic approach, tend to concentrate on the motivation of jazz musicians and the possible latent meaning to some very well-known and loved jazz compositions.

There is an even smaller number of papers which address and compare the experience of jazz with that of the analytic process. Of note, Lichtenstein (1993) develops a valuable comparison between free association and jazz improvisation in his paper, "The rhetoric of improvisation: Spontaneous discourse in jazz and psychoanalysis". His rich and stimulating contribution identifies a quality of jazz which has a bearing on both creative discovery as described by Sharpe, Milner, and Bollas while also implying technique similar to that within the independent tradition. Lichtenstein notes:

> there is an implicit musical structure behind all improvisation that functions analogously to psychic structure, setting both possibilities and limits. It includes the chord progression of the song, its rhythmic design, and its melodic nuances. But one can never say all of what it contains because in improvisation the musician finds something new, new possibilities that seem to emerge from the given structure. (Lichtenstein, 1993, p. 231)

The space must be present during an improvisation—space for surprise—for the arrival of the unexpected within the safety of both the psychoanalytic and the musical frame.

Knoblauch (2000), in "The musical edge of therapeutic dialogue", also considers that there is music in therapy and that the musical rhythms, tones, tempo, volume, gestures, and accent present in the patient's verbalisations communicate emerging meanings and desires. Moreover, he asserts that the analyst needs to immerse himself together with his patient in a shared dyadic musical performance (Knoblauch, 2000). This, he says, will facilitate the emergence, in the analysand, of unformulated experiences and establish mutual regulation between analyst and patient. He terms this listening technique a "resonant minding model".

The bridge

In a jazz standard the bridge can herald change. A very different tune, a melody change, part of the song may be in a new key, and certainly, the tempo often varies. The bridge in music is an apparent digression that attacks the theme from another angle, presenting it in a new light, often altering the mood drastically!

Returning to psychoanalysis I want to introduce the setting where focus on the capacities for listening, hearing, watching, feeling, not-feeling, thinking, absorbing, discovering and learning have a central possibility in psychoanalytic training. I refer here to a long-standing British Psychoanalytical Society focus on infant observation which provides candidates with a valuable potential space for experiencing the full complexity of the intra and interpersonal sound system, a place and space where the acoustic envelope/bath is multidimensional, dymamic, expanding and contracting like a muscle. The "orchestration" can be very sophisticated and it can be simple. Tuning into the sound system is not necessarily easy or comfortable and may stimulate the need for "ear training" to find a path into the keys, major, minor, natural or diminshed that characterise the experience.

In the British Psychoanalytical Society this experience involves the candidate finding an "observation family" while the mother-to-be is pregnant, and arranging to visit weekly to observe once the baby is born—a process which continues until the baby is a year old. There is widespread appreciation for the opportunity it affords candidates to learn about their own emotional reactions and responses to the "primitive", preverbal emotional development of infants and how this introduces the experience of countertransference as something to be encountered, borne and thought about in the safety of the seminar (Parsons, 2003).

Sternberg, a consultant clinician working with both adults and children, has produced detailed research which offers a comprehensive overview of the history, place, structure and value of infant observation in "At the heart of psychoanalytic training" (2005). It illuminates the growth of the specific skills needed to become a psychoanalytic psychotherapist. Interestingly, amongst her chapters Sternberg raises musical metaphors, writing of the therapist's instrument, the movement from this to melody and invites the reader to "feel the music". These poetic musical references are developed within an overarching and impassioned belief in the importance of the infant observation as a component of psychoanalytic training.

My own experience teaching this component certainly echoes and concurs with Sternberg's view. However there is, I think, an aspect that deserves further attention. I refer here to a movement beyond the privileging of the visual mode that is inherent in the description "naturalistic infant observation". I argue that auditory, aural, vocal, sonic dimensions play a significant part in the affective experience of both observer and observed alike. Infant observation heralds the candidate becoming a "feeling listener" and inaugaurates the process and art of psychoanalytic listening.

I will bring some observation material from one of the candidates to demonstrate the emergence of a "sonic motif" of sound, size, voice, and volume.

Baby Robert

Eight weeks, at home with mother and toddler sister Lily.

> Only a few minutes after his mother had left Robert began to stir. His face started to become red and he pursed his lower lip. This gave the impression of dismay. He started to writhe with his body and started to cry. This cry had a different quality from the last time I had heard him cry. I even felt his voice had changed from the coughing quality I had heard the last time to a more bell-like clear sound. There was also a different emotional quality. This was hard to describe, as if there was misery. But maybe there was also more of a sense that he listened to his own voice rather than it just coming out of him … Christina came into his room. She stroked him now very gently and made little humming noises. Robert made a farting noise. Christina said: Oh, is it a "wind"?. Are you pushing something out?

Robert nine weeks at home with father, Peter

Robert had not settled but had continued crying in an intermittent way. At one point Peter looked at him face to face holding him a bit further away as if he wanted to study what was going on or as if he wanted to communicate with him. Robert took his left hand and put it to his father's mouth several times. He then aimed with his hand at his own mouth and put four fingers in. Peter said: That's what he tries to do now. He desperately tries to find his thumb. He tried to help him to put just one finger in but Robert went back to putting nearly the whole hand. He also continued to cry.

Sometimes it sounded as if his voice could not find the place to produce a proper sound and it came out as air pressing through the mouth, sometimes he produced a clear sound of crying. He continued to put his fist into his mouth.

Robert, nearly fourteen weeks

Christina spoke to me pretty much continuously. At the same time Robert was in a dialogue without words with me, continuously changing expressions and movements as if telling a story as well. I was looking from one to the other and at times it was hard to follow both. However, I noticed how similar they were in their communication. They appeared so eager to be engaged and this had a friendly lively feel but made it hard to focus.

Commentary

From the beginning of her observation the candidate had felt welcomed by the family, as if there was enough emotional space between the couple to create a place for the new baby son and curiosity about whom he would become without undue anxieties about being observed or judged. The birth had been very quick and untroubled in ways that the parents had anticipated.

We had already, from the previous weeks' notes, found ourselves aware of listening to the rhythm of each parent's conversation with the baby and how each had by this time identified his internal "wind" as sometimes causing him discomfort. We may say that it had become a feature of sound in his personal sonic envelope. It also began to create in the student's mind a "motif" that she found herself wanting to trace "like a melody line in a song". This idea, taking shape as the weeks passed, also linked an internal process/cavity with an external element of weather, which could be powerful or calm and of course in-between. The candidate was becoming very thoughtful about actual voice qualities as much as the content of verbal communications and who said what to whom. Yet sometimes also found herself "in a bubble with the baby" as if cut off from all sound, or even feeling in a "bell-jar", just breathing with the baby in his pattern and rhythm.

The word "tone" is able to indicate a quality of voice as well as that of muscular body strength and appearance. Foreground music and noise, background sounds, from far away worlds sometimes competed for space in the soundscape. Thoughts about movement into sound and out of sound emerged in the candidate's accounts linked with feelings about closeness and distance in relationships together with images of emotional warmth, attachment, expressions of love and expressions of pain.

And on occasions the seminar discussions brought associations and images to mind rather like weaving thoughts around a dream, sometimes with musical accompaniment such as a nursery rhyme or snippets of song, enveloping all members in the group in a mutual gaze.

Coda

With permission from those in the infant observation seminar, I have included some observation material here which I hope has illustrated and conveyed something of the quality of imaginative perception, polyphonic listening, experienced within the acoustic "bath" enveloping infant and immediate caregivers as well as at times the observer.

The abrupt bridge in music is an apparent digression that attacks the theme from another angle, presenting it in a new light, often altering the mood drastically!

I too have found myself experiencing and building this bridge. There is no "control" with which to compare these fragments of observational material, these passages of everyday experience. Nor is it possible to say that the written accounts of these observation experiences directly echo the ideas of Ehrenzweig, Lecourt, Ogden, and the contributions of independent psychoanalysts on clinical technique. Yet, if the nature of the sonic dimension of listening experiences have in some measure been opened, generating a different and increased awareness of the nuances of emotional contact for the candidates, within themselves as well as with and between others, then there may be value in playing with musical metaphors, opening the musical horizon and even singing the blues.

My contribution is to suggest that the jazz groove and idiom has a close parallel to independent clinical technique. This analogy may encourage a particular kind of listening and this, in the context of the training experience of infant observation, can facilitate the development in the candidate of a creative authenticity, a gradual finding of one's own voice, in psychoanalytic identity.

Notes

I want to thank my infant observation seminar group, Esra Caglar and Anna Streeruwitz for their lively, creative, and imaginative work and generous permission to use their observation excerpts.

Itamar Levi brought polyphonic listening to my attention, providing a new way of thinking about sound.

My gratitude extends to Joan Raphael-Leff who provided her intelligence, creativity, and generosity to bring this chapter to life.

References

Antonis, B. (2002). Not his master's voice. In J. Raphael-Leff (Ed.), *Between Sessions and Beyond the Couch* (pp. 211–212). Colchester: University of Essex.

Antonis, B. (2004). Finding a voice of one's own. Paper presented at the 6th Cambridge Convention of the Independent Psychoanalysts.

Antonis, B., & Wolf, E. (2008). Affect and body. The contributions of independent women psychoanalysts. In: J. Raphael-Leff & R. Josef Perelberg (Eds.), *Female Experience: Four Generations of British Women Psychoanalysts on Work with Women* (pp. 316–329). London: The Anna Freud Centre.

Balint, E. (1993). *Before I was I: Psychoanalysis and the imagination. Collected papers of Enid Balint.* J. Mitchell & M. Parsons. (Eds.). London: Free Associations Books.

Blake, R. (2010). *Primacy of the Ear: Listening, Memory and Development of Musical Style.* Boston: Third Stream Associates.

Bollas, C. (2007). A theory for the true self. In: L. Caldwell (Ed.), *Winnicott and the Psychoanalytic Tradition* (pp. 8–23). London: Karnac.

Caldwell, L. (2007). *Winnicott and the Psychoanalytic Tradition.* London: Karnac.

Cohen, J. (2010). Turning to stone: Creativity and silence in psychoanalysis and art. *Bulletin of the British Psychoanalytical Society.* October, Confidential material.

Ehrenzweig, E. (1967). *The Hidden Order of Art.* London: University of California Press.

Faimberg, H. (1996). Listening to listening. *International Journal Psycho-Analysis, 77*: 667–677.

Gabbard, G. O., & Ogden, T. H. (2009). On becoming a psychoanalyst. *International Journal of Psychoanalysis, 90*: 311–327.

Joyce, A. (2011). *Infant Observation Guidelines for Candidates of the Institute of Psychoanalysis*. Curriculum Committee. British Psychoanalytical Society.

Kennedy, R. (2007). *The Many Voices of Psychoanalysis*. Hove: Routledge.

Knoblauch, S. (1997). Beyond the word in psychoanalysis: the unspoken dialogue. *Psychoanalytic Dialogues, 7*: 491–516.

Knoblauch, S. (2000). *The Musical Edge of the Therapeutic Dialogue*. Hillsdale, NJ: Analytic Press.

Lecourt, E. (1990). The musical envelope. In: D. Anzieu (Ed.), *Psychic Envelopes* (pp. 211–235). London: Karnac.

Levi, I. (2003). Polyphonic Listening. Paper presented at the 5th Cambridge Convention of the Independent Psychoanalysts.

Lichtenstein, D. (1993). The rhetoric of improvisation: Spontaneous siscourse in jazz and psychoanalysis. *American Imago, 50*: 22–252.

Meltzer, D. (1986). *Studies in Extended Metapsychology*. Strath Tay, Perthshire: Clunie Press.

Milner, M. (1952). The role of illusion in symbol formation. In: *The Suppressed Madness of Sane Men: Forty Four years of Exploring Psychoanalysis* (pp. 83–113). London: Tavistock Publications. (Originally published as Aspects of symbolism in comprehension of the not self. *International Journal of Psychoanalysis, 33*: 181–195).

Milner, M. (1956). Psychoanalysis and art. In: *The Suppressed Madness of Sane Men: Forty Four years of Exploring Psychoanalysis* (pp. 192–215). London: Tavistock Publications.

Ogden, T. H. (1998). A question of voice. *Psychoanalytic Quarterly, 67*: 426–448.

Ogden, T. H. (1999). "The music of what happens" in poetry and psychoanalysis. *International Journal of Psychoanalysis, 80*: 979–994.

Ogden, T. H. (2001). Conversations at the Frontier of Dreaming. *Fort Da. 7*: 7–14.

Parsons, M. (2000). *The Dove that Returns, the Dove that Vanishes: Paradox and Creativity in Psychoanalysis*. London: Routledge.

Parsons, M. (2003). The significance of mother–infant observation for a better understanding of our patients. Paper presented at the BAP Trainees conference, May, 2003.

Parsons, M. (2005). Psychoanalysis, art, listening, looking, outwards, inwards. *Bulletin of the British Psychoanalytical Society*.

Parsons, M. (2007). Raiding the inarticulate: The internal analytic setting and listening beyond countertransference. *International Journal of Psychoanalysis, 88*: 1441–1456.

Parsons, M. (2009). An independent theory of clinical technique. *Psychoanalytic Dialogues, 19*: 221–236.

Sharpe, E. (1937). *Dream Analysis*. Exeter: Hogarth Press. Reprinted, (1988). London: Karnac.

Sharpe, E. (1943). Memorandum on her technique. In: P. King & R. Steiner (Eds.), *The Freud–Klein Controversies 1941–1945* (pp. 639–647). London: Routledge. (1991).

Stern, D. (1985). *The Interpersonal World of the Infant*. New York: Basic Books.

Sternberg, J. (2005). *Infant Observation at the Heart of Training*. London: Karnac.

Urwin, C. (2002). A Psychoanalytic Approach to Language Delay: When Autistic Isn't Necessarily Autism ... *Journal of Child Psychotherapy, 28*: 73–93.

Whelan, M. (2000). *Mistress of her Own Thoughts: Ella Freeman Sharpe and the Practice of Psychoanalysis*. London: Rebus Press.

Winnicott, D. W. (1960). Ego distortion in terms of true and false self. In: *The Maturational Processes and the Facilitating Environment*. London: Hogarth and Institute of Psycho-analysis (1965) (pp. 140–152).

CHAPTER FOUR

William, did you say, "*Much Ado about Nothing*"?

Juan Eduardo Tesone

A natomy is no longer destiny and sexual identities do not depend on any aesthetic. The notion of gender has de-reified the biological and, after a long period of gender binarism, *queer* theory questions it and postulates multiplicity beyond the dichotomy of genders. The intersexuality and intergender that plead against binarism and in favour of flexible sexuality not assigned from birth question psychoanalysis and create a need for us to deconstruct and reformulate several of our paradigms. In psychoanalysis it is nearly impossible to speak of a woman or a man, not only because we need to use the plural but most of all because it is impossible to consider it from a-historical or a-cultural perspectives. No naturalistic essentialism of woman or man is able to transcend the symbolic construction of its era.

Therefore, speaking about "women and creativity" is a challenge that is difficult to face in terms of psychoanalysis. I will therefore allow myself a detour, something like a tangential look; we know that a frontal gaze may "meduse" more than one of us, and looking back may turn us into a statue of salt.

It is well-known that the anatomic difference between the sexes initially poses questions for girls and boys ... and probably all adults for the rest of their lives. The drive to know or epistemophilia is rooted in this questioning. In his phallo-centric theory, Freud postulates the boy's fear of castration and penis envy in the girl as prototypes of the decline of the Oedipus complex. The girl thinks at first that it will grow and, disillusioned because her mother did not give it to her, she turns toward her father without better results. She finally leaves behind her Oedipus by the penis-child equation. Obviously, we remain in the dark regarding the fate of women who have not had at least one child and do not know whether those who have had more than one have resolved their Oedipus faster or whether they have had several children because they were unable to resolve it ... Freud considers only one libido that is essentially masculine. Although there is no difference between the sexes in the unconscious and in this sense human sexuality could never be complementary.

Little is said of the boy's envy of the girl, although several eminent authors have described something that those of us who have a clinical practice with children have been able to confirm, which is boys' envy of girls. Boys want to have breasts or to get pregnant, adhering later to the cloaca theory. As Lucile Durrmeyer (1999) points out, this envy is joined by another that boys may have: envy of the "ideal penis", meaning one that could always be erect (the Roman fascinus) or even make it longer, as so well described in Louis Pergaud's *Guerre des Boutons* (War of the Buttons) in which the boys compete with each other to see who can piss furthest. In recent years, multiple spam emails arrive via the internet promising their potential and unwitting clients the sexual panacea of lengthening their penis.

We could also mention men's envy of women's capacity for sexual pleasure as revealed by Tiresias, the memorable blind man who had been a woman before being a man and attributed nine parts of pleasure in ten to women and only one to men. (Tesone, 2006).

Jessica Benjamin (1995) postulates an "over-inclusive" conception of the genders: the girl or boy wishes to be and have everything, in a narcissistic omnipotence that no adult abandons completely.

Freud underscored the double possibilities of identification in every individual, from which psychic bisexuality results. Much was said about gender identity as if it were something stable, attained once and for all, whereas it seems to me that a precipitate of both genders often remains which removes it far from the fixedness of an immobile identity, thereby allowing subjectivisation that is much richer in complexity and movements inside the psyche. The contemporary ego is a fragmented and many-faceted ego, an experience unrelated to psychotic fragmentation but rather to different facets of the ego. The literary production of Pessoa and his multiple heteronyms that converse with each other, have diverse styles, fight over literary issues and even have different dates and places of birth is a good example of this potential richness that made Pessoa the greatest Portuguese poet of our time.

What is the impact of the anatomical difference between the sexes on human beings from the fantasmatic and symbolic perspective? Much has been said and much has been negated. Some theories function as veils and thereby acquire value as fetishes.

When Shakespeare wrote his play, *Much Ado about Nothing* in 1600, in the form of a comedy, a Renaissance conception of women was placed in tension. His text distills subtle irony regarding prejudices about women and men in his time. On the lips of Beatrice he sets incisive and provocative dialogue in a duel between equals with Benedick, unusual for his era; they mutually deny love but finally become spouses. Through Hero, the daughter of Leonato, all of men's fears concerning women's infidelity appear, as well as the seal of disapproval reserved for women if they are not virgins when they marry. We may assume that this play is a satire on the condition of women and that it was not worth making such "ado" about Hero's allegedly missing virginity or her false infidelity. However, "nothing" in Elizabethan slang means vagina. Therefore, "nothing" was intended to mean that women had nothing (no-thing) between their legs. I would like to discuss this term *nothing* in greater detail.

The slip from the penis to the phallus proposed by Lacan (this concept is complex and requires further development) enabled at least a desacralisation of anatomy, but still positions both genders in relation to the phallic order. "The male position is ruled by having and the feminine position is based on lack in being. For men it is a question of having the phallus in order to be in a position to give it, and for women not to have it in order to be able to desire it" (Chaboudez, 1994, p. 27). Tension is produced between being and having, but the order still turns upon the phallus, the only symbol of desire for both sexes, although Lacan also spoke of gender, departing from biological binarism, when in his famous formulation about sexuation Lacan (1972–1973, p. 67) he spoke about the feminine position and the masculine position. He cites the mystics to exemplify it: Saint John of the Cross occupying a feminine position in his poems. However, he does not discard binarism, although he does drop the idea of complementarity between the sexes. Leticia Glocer (Glocer-Fiorini, 2001) proposes understanding the feminine position with the help of Edgar Morin's notion of complex thought, which consists in considering two propositions recognised as being true but that seem to exclude each other mutually as two faces of a complex truth in a relation of interdependence. This author reminds us that since the origins of psychoanalysis the feminine has appeared to be an obstacle to any hope of coherence and integration of the theory. In this point of view, Freud's dark continent would be an expression of the unexplored and the enigmatic, but also of complexity exceeding the phallic register.

In relation to the phallic order, is there nothing in the sense of a void … or does nothing acquire existence? The invisibility of female sex organs has often been compared to nothing, to negativity, to the point that debates about whether girls had a notion of the existence of their vagina before or after puberty were interminable. A famous controversy was raised by Karen Horney (1967) in 1926 when she questioned Freud's hypothesis: unlike him, she stated that this alleged ignorance of the vagina was a product of repression.

Before continuing with this representation of the female sex, I will take a detour through the notion of nothing in Heidegger. What is nothing? asks the philosopher in his text, *What is Metaphysics?* (Heidegger, 2000). Any metaphysical question, he explains, may only be formulated in such a way "that the person who asks—as such—is also included in the question, that is to say, is also questioned in it." (Heidegger, 2000, p. 94). Why does Heidegger ask about nothing? Precisely because science rejects nothing and discards it because it is nothing. For science, nothing is nothing more than a reason for horror and a phantasmagoria, he deduces. Boys and girls behave just the same way, as if they were investigators perturbed by their object of study. If thinking is always thinking about something, then thinking about nothing would essentially be a logical contradiction. "Would there only be nothing because there is a no? Does nothingness represent the no and negativity and therefore negation? Or is it the other way around? Is there negation and the no because there is nothing?" (Heidegger, 2000, p. 95). A methodological inversion that subverts reasoning and thinking about nothingness and negation. However, if "come what may, nothingness must be questioned, then previously it has to have been given." (Heidegger,

2000, p. 95). In French, nothingness is "le néant", which is to say "non-entity". In consequence, if nothingness is not considered, we could only believe in the existence of the entity. When we leave behind the existence of entity and come close to the nothingness that is non-entity, this generates anxiety: "Anxiety reveals nothingness," states Heidegger (Heidegger, 2000, p. 3). Anxiety "leaves us without words." Since entity completely escapes us, this would be the way nothingness questions us. In the face of nothingness, "all pretense of saying that something 'is' falls silent" (Heidegger, 2000, p. 104).

The German philosopher maintains that nothingness does not attract but due to its essence repels. How can we help thinking about the boy's reaction, but also the girl's, to castration anxiety when they confront the invisibility of the female sex? "Dasein" (being there) means being immersed in nothingness. Without the originary manifest quality of nothingness, there would be no being-oneself or any freedom at all. In this sense, "nothingness is not the concept opposite to entity but pertains originarily to being itself" (Heidegger, 2000, p. 106). For psychoanalysis, it is not a matter of indifference to follow the development of his thought when he states that nothingness is the origin of negation and not vice versa. However, negation is not the only component of entity's desisting supremacy; bitterness is also produced "in deprivation and in renouncement" (Heidegger, 2000, p. 107). Paraphrasing Jessica Benjamin, we would say that giving up the narcissism of being and having everything is not a simple thing for human beings or something that can be entirely resolved.

Originary anxiety, related to nothingness, as Heidegger states, may awaken at any moment in the Dasein. He quotes Hegel when he thinks that pure being and pure nothingness are the same, that is to say, being and nothingness mutually pertain to each other.

Therefore, we propose that the discovery of the difference between the sexes involves including nothingness in the two sexes as a logical necessity. Historically, male bias pushed nothingness into the female sex with the facilitation of the non-visibility of the woman's sex, folded inward. The female sex came to represent nothingness as a projection of masculine cultural dominance that was too preoccupied with projecting into women lack, emptiness, nothingness and the negative of "having" the phallus venerated by all cultures as a symbol of fertility. Plutarch (cited by Quignard, 1994, p. 98) writes that the ithyphallic amulet attracts the gaze of the fascinated. Hence, the incredible arsenal of amulets, burlesque dwarves, in gold, ivory, stone, bronze, all in priapic form, essential in archeological explorations.

Mariam Alizade (1992) praises nothingness and emphasises nothingness in women, both in their biological dimension and in the fantasms based on this biology. She states that "the concept of nothingness in psychoanalysis is on the opposite side of the street from the phallus" (Alizade, 1992, p. 27). Her position is close to Heidegger's, given that he maintains that this is "a nothingness that has a name. There is positivity and participation in nothingness. Nothingness exists. The second way to consider nothingness places it beside the impossible, the unnameable, the unrepresentable and the unthinkable" (Alizade, 1992 p. 32).

However, for Alizade, this nothingness is a productive and fertile nothingness, even though the human subject tries to avoid the "encounter or contact with these effects of nothingness by means of excessive discrimination, fixedness of oppositions and certainty of concepts" (Alizade, 1992, p. 45). In reality, it is nothingness that insists and finds the subject, evoking the archaic, the uncanny and the demonic, leaving an invisible and mute trail. She adds the "nothingic" order to the phallic order. It is characterised primarily by the installation of knowledge of lack, knowledge supported beyond anxiety. This order constantly touches on the real where the psychic uproar of the phallic is. All phallic power allows avoidance of confrontation with lack and finitude. It is on the woman's body that the horror of the truth materialises, "the *horror feminae*, designated an enigma" (Alizade, 1992, p. 56). Both mystery and death are condensed on the woman's body. Having the phallus facilitates projection of the representation of absence. As extreme solutions to the anxiety aroused by nothingness, the fetish object sutures the place of lack and erotomania fills lack with certainty of the object's love. When disavowal seizes the throne, the pleasure ego disavows the traumatising perception. In this sense, phallic value acquires the power of reassurance to ward off anxiety of lack in both sexes.

Behind the phallic order lies hidden a narcissistic omnipotence that would conceal "a deeper, subjacent and silent order" (Alizade, 1992, p. 65) where Eros and Thanatos are intimately fused, in which incompleteness is conceived as circulating in a creative way. What is important for Alizade, and I concur, is that nothingness should not be expelled, both sexes accepting that nothingness concerns them equally, that this nothingness includes the mystery of life and death for both sexes in the same measure.

It is no coincidence that the outset of life is represented as the figure of a woman, as creating, and the end of life as one of the Fates. "The Origin of the World" by Courbet, which represents the vulva as a painting, probably provoked questions in Lacan who nonetheless in some way concealed it by not making it public although he was its owner, and by restricting it to his country house. After his death, as payment of death taxes, it was turned over to the Musée d'Orsay, where it continues to provoke questions in its numerous viewers.

The world, things, the other and each part of the other have no other presence "than the painting that is made out of them" in the words of Corinne Enaudeau (1998), who adds, "All that is authentic is only a substitute, image or word" (Enaudeau, 1998, p. 54). Courbet's image, like a mirror, duplicates the representation of the female sex. But the image does not judge: it illustrates the thing.

In his article on negation, Freud (1925h) states that judgment of attribution precedes judgment of existence: "The function of judgment is concerned in the main with two sorts of decisions. It affirms or disaffirms the possession by a thing of a particular attribute; and it asserts or disputes that a presentation has an existence in reality" (Freud, 1925h, p. 236).

It is inherent to thought to rise above pure activity of representation, but there is no thought that is not influenced by perception and vice versa, perception is not a purely passive process. Caravaggio (cited by Quignard, 1994, p. 23) said in the seventeenth century that every painting is a Medusa's head. Terror may be defeated by the image of terror. In this sense every painter could be considered as Perseus, and Caravaggio painted a Medusa. Did not Freud (1940) say that the representation of Medusa's head with its phallic abundance helped to deny castration anxiety in the confrontation with the female sex and consequently with the difference between the sexes? We see that, at least for Caravaggio, the first image that confronts the subject with the difference between the sexes produces terror or, in psychoanalytic terms, produces a disruptive effect (Benyakar, 2005) in human beings, provoking a potentially traumatic affect that forces the psyche to work on the lifelong Oedipus complex. The representation is given us by pure immediate perception; more precisely, it is a conquest for Enaudeau (1998) who cites Green (1987) when he writes: "Psychoanalysis is work on representations (unconscious and preconscious) that, at least in certain cases, becomes a labor of representation" (Enaudeau, 1998, p. 141).

I suggest that, even though the genesis of the judgment of existence follows that of attribution, it resignifies the latter *a posteriori*, and the ego's initial good and bad—pleasure–again becomes good or bad *a posteriori* in function of the judgment of existence as filtered through the Oedipus complex.

My hypothesis is that the possibility of creativity in both sexes involves the possibility to sustain within the psyche a never resolved tension between the *phallic order* and the *nothingic order*, forces in tension whose dynamics and fluidity determine whether the subject will exhibit greater or lesser porosity in the work of representing into which the streams of all psychic agencies flow, both in the work of representation and in the vicissitudes of the concomitant affect. Two images provoke questions in human beings and produce a more or less traumatic effect depending on the individual. One is an image we have never experienced and from which we have been excluded forever: the primal scene. "We originate in a scene we were never in: an image lacking in human beings," states Pascal Quignard (1994, p. 22). The other is the image of the difference between the sexes whose confrontation is inevitable. Both provoke questions in human beings throughout their lives. I cite a passage from Quignard that I consider most revealing of the work of representing in human beings:

> Whether they close their eyes or dream at night, open their eyes or closely observe real things in light shed by the sun, whether their gaze wanders afar or is lost, whether they turn their eyes to the book in their hands, whether sitting in the dark they watch the development of a film or let themselves be absorbed in the contemplation of a painting, human beings are a desiring gaze that is seeking another image behind everything they see. (Quignard, 1994, p. 34)

I would add that, in my opinion, this work of representation that is the core of all psychic work of working through is also the core of every creative process. When I refer to "work" I am not referring only to the sustained labour involved in creative activity, in the solitude of the studio or when facing the anxiety of the blank page, but in particular the psychic work that supports it as a basement. This basement is not static or immobile, nor a fixed baseboard of creativity forever given. Like a moving sculpture, or even more, like interactive art in which the spectator is both passive and active in relation to the work of art, in the creative subject the life drive (desire to desire) and death drive (desire to not desire), the psychic agencies, the multiple sexual identifications, passivity and activity, libido and inertia, all interact and converse with each other. Here, Eros finally triumphs, having succeeded in deactivating traumatic effraction and transforming it into the sensuality of a text, the palette of colours in a painting or the movement that animates a sculpture.

Murielle Gagnebin (1994) suggests approaching the work of art avoiding any pathography or psychobiography of the author, but instead proposes four metapsychological causes that enable the work of art to emerge. In the first place the artist's capital of drive: "the richer and more available it is, the denser the work will be materially" (Gagnebin, 1994, p. 31); second, the working through of absence; third, the artist's possibility to introject harmonious bisexuality and fourth, the sublimation of part drives. The free circulation of these four causes determines the poietic of the work of art. But, she states, not so much in a sublimatory act as in a movement of metonymic displacement or perhaps of reaction formation.

Didier Anzieu (1981) considers that in the author pierced through by creation, psychic work is similar to dream work or the work of mourning. What is common to these three is that they constitute phases of crisis for the psychic apparatus. He establishes a difference between creativity, within the reach of many, from creation characterised by contributing something new (something never done before) and by public recognition of the creator's work sooner or later. Anzieu attributes the larger quantity of male creators compared to female creators to the struggle against death that is creation, in which men, unable to engender, find compensation for their desire to transcend. However, he suggests, a hypothesis that interests me, that creation involves a combination of the maternal, the paternal, the feminine and the masculine, but also the sexually indeterminate. The creator is one "who has free play of all the variables of the sexual in thought and who has the luck or intelligence to use at the right moment whatever is required in each phase of the work" (Anzieu, 1981, p. 19).

Traditionally, women are assigned the place of the muse of the creating man, and in figurative art in particular, the place of the model either of the beautiful, the voluptuous or the uncanny. As highlighted by Marian Cao (2000), the history of art, through the representation of the woman, has stated a certain conception of the woman and has denied women. "The different vanguards have treated the image of the woman either as part of a landscape, irreducible to itself—as in Fauvism, Cubism and Surrealism—or as the vampiress, a threatening spider that weaves its web to eat the man" (Cao, 2000, p. 23). In the images of abductions and rapes, Cao continues, "that plague Western imaginary, women do not appear as victims but as voluptuous, lascivious beings" (Cao, 2000, p. 25). These images have passed on to publicity, which drinks from sources of artistic iconography that remain alive. In iconographic representation, the woman is either viewed directly or is looking at herself in a mirror.

Many creative women were recognised because they were someone's daughter, as was Artemisia Gentileschi at the beginning, or somebody's lover, as in the case of Camille Claudel. It took Frida Kahlo great courage to make her work be valued independently of her husband Diego Rivera. However, as Cao stresses, when we read about Frida Kahlo, the sad and tragic facts tend to overshadow the definition of her works. Maria Sklodowska, in spite of having won two Nobel Prizes, one in physics and the other in chemistry, was better known by the name of her husband, Mr Curie. Many paintings by Artemisia Gentileschi were attributed to her father or to Caravaggio, not to speak of the public humiliation and tortures to which she was subjected after being raped. In the anthological exhibition of this artist, held in Florence in 1991 (cited by Cao, 2000, p. 35), it stated: "Proven and truly exceptional mastery for a womanish brush" only to add "Artemisia, lascivious and precocious young woman". An incredible summation of prejudices and injuries on the creative condition of women. I quote Lacan when he says, in a subtle and evocative play on words: "on la *dit-femme*, on la *diffâme*" (you call her woman and you defame her) (Lacan, 1972–1973, p. 79).

The psychic topics need to enter into an effervescent tension if creativity is to emerge. However, the necessary condition is the production of a fertile subjectivisation. It is in the conquest of her condition as subject, in her ability to run through drive circuits fluidly, to oscillate past the "three modalities of satisfaction, the active, the auto-erotic and passivization" (Penot, 2006, p. 1590) described by Penot. This subjectivisation cannot be attained if social and cultural conditions are unfavourable: the ego and its circumstances, in the words of Ortega y Gasset. I am sure that for creativity to emerge freely from the unconscious, certain trans-subjective social circumstances are also required.

Concerning the subjectivisation that is necessary as a conquest, some words follow about a contemporary artist who is of great interest for psychoanalysis since she associates her work with letters, notebooks and commentary, sometimes on the back of her drawings, with her states of humour and feelings during her creative process. Works primarily conceived by work of subjectivisation achieved by means of her art and her personal analysis in a highly intricate way. I refer to Louise Bourgeois.

Thus we read, in reference to traumatic effraction and her effort at subjectivisation:

> I have dragged Louise Bourgeois around with me for over forty years. Each day I brought her wound along with me and I have carried my wounds ceaselessly, without rest, like a piece of leather with holes in it that cannot be repaired. I am a collection of wooden pearls forever unstrung. (Bourgeois, 2011, p. 4)

In one of her notes, she summarises the place of the death drive in all works:

> in sculpture, voluntarist attempts lead to formlessness or incoherence. Sculpture may incorporate a lot of blind and formless aggression but it demands more than that—aggression is necessary and useful but not sufficient. Although rage leads to destruction, sustained fury may be productive (Bourgeois, 2011, p. 65)

Perhaps she is speaking of the need of the death drive in the creative act that destroys forms to allow Eros to generate other representations more concordant with the working through of the traumatic that we proposed at the beginning of this chapter. In a humorous vein, Bourgeois describes the involvement of the drive and the body, sometimes laid bare, in view of the artist's perceptual intensity in relation to the world, and the way it is transformed into representation: "luckily we have only five senses, what a lot of problems and suffering this saves us! Imagine if we had fourteen!" (Bourgeois, 2011, p. 72).

"Being-in-the-world means", in the thinking of Emanuelle Coccia "above all, *being* in the sensitive, moving in it, doing or undoing it without interruption." (Coccia, 2010, p. 10), I believe that there is no creativity without suffering during the creative process, whether in the writer's confrontation with the blank page, the painter's with the empty canvas or the sculptor's with formless matter.

The elusive is the adequate expression of suffering since it puts artists in contact with their own penury in relation to the magnitude of the senses. Perhaps also because the contact with the primary process demanded by creativity is a source of anxiety, censure is not lifted without consequences.

I do not draw conclusions but I do however insist that for creativity to emerge, in men or in women, it needs their psychic agencies and repression to be porous enough, the dialogue between their life and death drives to be free of fear, for their multiple identifications, both feminine and masculine or indeterminate to refract freely, for the psychic work of working through the traumatic to find a livable and fertile solution in creative work.

I will let Louise Bourgeois be my spokesperson in closing: "The work of art is barely acting-out, not understanding. If we understood it, there would no longer be any need to create the work" (Bourgeois, 2011, p. 81).

References

Alizade, M. (1992). Nada de mujer. In: *La Sensualidad Femenina* (pp. 27–65). Buenos Aires: Amorrortu.

Anzieu, D. (1981*). Le Corps de l'Oeuvre*. Paris: Gallimard.

Benjamin, J. (1995). *Like Subjects, Love Objects. Essays on Recognition and Sexual Difference*. New Haven: Yale University Press. (Spanish translation by Jorge Pitiagorsky Buenos Aires: Paidos, 1997).

Benyakar, M. (2005). *Lo Traumático*. Buenos Aires: Editorial Biblos.

Bourgeois, L. (2011). *El Retorno de lo Reprimido*. Catalogue of the Exhibition of Works of Art and Writing of Louise Bourgeois organized by Fundación Proa, Buenos Aires.

Cao, M. L. F. (2000). La creación artística: un difícil sustantivo femenino. In: *Creación Artística y Mujeres* (pp. 23–36). Madrid: Narcea Editorial.

Chaboudez, G. (1994). *Le Concept du Phallus dans ses Articulations Lacaniennes*. Paris: Lysimaque.

Coccia, E. (2010). *La Vita Sensibile*, Spanish translation by M. T. Mezza. Buenos Aires: Marea Editorial.

Durrmeyer, L. (1999). Et changer de plaisir. In: *La Féminité Autrement* (pp. 15–25). Paris: PUF.

Enaudeau, C. (1998). *Là-bas comme ici. Le paradoxe de la représentation.* Paris: Gallimard.

Freud, S (1924d). *The Dissolution of the Oedipus Complex. S. E. 19.* London: Hogarth Press.

Freud, S. (1925h). *Negation. S. E. 19.* London: Hogarth Press.

Freud, S. (1925j). *Some Psychical Consequences of the Anatomical Distinction Between the Sexes, S. E. 19.* London: Hogarth Press.

Freud, S. (1940 [1922]). *Medusa's Head. S. E. 18.* London: Hogarth Press.

Gagnebin, M. (1994). *Pour une Esthétique Psychanalytique.* Paris: PUF.

Glocer-Fiorini, L. (2001). *Lo Femenino y el Pensamiento Complejo.* Lugar Editorial: Buenos Aires. (English translation, Deconstructing the Feminine. London: Karnac 2010).

Green, A. (1987). La représentation de chose entre pulsion et langage. In: *Propédeutique (la métapsychologie revisitée)* (pp. 135–155). Paris: Champ Vallon, 1995.

Heidegger, M. (2000). *¿Qué es la metafísica?*, Spanish translation by H. Cortez & A. Leyte. Madrid: Editorial Alianza.

Horney, K. (1967). *La Psychologie de la Femme.* French translation, Paris: Payot, 1969.

Lacan, J. (1972–1973). Le Séminaire, Livre XX, *Encore.* Paris: Seuil, 1975.

Penot, B. (2006). La position féminine dans les échanges premiers. *Revue Française de Psychanalyse, LXX:* 1585–1593.

Pergaud, L. (1912). *La Guerre des Boutons.* Paris: Gallimard, col. Folio, 1994.

Quignard, P. (1994*). Le Sexe et l'effroi.* Paris: Gallimard.

Shakespeare, W. (1600). *Much Ado about Nothing.* In: *The Complete Plays of William Shakespeare* (pp. 110–132). New York: Chatham River Press, 1984.

Tesone, J. -E. (2006). La divine jouissance: Le narcissisme féminin et les mystiques. *Revue Française de Psychanalyse, LXX:* 1523–1528.

CHAPTER FIVE

Discussion of "William, did you say: '*Much Ado about Nothing*'?" by Juan Eduardo Tesone

Ingrid Moeslein-Teising

I very much thank Juan Tesone for being so creative in giving us such a rich text. Like in great pieces of art, everything is said and at the same time many questions are raised. I just want to add some aspects and comments.

Female core

Juan Tesone refers to classic theories on the origin of libido, penis envy and the pre-feminist debate against phallic monism. In the twenties and thirties, starting in Berlin with Karen Horney's (1923, 1924) rebellion against the view that women felt themselves constitutionally inferior, a series of contributions mostly by female authors (Helene Deutsch (1925), Melanie Klein (1928), Jeanne Lampl-de Groot (1927), Josine Müller (1931), Lillian Rotter (1932), and others), in which Jones (1927) joined in, sought to enlighten Freud's "dark continent". The discourse went on internationally, was especially taken up in the seventies and eighties within the feminist movement, and today we are able to have more insight into these complex issues, although, interestingly, the alternative findings disappear again and again from the stage of scientific psychoanalytic debate.

Elina Reenkola (2002) raises the interesting idea that this ignorance is due to the human tendency to carefully hide a woman's specific characteristics, her most valuable treasures, her fertility, her desire and her pleasure, to which a woman's core anxieties relate.

> It has been kept a carefully guarded secret that the woman's body as such would be a source of enjoyment and pleasure ... and that motherhood could be a primary value for her, not just cold comfort for lacking a penis. (Reenkola, 2002, p. 134)

The lack of an illusionary penis does not touch upon a woman's core in the same way as imaginary or real damage to her own genitalia or fertility; in our context here we may say: her core creativity.

So women allow men to talk about penis envy, as penis envy is not their foremost concern (Reenkola, 2002, p. 134). As Juan Tesone observes, *"men's envy of women's capacity for sexual pleasure"*, (citations taken from Chapter Four are in italics) we may add: this is to not arouse men's envy of women's unique capacities.

Gender tension (Geschlechterspannung)

Already in his definition of a constitutional, innate bisexuality, Freud states that

> ... in human beings pure masculinity or femininity is not to be found (either in a psychological or a biological sense.) Every individual on the contrary displays a mixture of the character-traits belonging to his own and to the opposite sex; (and he shows a combination of activity and passivity whether or not these last character-traits tally with his biological ones). (Freud, 1905d, p. 219)

In the psychoanalytic gender discourse we have on the one hand phallic monism etc. in classical psychoanalysis and, on the other hand, a differentiation theory in feminist-oriented psychoanalysis, which creates a positive concept of femininity which is placed as the "Other" opposite masculinity. Thus the concept of "deficit"—no-thing!—has been overcome and femininity has also been provided with aspects which were reserved only for masculinity, and vice versa.

Juan Tesone proposes that the *"discovery of the difference of the sexes involves including nothingness in the two sexes as a logical necessity. Historically male bias pushed nothingness into the female sex with the facilitation of the non-visibility of the female sex, which came to represent nothingness as a projection into women lack, nothingness and the lack of the phallus, the symbol of fertility"*.

As discussed above, women could easily turn the tables!

Tesone refers to Alizade (1999), who states that *"the concept of nothingness in psychoanalysis is on the opposite side of the street from the phallus* and adds *the 'nothingic' order to the phallic order"*.

This links to Reimut Reiche's (1990) understanding of bisexuality, for which he uses the term gender tension, not related to interpersonal but intrapersonal forces, to the tension-laden state with*in* a man, or with*in* a woman, which results from the two-sidedness of gender, or the difference between masculinity and femininity. In his concept of gender ambiguity, emphasising the unconscious drive dimension of gender identity and gendered relationships as a central aspect of psychoanalytic theory, he questions gender dichotomy: "The correct formulation should be as follows: gender can be found in two forms (= dimorphic)" (Reiche, 1990, p. 46; see also Quindeau, 2013).

I follow Ilka Quindeau (2008) when she replaces a reductionist dichotomy of masculinity and femininity with gender tension—a conflict-laden status of male and female identifications within each individual. "Sexuality offers this gender 'ambiguity' an excellent *locus*—however, not between the individual persons concerned, but within every individual, a continuum with masculine and feminine poles" (Quindeau, 2008, p. 224).

Creativity

Tesone's consideration that *"the possibility of creativity in both sexes involves the possibility of sustaining within the psyche a never resolved tension between the phallic order and the nothingic order"*, his picture of the *"forces in tension"* and their fate, gives a very important aspect in addition to the concepts of creativity.

What is a human being's need to be creative? An artist once told me: "When you can't express something with words, you become creative."

(This can be a good solution; as analysts we know that there are worse solutions, such as developing, for example, bodily symptoms).

Hanna Segal (1991) conceptualises that the origin of the creative impulse lies in the need for reparation and that symbol formation is the very essence of artistic creativity. "The artist's need is to recreate what he feels in the depth of the internal world" (Segal, 1991, p. 86). She states that it is the inner perception of the artist's deepest feeling of the depressive position that his/her internal world is shattered, which leads to his need to recreate something that is felt to be a whole new world, and in the creation of the inner world also a recreation of a lost world, a harmonious internal world. Furthermore, the artist has not only to create something in his inner world corresponding to the recreation of his internal objects and world, but also has to externalise it to give it life in the external world.

Tesone is right in pointing out the suffering in the creative act. The process of creation of a piece of art, or text, or ... is a painful act, in the pregnancy of which phases of great despair appear, labour pains, and in the exhaustion as well as satisfaction with the newborn baby there may also be despair at not having reached perfection. (We know of many artists, who destroy their work in despair, or finish their life with the deep conviction that they did not create anything of value, as Giacometti is said to have done).

But this is not only, as Tesone said, "*because censure is not lifted without consequence, the contact with the primary process demanded by creativity is a source of anxiety*". Creating a new baby requires, but does not always succeed in a shift from a narcissistic position, where the created artistic product (be it painting, sculpture, text) is put forward as self-created faeces with the constant terror that one's product is going to be revealed as shit, to the genital position in which the creation is felt to be a baby resulting from meaningful internal intercourse. The work of art then is felt to have a life of its own and one which will survive the artist (Segal, 1991).

You will have noticed that I have used words like "baby" and "birth". Although these words are used to describe circumstances of creative processes, and those of both men and women, having labour pains and giving birth to real babies is a woman's and despite modern medical techniques only a woman's task and possibility. We acknowledge men's envy because they cannot experience this complex occurrence on the practical level, although our task is to move beyond. One of many ways for a woman, not always the healthiest ones, as for example Estela Welldon (1988) shows, to become creative, is by creating a baby.

Woman as artist

Juan Tesone reminds us of the *"traditional role of women"* in the arts *"as muse or model"*, and he honours the female artist by mentioning some.

Since the feminist movement in the seventies, exhibitions were set up showing "Woman in the arts as subject and object", museums were founded such as the National Museum of Women in the Arts in Washington, installations of art were designed such as Judy Chicago's famous "Dinner Party", with the goal of ending the ongoing cycle of omission in which women were written out of the historical record. Throughout the history of Western society, women artists have been ignored and devalued. We do not know who created the very early paintings and sculptures, such as the forty thousand year old Venus of Hohle Fels. In the ancient world of Greeks and Romans woman artists were celebrated (and in 1600 it was a goal in Italy to become a painter, even a sculptor).

Today, as we saw at the Documenta, the famous art exhibition in Kassel, Germany, directed in 2012 by a woman, women are represented in the arts and we can focus on their special aspects instead of emphasising that they are there at all. Women have at all times become creative by working through their own topics. Frida Kahlo's work for example, besides other aspects, gives testimony to her struggle to become a mother and create a child. In Artemisia Gentileschi's famous "Judith and Holofernes" everything is said, her taking revenge for humiliation being only one aspect.

Lady Macbeth

I shall now use Shakespeare as an analyst of complex issues (Saottini, personal communication), although not as lovely and light as in *Much Ado about Nothing* …

In literature and other arts we meet couples who represent within themselves the dichotomy discussed above, mingling as well as projecting feminine and masculine aspects: think of Catherine and Heathcliff Earnshaw in Emily Bronte's *Wuthering Heights,* for example. Especially in Shakespeare's couple, Lady Macbeth and Macbeth, the mingling of, or conflict between, femininity and masculinity, we now may say the nothingic and phallic order, and their representation within the characters, the life drive and the death drive are brought onto the stage of awareness; we remember that *"both mystery and death are condensed on the woman's body. Both sexes have to accept that nothingness concerns them equally, it includes the mystery of life and death for both sexes in the same measure"* (Alizade, cited by Tesone). The powerful acceptance of this play shows its relevance to unconscious core issues. Freud (1916d) also documented his reflections and refers to Jekels (1917), who suggested that Shakespeare split one person into two for dramatic reasons.

I come to the play, to some parts that are relevant for this topic. Lady Macbeth claims that her husband is womanish:

> ... thy nature;
> It is too full o' th' milk of human kindness. (*Macbeth*, 1.5.15/16)

So she has to suppress her instincts toward compassion, motherhood and fragility, and creativity—associated with femininity, in favor of ambition, ruthlessness, violence, and destructivity—associated with masculinity. She is pleading to be unsexed, defeminised. She asks her menstrual cycle to stop to become like a man, stopping her means of becoming generative. Her woman's breasts still reveal her femininity, but her milk shall not be of human kindness but become gall. She says:

> Come, you spirits
> That tend on mortal thoughts, *unsex me here,*
> And fill me from the crown to the toe top-full
> Of direst cruelty! make thick my blood;
> Stop up the access and passage to remorse,
> That no compunctious visitings of nature
> Shake my fell purpose, nor keep peace between
> The effect and it! Come to my woman's breasts,
> And take my milk for gall, you murdering ministers,
> Wherever in your sightless substances
> You wait on nature's mischief! Come, thick night,
> And pall thee in the dunnest smoke of hell,
> That my keen knife see not the wound it makes,
> Nor heaven peep through the blanket of the dark,
> To cry 'Hold, hold!' (*Macbeth*, 1.5.39f)

Macbeth, of whom we know that "(He) has no children" (*Macbeth*, 4.3.217), wants his Lady to:

> "Bring forth men-children only! For thy undaunted mettle should compose nothing but males". (*Macbeth*, 1.7)

But deeply mourns his childlessness: "No son of mine succeeding" (*Macbeth*, 3.1.60)—and gives the order to kill babies—those of others. Whether Lady Macbeth experienced the loss of her child which causes such a deep disturbance in her—her rage—or whether she was not able to become creative herself (and the following lines about suckling come out of her fantasy), she was not able to defend against the death drive that dominates the play, and conjures her masculine toughness:

> I have given suck, and know
> How tender 'tis to love the babe that milks me:
> I would, while it was smiling in my face,
> Have plucked my nipple from his boneless gums
> And dashed the brains out, had I so sworn as you
> Have done this. (*Macbeth*, 1.7)

In the end, the power of a man, for none of woman born/did harm Macbeth (*Macbeth*, 4.1.81, rev.) "Macduff was from his mother's womb/ Untimely ripp'd" (*Macbeth*, 5.8.15–16), perhaps by a male doctor through a caesarian. Men conquered this very female field long ago.

"The Origin of the World" by Gustave Courbet

This work of art was owned by Lacan, who not only somehow hid it by keeping it in his country house, but also hid it behind a sliding wooden door, which itself was a painting (by Lacan's stepbrother, Andre Masson). This picture was a landscape, designed in the lines of the "Origin of the World", so that in a certain way "the Origin of the World" was visible, at least and best of all in the imagination of someone who knows the picture behind this mask. The artist does not create, he reveals, says Segal, and, when we look at a painting, we are drawn into a new world. How meaningful especially for this picture.

Conclusion

I see the special merit of Tesone's contribution in his conceptualising what men and women have in common, which is our contemporary challenge, as outlining the differences in a non-hierarchical way seems to be widely solved. In spite of all the forces I have described within each individual, call it gender tension, or phallic and nothingic order, despite all our technical development, man and woman have to come together to become creative in the very pure sense of the word.

References

Alizade, M. (1999). *Female Sensuality*. London: Karnac.
Deutsch, H. (1925). *Psychoanalyse der Weiblichen Sexualfunktionen*. Leipzig, Wien: Internationaler Psychoanalytischer Verlag.
Freud, S. (1905d). *Three Essays on the Theory of Sexuality, S. E., 7*: 219–246. London: Hogarth.
Freud, S. (1916d). Some character types met with in psycho analytic work. *S. E., 14*: 309–330. London: Hogarth.
Horney, K. (1923). Zur Genese des weiblichen Kastrationskomplexes. *Internationale Zeitschrift für Psychoanalyse, 9*: 12–26. In: Horney, K. (1989): *Die Psychologie der Frau*. Frankfurt am Main: Fischer.
Horney, K. (1924). On the genesis of the castration complex in women. *International Journal of Psycho-Analysis, 5*: 50–65.
Jekels, L. (1917). Shakespeare's Macbeth. *Imago 5*: 170. English version: The Riddle of Shakespeare's Macbeth. *Psychoanalytic Review, 30*: 361 (1943).
Jones, E. (1927). Die erste Entwicklung der weiblichen Sexualität. *Internationale Zeitschrift für Psychoanalyse, 14*: 11–25.
Klein, M. (1928). Frühstadien des Ödipuskomplexes. *Internationale Zeitschrift für Psychoanalyse, 14*: 7–21.
Lampl-de Groot, J. (1927). Zur Entwicklungsgeschichte des Ödipuskomplexes der Frau. In: M. Mitscherlich & Ch. Rohde-Dachser (Hrsg.), *Psychoanalytische Diskurse über die Weiblichkeit von Freud bis heute*. Stuttgart: Internationale Psychoanalyse, 31–47, 1996.
Mueller, J. (1931). Ein Beitrag zur Frage der Libidoentwicklung des Mädchens in der genitalen Phase. *Internationale Zeitschrift für Psychoanalyse, 17*: 256–262.
Quindeau, I. (2008). *Verführung und Begehren*. Stuttgart: Klett-Cotta. (2013): *Seduction and Desire*. London: Karnac.
Quindeau, I. (2013). Female sexuality between gender dichotomy. In: I. Moeslein-Teising & F. Thomson-Salo (Eds.), *The Female Body—Inside and Outside* (pp. 223–241). London: Karnac.

Reenkola, E. (2002). *The Veiled Female Core*. New York: Other Press.

Reiche, R. (1990). *Geschlechterspannung—Eine Psychoanalytische Untersuchung*. Frankfurt A. M: Fischer.; new edition 2000: Psychosozial-Verlag, Gießen.

Rotter, L. (1932). Zur Psychologie der weiblichen Sexualität. *Internationale Zeitschrift für Psychoanalyse, 20*. In: M. Mitscherlich-Nielsen, *et al.* (Hrsg.), *Psyche. Zeitschrift für Psychoanalyse und ihre Anwendungen*. 42. Jahrgang. Heft 1. Stuttgart (Klett-Cotta), 365–375, 1988.

Segal, H. (1991). *Dream, Phantasy and Art*. Hove, UK: Brunner-Routledge.

Shakespeare, W. (1606). *Macbeth*. In: *The Complete Works of William Shakespeare* (the Alexander text) (pp. 1049–1078). Glasgow: HarperCollins.

Welldon, E. (1988). *Mother Madonna Whore*. New York: Other Press.

CHAPTER SIX

Female elements and functions in creativity

Maria Adelaide Lupinacci

As a psychoanalyst, my first thought inevitably goes to Freud (1932) when discussing femininity. I went back to read his last work on the subject, which marks the climax of his thought: lecture 33 "Femininity" in *New Introductory Lectures on Psycho-analysis and Other Works*.

In this lecture, Freud reaffirmed that the origin of femininity lies in castration—hence, in the absence of something—and that passivity, as one of the characteristics of being feminine, is a consequence.

Therefore, femininity appears to be organised around this "absence".

Moreover, when speaking of libido, understood as the driving force of sexuality, he concluded saying:

> There is only one libido, which serves both the masculine and the feminine sexual functions. To it itself we cannot assign any sex; if, following the conventional equation of activity and masculinity, we are inclined to describe it as masculine, we must not forget that it also covers trends with passive aim. Nevertheless the juxtaposition "feminine libido" is without any justification. Furthermore, it is our impression that *more constraint has been applied to the libido*

when it is pressed into the service of the feminine function, and that Nature takes less careful account of its demands than in case of masculinity (italics added). (Freud, 1932, p. 131)

As a theorist, Freud seemed to be absolutely convinced of this; however, being the extraordinarily acute and honest empirical observer that he was, he did have doubts, so he left a door open. In doing so, he even resorted to subtle self-mockery: "If you … regard my belief in the influence of lack of a penis on the configuration of femininity as an *idée fixe* …" (Freud, 1932, p. 132). His conclusion was, "If you want to know more about femininity, enquire from your own experiences of life, or turn to the poets, or wait until science can give you deeper and more coherent information" (Freud, 1932, p. 135).

Of course, psychoanalysis too is a science.

Unsurprisingly, it was a woman and a great child psychoanalyst, Melanie Klein, who strongly asserted that femininity was a quality *per se* when speaking of the "receptive" nature of female genitalia (and of the psychosexual constitution of women), of little girls' insight and unconscious awareness of having potential babies inside themselves, and of the wealth and internal abilities of their own body (though haunted by doubts and fears). Melanie Klein was supported in her ideas by Ernest Jones (1935). "We consider that the girl's attitude is already more feminine than masculine, being typically receptive and acquisitive" (Jones, 1935, p. 265).

Clearly, this shift from the idea of "lack" and "passivity", and hence of femininity as an identity to be built and accepted starting from this "minus", to the concept of "receptivity" and femininity as a primary psychobiological fact is groundbreaking. "The ultimate question is whether a woman is born or made" (Jones, 1935, p. 273).

A patient who was recovering poorly developed or undeveloped aspects of her femininity suddenly remembered, in a surge of intense emotion, a song by an Italian singer that she had loved as a teenager:

> *C'è una linea sottile*
> *Fra star fermi e subire*
> *Fra andare e venire*

> There is a fine line
> Between being still and submitting
> Between coming and going

Incidentally, it is my opinion that masculinity too can benefit from this: the penis is desired and admired for its power as a bearer of gifts and pleasure and not as something that narcissistically completes a woman. I believe that the complementary and opposite of female receptivity is not "activity" (according to the classic combination), but the penetrating nature, the sharpness and forward thrust of the masculine.

However, is there such a thing as specificity when speaking of female creativity? Clearly, creativity is linked to a variety of factors. These include the feminine and the masculine and both contribute, each for their own part, to the forms and issues of creativity. However, the psychic structure of every individual features feminine and masculine elements that are combined in varying degrees and intersect with one another as a result of an innate predisposition (bisexuality), which is then shaped by experience and identifications. For this reason, I tend to believe that creativity belongs to the couple. Better yet, it belongs to a good and harmonious relationship of the female/male dyad, a "convivial" relationship as Bion (1970) defines it, both within an individual and in a couple.

I would rather place creativity in the harmonious relationship between "Two different Others".

As Fornari (1975) argued, in an adult sexual relationship there is a move from a condition of narcissistic closure and self sufficiency to a condition of reciprocity and mutual exchange as "The constitution of heterosexual identity implies that each sexual partner has a sex that the other does not have" (Fornari, 1975, p. 11). Put otherwise, each partner has a prevailing sex that the other does not have to the same extent. In this vision of couple, the woman has a "plus" of femininity that she gives the man, enriching him and making him freer to express himself as such, in exchange for a "plus" of masculinity that the man gives to the woman to make her richer and complete. Each needs the other to be complete in a genuinely libidinal and object relational view (indeed, social *vs.* narcissistic).

This does not mean that men and women, taken as individuals, cannot be creative in qualitatively different ways that are typical of their gender.

Therefore, I would like to explore the feminine elements of creativity in women, alongside the masculine ones, which are absolutely necessary for a personality to be rich and complete.

So I will speak of masculinity and femininity. I would like to start with a typical scene taken from the psychopathology of everyday life.

You may have noticed what happens when a family is leaving for a trip and you need to make the passengers and luggage fit inside a car. Usually, the husband sighs (or grumbles) that there are too many bags, too many useless things and that everything will never fit inside the car, and so on. The wife argues that everything is absolutely necessary and she is sure that they will manage to find room for everything. In the end, the car usually ends up fitting in the luggage arranged, often with the wife's help, because she manages to see the arrangement in space better and finds the tiny free recess that is best suited for "that little pack over there"!

The sense of space as inner space and of the potential of this space is one of the feminine elements of personality. The feeling that later becomes awareness of an "inside" one's own body where unseen processes unfold saturates femininity reducing its need to adhere to what is precise, defined, and visible and perhaps expands its imagination.

The container as a female symbol and containment as one of the basic maternal creative functions, alongside nutrition, have become all too familiar to psychoanalysts. However, this sense of space would be useless if it were an empty space or, on the contrary, boundless. The woman in our scene could not have had a "creative" departure without a husband and possibly children (a content for the affective space of her life as well as for the car) and without an inner sense of limits: both of the car's capacity and of her husband's ability to bear (a feminine quality that even men need) his spouse! I am referring here to the limit as a male/paternal quality, a limit to the almighty fantasy of an infinite feminine space/capacity, and finally a limit imposed on the children by the presence of their father through the possession of their mother.

Two other concepts linked to space and containment are softness and flexibility. What is softness if not a full, yet yielding space that surrounds and protects, that can be imprinted and shaped, that receives the image of the other? Softness is also expressed by the soft lines of the female sexual body that arouses and welcomes the male, while the bosom and womb give a baby safety and warmth, while a mother's pliability seeks to grasp and to paint a picture of the peculiarities of her child's "true self". But up to a certain point. Resoluteness and courage are also needed (masculine qualities?) to put up with the little tyrants and not to wait for their father to raise his voice (according to a certain male-chauvinistic/hyper-maternalistic stereotype). A solid sense of the self and of one's own needs and limits (of endurance?) to cope with expansionary and propulsive male tendencies.

Another element of female creativity regards the value of what is small, minute, the value of the detail and the creative ability to get much out of little.

Let us turn to the poets, as Freud suggested. We owe a delightful scene to Jane Austen's (1815) pen in *Emma*. Emma is waiting patiently for a friend who is lingering in a shop:

> Emma went to the door for amusement. Much could not be hoped from the traffic of even the busiest part of Highbury ... and when her eyes fell only on the butcher with his tray, a tidy old woman travelling homewards from shop with her full basket, two curs quarrelling over a dirty bone and a string of dawdling children round the baker's little bow-window eyeing the gingerbread, she knew she had no reason to complain, and was amused enough. ... A mind lively and at ease can do with seeing nothing, and can see nothing that does not answer. (Austen, 1815, p. 208)

Jane Austen was a master in the art of narrating the little big affairs of small towns in the English countryside in the early nineteenth century. But would she have been equally creative (the creativity that would have later enchanted Virginia Wolf) without the acuteness (masculine quality) of her sense of humour and irony that reveal a remarkably penetrating ability (once again masculine?) to observe environments, situations, and especially characters of whom she creates merciless portraits?

Emma's father is the foremost example. An imaginary invalid, a hypochondriac, blindly and childishly self-centred, his idiosyncrasies are described without reserve. Yet the author tells us that he was widely loved and respected in his circle and many were willing to tolerate and to keep him company. Even more amazing is the fact that not even readers can come around to disliking him. However, would this have been possible if the writer's intellectually lucid and sharp criticism (masculine qualities) had not been expressed in a gentle and good-natured style, if she had not used warm halftones to depict the nuances highlighting the candour of this wisened child, whose heart is good and affectionate in essence and hypochondriacally concerned about others as he is for himself? This is a superb example of female and male qualities, of container (the style) and content (the character), in fruitful harmony with a way of writing that, in my opinion, only a woman could have created.

Speaking of representation, nuances and halftones: I had the fortune to visit an exhibition of paintings made by boys and girls aged between eleven and fourteen years from a school in Rome. The teacher had given everyone the assignment of reproducing paintings of various styles and by various artists. At a glance, you had the chance of seeing how the same painting was reinterpreted over and over again.

I was immediately struck by the difference in style between the boys and the girls; it was quite evident not only to me, but also to a friend of mine who is not a psychoanalyst. The girls generally used lighter and more nuanced colours. The figures were more shaded and featured more details. The boys' colours were much more vibrant, at times violent, the lines were sharper, the outlines thicker and darker, the strokes bold, with fewer nuances and details. They aimed for the essential! In a study on perspective, where the assignment was less constrained (an urban landscape with a church in the background), yet more technical, the differences were less evident, but in a way more complex. The girls had chosen mostly churches with a dome and at times colours that were very bright (warm rather than acidic), as if a more technical than aesthetic assignment had called for more masculine elements or as if they had felt the need to offset a more technical task with liveliness and imagination. The boys had chosen churches with triangular pediments and their style featured the same characteristics described above.

I would like to conclude by recalling the work of a male psychoanalyst on masculinity. Karl Figlio (2010) in a paper on phallic and seminal masculinity interestingly observed that some aspects of male identity and creativity (testes, sperm, semen, and "seminal" structures and functions) are often scotomised in favour of the penis and phallus. I wondered why. Could it be that this impressive scotomisation is linked to the container structure (therefore, "feminine") of the scrotal sac which is its most conspicuous feature? The content and the internal function of the testes (sperm production) for a male are less visible and concern the "smaller" particles (spermatozoa), which are so little regarded by men (or taken for granted at a conscious level). Could it be that this creates a sort of narcissistic "shame" in men, giving rise to scotomisation? In Italy, the slang term for testicles is *coglioni*. However, calling someone a *"coglione"* is a rather grave insult meaning idiot, wimp.

In addition, the author rightly speaks of a denial of male interiority in itself, as if it were an exclusive prerogative of women. This seems to be yet another example of the terrible confusion existing between receptivity and passivity. On the contrary, in order for masculinity to express itself in all its manhood, it must also integrate feminine aspects and functions, acknowledging their creative value, without fearing that these are the result of castration, of a *minus*. The scrotal sac could actually be an example of this, since it contains a man's precious testicles and sperm.

Returning to the song:

> *There is a fine line*
> *Between coming and going*

Between *going* to explore and conquer the outer world and the *coming* to the realisation and experience of interiority which also contains expressions of delicate and minute emotions, as is unashamedly natural for women.

References

Austen, J. (1815). *Emma*. World's Classics. Oxford: Oxford University Press, 1990.

Bion, W. R. (1970). *Attention and Interpretation*. London: Tavistock Publications.

Figlio, C. (2010). Phallic and seminal masculinity: A theoretical and clinical confusion. *International Journal of Psycho-analysis, 91*: 191–199.

Fornari, F. (1975). *Genitalità e Cultura*. Milano: Feltrinelli.

Freud, S. (1932). Lecture 33 Femininity. In: *New Introductory Lectures on Psychoanalysis and Other Works, S. E., 22*, (pp. 112–115). London: Hogarth Press.

Jones, E. R. (1935). Early female sexuality. *International Journal of Psycho-analysis, 16*: 265–273.

Klein, M. (1932). *The Psychoanalysis of Children*. London: Hogarth Press.

CHAPTER SEVEN

Women and creativity

Maria Pia Conte

Let us look at a baby girl, a baby girl of a few months, she is on the changing table, mother undresses her, they look at each other and smile. The little girl moves. What has she got between her legs? A small pink mound, two soft folds that cover a precious little button and create a fine vertical line that dips into the access to a passage. Where does it lead to? To a small chamber, empty now, but potentially vital for our species.

When it occurred to me to begin this paper describing a little girl's genitals I thought I would never dare.

But as I was reading all I could to prepare for writing this chapter I came across Nancy Kulish and Deanna Holtzman's (2007) paper, "Baubo: rediscovering woman's pleasures". Who is Baubo? She is an old woman in Demeter and Persephone's myth. Demeter bereft and grief-stricken, has caused drought and famine to plague the world until her daughter is found. She is so full of grief she refuses food and drink. An older woman, called Baubo or Iambe, jests and pulls up her skirt, showing her genitals; Demeter begins to laugh and lifts the coat of depression that had fallen on her and on the world. The sexual jesting, the intimate communication between the two women allude to female sexuality and a woman's pleasure in her sexed body.

69

In this female body, through this passage and in this chamber we have all been conceived, we have developed and we were born. These female outer and inner genitals play a decisive part in the shaping of our physical and mental life, of our inner world and of our mind. We all share the experience of depending on this reasonably safe space, of being nurtured and cleansed of our waste products so that we could grow and become sufficiently equipped to face the outside world.

According to Freud (1923b) our ego is first and foremost a bodily Ego, this understanding is developed through Klein's concept of unconscious omnipotent phantasy, described by Susan Isaacs (1948) in "The nature and function of phantasy". I would like to focus on these early experiences and the unconscious phantasies through which we try and represent them in our mind.

The growth of the embryo into foetus occurs thanks to the development of the umbilical cord and the foetal part of the placenta that reaches out to the corresponding maternal part. Through this early connection the mother's body tunes into the foetus's necessities. One of my first patients, a woman with a very personal view of life, during our work together, gradually gave me the impression that she was experiencing herself as a foetus who has given rise to a mother all around her.

While I was reading for the nth time Melanie Klein's "The Oedipus complex in the light of early anxieties" I was looking at one of Richard's drawings. The one with a battleship called Rodney cruising with a submarine called Sunfish underneath and connected with her through the periscope. Underneath the submarine there are plenty of fish and two starfish rest near the bottom of the sea amongst the seaweeds. Following Klein's interpretations, I recognised Richard's wish to keep his father and brother as babies at the bottom of the sea and to put himself in the central position as the submarine connecting with mother's battleship through his penis. But it occurred to me that the drawing could be seen as one of those pictures that can be interpreted in two different ways, like the famous one of the two profiles or the vase.

The picture represents the sea, and it can be interpreted as the environment surrounding Richard, his mother and all the family. In this case we can see the link between mother and Richard phantasised as happening through the penis, as between adults, and this exposes Richard to oedipal anxieties. On the other hand the sea could represent the inside of mother's body; in this case the link would be through the umbilical cord and the placenta; father's presence inside mother is still recognised but the anxieties involved would be more connected with a dependency relationship and the foetus's feelings of total dependency or, as in my patient, of omnipotently giving rise to mother's body through his or her powerful umbilical cord.

According to some psychoanalysts the "phallus" represents an illusory wholeness, a state free of need and desire. I wonder whether at the root of so much importance given to this notion lies the omnipotent phantasy of the permanence, in the male's erect penis, of a turgid umbilical cord that creates the mother around, the world around. The early connection between mother and foetus is the first meaningful link in our life. How and what passes through it shapes not only our body but also our mind.

Being in a container that grows with us, but then gets tight and we have to get out, feeling safely held or disposable, sheltered from outside disturbances or exposed to aggression directly from the inside, abundance or famine, sharing richness or competing from the start for the little there is, being cleansed from waste products or being invaded by toxic substances, I am sure makes enormous difference in the unconscious phantasies that take shape even from our prenatal experiences.

As psychoanalysts we are aware of the importance of the recognition of the parental sexual relationship in the development of our capacity to think. Acknowledging the link between our parents requires the relinquishment of the idea of sole and permanent possession of mother and the tolerance of the profound sense of loss it leads to.

This involves also the recognition of the relationship between parents as distinct from the relationship between parent and child: the parent's relationship is genital and procreating; the parent–child relationship is not. I have the impression that in this formulation another fact of life, just as important, is omitted in the neutral term, "parent".

After the procreative intercourse of the parental couple, another link just as important is formed through the placenta and the umbilical cord between mother and foetus in the womb during pregnancy and through breast-feeding in the first period of life outside the womb. Those who are excluded may not accept this very intimate connection of mother and child and this can give rise in father, siblings, and other women to grievance and competition with both members of the mother–child couple. The incapacity to recognise this special link restricts the mind to a narrow corridor like the road in which Laius and Oedipus met, and gives it an overwhelming one-eyed perspective that leads to abuse and violence. After all, the tragedy of Oedipus started with Laius fearing that his son would take his place. For this reason he wanted him dead but in the meantime he also wanted the child of his wife dead.

In the centre for abused women where I have been working for the past few years, in most cases I have come in contact with, the actual beating started during the first pregnancy of the woman. The man seems to attack the link between the woman and the baby inside; behind the big man hides the persisting foetus that cannot accept the arrival of a new baby seen as a threat to his own survival.

The sexual intercourse of the parental couple that leads to conception and the development of the new baby both happen inside a woman's body, in two ajacent spaces. In this body two living cells come together to form a third new being who will develop there.

Ron Britton (1995) has talked about "the other room" where parental intercourse occurs, different from "this room" where he and his patient are in a dependent relationship. A kind of awareness of "the other room" may begin while we are in "this room", our mother's uterus, and sexual intercourse may happen in the vagina. The interference may have a very happy ending with a flood of endorphins in both mother and foetus, or a very worrying one if there has been imposition. It seems to me that this prenatal experience could be at the root of the unconscious phantasy of the presence of father's penis inside mother's womb, so frequent in children.

Our mind needs space for all these relationships: the one in which we depend on mother, sheltered in a private and intimate room, and the one between mother and father with its qualities of respect and mutual exchange or of force and contempt. It is the acknowledgement of these relationships and their qualities that opens our mind and we may feel invited to explore the world in joyful expectancy, or feel restrained by fear or no interest.

As women we not only identify with the baby inside but also with the mother outside. I remember, when I was a little girl, I was sure of the importance of my navel, it felt so central and so interesting. I thought my children would be connected with it from the inside of my tummy, and I was very disappointed when I realised it would have no further use in my life.

Since we are little girls we know that to become important like mother we need someone like father. "Mummy, when I grow and I get married, I would like a handsome guy like father", said a little four-year-old girl, and a few months later: "Granny, granny, someone arrived in the night, and now there is a baby in mummy's tummy". We know that to have children we need a man with a penis, not a penis of our own.

A patient in analysis told me one day with a rather sad voice that her husband loved snails and, to clean and cook them, used her cooking pot. She seemed rather disgusted and added that she did not eat them, and what is more she was the one who had to clean the pot. It occurred to me that she might be referring to a kind of intercourse, creative, yes, but in which she participates only as a part object and so feels cheated of the joys of life and is left with the chores. An intercourse in which not only the pleasure is one sided but also the babies are a kind of transformation of the penis and the vital contribution from the mother is not recognised. The mother is downgraded to a lifeless container.

In truth, through the connection between penis and vagina, two living cells come together, one from father, one from mother. Through the joining of these cells life passes on to the new being that will eventually become capable of an independent life of her or his own. The mother's living contribution to the psychic development of the child is often denied in the same way, and some psychoanalysts even claim that it is exclusively the "phallus" or the more gentle expression of "penis as a link" which introduces us to the symbolic function, not the link between both members of the parental couple.

To me this rings a bell in connection with women's condition in our societies. As women we are at the receiving end of powerful projective identifications that deny our capacity for a creative intercourse on a peer level and for another kind of creative relationship that promotes development in a dependent object while at the same time maintaining our independence as individuals. As women we struggle to identify with a living being who has enough space inside to mate, to introject, to allow transformation while remaining herself. The gradual acknowledgement of all these functions opens and structures our mind.

At a level of concrete part objects the penis has two functions: to introduce the sperm in the vagina and to evacuate urine. Many of the women that come to the centre for help are forced regularly to suffer sexual intercourse as if they were a container in which the partner omnipotently phantasises to get rid of all his unwanted feelings of fear, need, frustration and impotence, all felt as unbearably humiliating and menacing his own survival. The abuser also expects the woman to dispose of these bad feelings so that he has never to face them again. On the contrary these women find themselves flooded and overwhelmed by these feelings and try desperately to regain equilibrium, but often in the struggle they lose touch with their own and their children's needs.

In a peer relationship among members of a creative couple, something alive is contributed by both members and each provides for its own nurturing and cleansing. A couple in a dependency relationship is also reciprocally enlivening, but only one of the members provides nurturing and takes care of the waste. Our caring instincts need an object and sometimes they can get the better of us. Some of us may remain stuck in ever providing for others. This sometimes reminds me of the couple of small birds in whose nest the cuckoo lays her eggs. When the bigger cuckoo chick hatches from the egg, it throws out all the other chicks and the poor birds exhaust themselves trying to raise the monstrous cuckoo chick. Many of the women I meet at the centre remind me of these smaller birds, emptied and consumed by the impossible task and yet showing enormous capacities of endurance and resilience. We women should beware of the appeal of the cuckoo and refrain from sheltering, nourishing, cleansing anyone beyond the right size. Our real children and our dependent self get thrown out while we feel enormously important in providing for the big cuckoo's chick and have no space for ourselves.

Preoccupations with the state of our inner organs and with the availability of a man's penis and a potentially ever pregnant uterus feature early in our female lives and, in some places of our mind, we can go on having them concretely present as part objects. I believe these preoccupations are aggravated by the actual unfair conditions in which we and our mothers have lived and still live, giving rise to a vicious circle of devaluation of our qualities, even though we are beginning to get out of it.

A patient of mine told me a dream the other day.

> She was in the best shop in town and she was buying a bag for a really long journey she was happy to make. The manager showed her a few and she chose the one she liked most, it had three zipped pockets. She immediately started to fill them, but realised it would never be big enough for all the things she wanted to put in. She asked the manager for a bigger one, he brought it and she took it.

Let us look at a baby boy, he is eight months old. His mother is feeding him in a quiet corner of the living room. He is caressing the breast with his free hand and looking her in the eyes. He is taking her in whole, with all her other pockets: his father making noises while he gets supper ready, his sister watching TV and talking to granny on the sofa. Her relationships become his; we all need space in our minds for each other, like in my patient's big bag.

Back from the weekend and facing a longer break, my patient dreams that a female doctor finds three wounds deep inside her. She is worried but the doctor is confident they are not fatal. A woman's life is a continuous cycle of beginnings and ends, of fulfilment and loss. The same relationships that fill and enrich us cause us worry and pain, the wheel of life moves on.

References

Britton, R. (1995). Psychic reality and unconscious belief. *International Journal of Psycho-Analysis, 76*: 19–23.

Freud, S. (1923b). *The Ego and the Id. S. E., 19* (pp. 19–27). London: Hogarth Press.

Isaacs, S. (1948). The nature and function of phantasy. *International Journal of Psycho-Analysis, 29*: 73–97.

Klein, M. (1945). The Oedipus complex in the light of early anxieties. *International Journal of Psycho-Analysis, 26*: 11–33.

Kulish, N., & Holtzman, D. (2007). Baubo: rediscovering woman's pleasures. In: A. M. Alizade (Ed.), *The Embodied Female* (pp. 109–120). London: Karnac.

PART II

CREATIVITY IN PSYCHOANALYTIC PRACTICE THROUGHOUT THE LIFE CYCLE

CHAPTER EIGHT

When creativity restarts: distorted and adaptive forms

Frances Thomson-Salo

I want to explore an idea that when creativity has been stifled for a long time it may first start again in a distorted form like a blade of grass in a desert at first growing sideways, and in analysis this needs not to be disparaged; and to consider this in conjunction with the independent tradition of being the analyst whom the patient needs rather than always interpreting with a focus on the negative transference. I will illustrate with vignettes from child, adolescent, and adult patients all deidentified or composited, describing how female patients made a creative use of creativity and how creativity is sometimes cocreated as a female analyst with a male patient. James Grotstein (1997) suggested that the development of ontological courage—to accept one's life as a life to live and to create—is related to Klein's epistemophilic and sadistic propensities, and to Winnicott's creative ones.

I will begin with an artist's thirty year struggle against depression with an early image of Joan Rodriquez, whose work is in the Cunningham Dax collection of artworks by people with an experience of mental illness and/or psychological trauma for which I am the honorary psychoanalyst. Joan now in her seventies remembers from the age of four using any crayons she could find to make drawings. Decades later she painted Figure 1. The pain in the face of the mutilated person who

Figure 1. *Vinegar Woman* by Joan Rodriquez.

gazes at the trapped one, *Vinegar Woman*, is palpable. Rodriquez wrote at the time, "I've got her contained! But she is cut off! which paralyses her—I was battling with the 'conflict of opposites'".

An overwhelming theme here is of feeling trapped. There is horror at the figure cruelly cramped in the jar, mirroring the other figure. They seem trapped in a nightmare of horror, of deformity and pain, continual rejection, like trauma in childhood. The dismembered limb signals castration, echoed by the gazer's deformed arm. Being trapped even in an open jar there is no escape, it is a cruel tease. The window frame is a reminder of escape but there is no sunlight for hope. The sense of being depressed is suggested by the black. They are trapped with the other. Their gaze will never meet, despite attunement of their limbs, suggesting being trapped forever in a parallel universe with an unseeing gaze.

Does vinegar woman represent a part of the gazer, the one gazing at the artworks? When an infant may feel that a rejected part of them was not taken in by the mother, they have to take it back. Who has the power in gaze? The infant may feel the mother has the power but she may feel her baby does. But to gaze and not see! This artwork speaks of gazing with painful longing and never feeling "seen". If the self feels depleted, it looks for the missing mirroring gaze, depending desperately on another to mirror its internal states and for self preservation. Jacques Lacan has pointed to the power of gaze when a child sees the mother breastfeeding the sibling and casts the evil eye on the baby whom the child envies and wishes to kill and petrify. That the experiences shown in the picture can never come together is central, as if pain and unconscious experience cannot be integrated.

I shared these thoughts with Rodriquez. She felt that the artwork represented two aspects of herself, her frustration at domesticity as though she had lost her arm (reminscent of feeling trapped as described by Louise Bourgeois in Chapter Sixteen). She saw the figures as friends. She said that her mother's mother died when she was young and her own mother had been very busy running a farm single-handed when she was a child; Rodriquez felt that at some time we must explore and "own" areas of one's life that have not been previously owned. She has painted mothers with black eyes, one titled "Un-mothered", as though sadly haunted. She talked of reworking things at different stages of her life.

I think a child who feels that a maternal presence is unavailable, could feel unprotected, perhaps abused,

The Cunningham Dax Collection "This 'Woman in the Vinegar Bottle' is contained but 'cut off' which paralyses action …", "I was battling with the conflict of opposites."—Artist Statement and facing a black despair of meaninglessness.

Rodriquez summarised her work from 1963 to 1993 as a "struggle to define identity. The old work shows the bottled up energy of the unconscious situation". She said that she explores the use of art in the process of self-realisation, a method of healing in the transforming process and she drew from a personal experience of loss, with a recurring theme of a mother/child split. Currently she illustrates beautiful children's books.

Creativity bubbles out of children in their play and imagination, beginning, Winnicott suggested, in mutual gaze at the breast, with a mother allowing her baby the sense of creating the milk, and to trust their capacity to create. Is the artist's creativity reparation for destructive wishes, a containment the parents were not felt to provide, or part of creating the self and feeling alive? Creating artwork may give an illusion of oneness with the mother at the same time as facing the painful reality of separateness. The artist's creativity in integrating their destructiveness and contact with deathliness does something very valuable for us, because as Winnicott (1971) thought, artists constantly create new forms and enable us to stay alive. Creativity can be seen as an antidote to the struggle in life and it is also joyful (Leunig, 2013).

I want to turn to three early drawings of a six-year-old girl, Louisa, whom I saw in five times a week analysis. She was referred because her adoptive parents thought that she might be autistic, with considerable regression. She appeared frozen and to be almost completely inhibited in her thinking. She was conceived while her parents were patients in a psychiatric hospital, her mother with a schizophrenic episode. At ten weeks of age Louisa was placed with a foster mother and adopted at two years by relative strangers. A three-year-old adoptive brother tried murderously to smother her. The adoptive parents found it was too difficult to tell Louisa the truth of her biological mother. They said that her foster mother was her birth mother, that their son had wanted a sister and they had a nice room for her. That makes no sense as a reason why a family would take a child from another family so Louisa in not being told the truth shut down her curiosity. When I first saw her, she was strikingly like a two-year-old. A few immature words poured out of her incoherently. She said it was sunny at night. She asked, "Where's the mudder (mother) doll? She's lost ..." She sat on the floor sucking her thumb. She drew the thin lips of a mouth on one piece of paper and on a separate piece of paper she drew a red eye and said she had nearly drowned. (See Figure 2 and Figure 3). She dipped her paintbrush in the paint, then in water and was puzzled that there was no colour. With her mother lost, she nearly drowned psychically and the world lost both colour and sense. Giving me these psychotic-like fragments was her attempt to join up what could not be joined up.

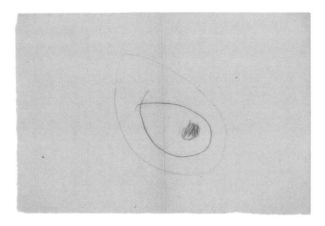

Figure 2. An eye-I nearly drowned.

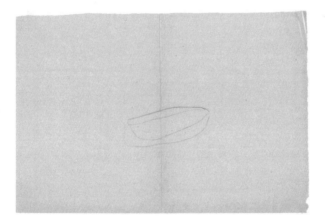

Figure 3. A mouth.

Two weeks after starting analysis she drew herself and me sitting together. (See Figure 4). It was very different from the drawing of the two body parts and quite colourful. She "accidentally" drew herself wearing my shoes, and our sleeves were coloured the same. While seeming perhaps adhesive, I think that the containment of another mind allowed hers some integration. In her drawings she found herself as an agent in her relationship with me and a few weeks later she was able to use words, saying, "I have a first mummy and a second mummy. I like my second mummy, but I love my first." And then painfully she said,

Figure 4. You and me.

"I don't understand. Why did it happen?" She shouted "WHY?" and lay down and said, "I'm dead. You should …" she trailed off, as if I should have looked after her and prevented a loss. If her foster mother was dead, Louisa felt dead also. Here, the creativity expressed in the drawings allowed her to face the psychic murder of the adoptive mother and to recreate the beloved other.

Now I want to move to the end of an analysis of an older woman, Mrs G, and a trio of dreams, effectively a canvas that allowed some vital working through, Quinodoz's (1999) dreams that "turn over a page". Mrs G felt that she had not got it right with her daughter. Her transference included aspects of her lonely embittered mother and I was at times an empty-eyed snake-headed Medusa, whom she envied for being fertile. Three months after her granddaughter's birth, Mrs G was angry with her daughter, whom she felt did not reach out to Mrs G. Mrs G could reflect that her daughter was able to *think* about the meaning of her baby's experience, which was different from how Mrs G had been as a mother. It seemed that Daughter G might still be hurt and angry about her painful infant experiences but did not need to repeat these with her baby daughter. The ghosts from the past had not captured her.

Mrs G's anger with her daughter—a good-enough mother who could not repair the rift with her own mother—was brought in a dream of a young woman who grew an amazingly fertile garden full of Mrs G's favourite flowers. Mrs G had previously had rather restricted, one-line dreams. Mrs G's association was that it was her envy of her daughter, although consciously she did not want to spoil things for her. She was in touch with painful feelings saying, "When I see my daughter get it right I feel ashamed I didn't get it right." She dreamt that she and I were at a meeting and I left without her; she wanted to follow me but couldn't find her way to her car. The central disconnection which this patient had suffered all her life was fully in the transference and this was followed by a session that "turned a page". She dreamt of a devastated house with empty windows and a sense of impending catastrophe although there was a "second chance" of survival with a woman in a business-suit telling them to flee from Fiji. In association, she said that the previous session I had smiled about something, which she felt I did very rarely, and she said it felt like "sunshine entering my soul, it was heart warming." I had worked many times with her feelings in the transference that I was withdrawn. On this occasion I simply suggested that the catastrophe had been her mother's eyes, their emptiness, and Mrs G started to cry. I do not know if this would be included in Leon Hoffman's (personal communication, 2009) suggestion that the analyst embrace a commitment to be creative, but it seemed to open more potential space.

For the first time Mrs G said she wanted to face away from me to be alone with the pain. She had always used the couch until this time when she wanted to sit up to prepare for ending the analysis. She half turned away and raised her handkerchief to her eyes so that we could not see each other. She said that the smiling look was something that her granddaughter got all the time from her mother. (We could now link how Mrs G had identified with her own mother: Mrs G had her own "snake eyes" when she went "far away" and also had a phobia of snakes, symbolising her own snake-mother who was felt not to hold her.) Mrs G now felt sad for the first time for her mother, wondering what had happened to make her the way she was.

These were the tears and pain that Mrs G had held all her life and never allowed herself to feel with me. It was the pain her daughter had carried for her. As Mrs G felt that there was an enlivening place in my mind, not an empty one for which she was responsible, her sense of self-worth consolidated. She was more generous with her daughter and creative in her relationships. She felt her daughter had a love affair with *her* daughter which she had not had. I thought that Mrs G was working things out with her so that the hate and conflict did not have to pass transgenerationally down the line from the great grandmother who had eyes like coffins. The trio of dreams, a new feature, perhaps represented the three generations. This new creativity in the dream facilitated a new level of working through.

I have looked at creativity in female artist and patients and I want to finish with some transition points in an adolescent boy's analysis, exploring the creativity that a female analyst may bring in the patient-therapist interaction in trying to see an adolescent's fantasying while using pornography as creative. Having worked in an adolescent centre in London which offered analysis I have drawn on that work for this vignette which I will give without background in order to focus on the adolescent's sense of self. He was referred as a thirteen-year-old for concerns about autism and possible psychotic breakdown. Only when he had started analysis did he disclose that he had previously tried to hang himself and cut his wrists. For years he tried to be a good boy. Bowed down by the weight of a backpack this tiny boy trudged to school. He was anxious, inhibited, had a learning disorder, extensive obsessive doubt, looked like he had Tourette's syndrome and was badly bullied. He had little sense of self and was despairing about integrating the different states of mind he lived in.

We began face-to-face analysis four times a week. After about nine months, in an important session unlike any other, he brought a number of questions and was surprisingly inarticulate. He asked if I thought that it was odd that he did not like wearing sandals in the summer. I took up that he seemed to feel that he would not be him (if he wore sandals) and he agreed. He would say, "Yes", there would be a long pause and then another "yes" as if he was being half-heartedly polite and when he said "yes" it seemed to be almost mechanical and dying away. I thought of the beeps in a humidi-crib, an anxious maternal heart-beat and how anxious he had been as a foetus pulling away from the amniocentesis needle. He said, "I just wouldn't be me if I wore sandals" as though only wearing sneakers would ground him and not lose his fragile sense of self. The silences punctuated with an occasional "yes" continued throughout the session. He asked if I thought watching violent movies was weird. I said that perhaps he felt grounded in himself when he watched them and he agreed. I felt it was important that my gaze at him should not be felt to intrude on him. He eventually commented that it was a long pause, I said "Perhaps an important one", and he beeped "yes". In the countertransference I had a sense of sadness at how painful life in his mind must be—feeling in a fog and persecuted. He asked, "Could liking violent movies be how I saw myself?"

I said he had asked some important questions and perhaps wanted to know if he was liked. He asked, "Am I gross?" about being gross. In the countertransference I again felt a wave of sadness and wondered whether what he felt was his grossness partly defined his sense of self, but then he felt so bad that he wanted to get rid of it. I put some of this into an interpretation and he agreed with me vehemently. He cracked his back, his hands and his neck looking at me to see if I found this gross. He then said as if trying to accept himself, "I'm gross, that's who I am, that's me, I am gross". Two last questions were why people wear black at funerals which I linked with his sadness, and he took his helmet off and asked why analysts could not hug their patients. I talked of coming to try to understand his mind, and if there were hugs he would not know if he was here for something sexual. I thought he was reaching towards a sense of himself.

As he went into adolescence he would talk about films with encyclopaedic knowledge but also a flavour of Asperger syndrome, boring other people. He obsessionally felt that he had to use every minute of every session. He was frightened of his parents, disclosing with shame that his father beat him until he was thirteen years old. Suppressing his hatred of them, he was very anxious if I interpreted anywhere near his fear. Containment often seemed more helpful as he faced trying to detoxify the atmosphere at home. With analytic work there was a sense of his self having a little more emotional muscle and he moved to use the couch.

He became driven to watch film pornography and I heard about the stuff of nightmares. He described extreme sadism, voyeurism, bestiality, cruelty to animals and snuff movies in which people are watched as they die. With shame he wondered if he identified with neo-Nazis raping two girls. The pictures were palpable in the room. He was in thrall to a dark world and I had to be too. I felt I was in a sewer with him that I had not agreed to, hating this. In the transference at times, however, he saw me as leading him on to become a cock teaser and he attacked me using film pornography. I wondered, continuing to listen to him, whether I was colluding. Once when his mind seemed to be blown by these images, and his parents unable to see what was happening, I like a father offering a benign holding verbalised that these images were very hard for his mind to contain at this point and he used that to prevent himself being further flooded. In this distorted half-life, talking with me about sexuality seemed to be where he could discover an authentic and more integrated self.

There are many ways of understanding the pornography and I will only concentrate on possible creativity. Could there be any fantasying that was not sterile? He was using fantasy in the process of trying to unblock his creativity (Sugarman, 2009). In the pornography he was caught in a mousetrap vice, he also projected his aggression into it. In the freedom to explore it with me, hit me with it, and at times I felt raped me, and still be accepted I helped him to see that it was his and to take it back. I think in continuing to try to think clinically may be a kind of creativity.

His learning difficulty had been so pervasive that I had doubted that he would graduate from school. But he was admitted to college. Unable to stand up to his parents for years he was gradually able to tell them to back off. After his first sexual encounter in group sex with mild sadism, he found a girlfriend with "granny boobs" (breasts like a grandmother, a transference reference to me?) with whom he had a short-lived relationship and then broke it off. He wanted to snuggle forever with a girlfriend *and* to be "free to fuck everyone". At the same time he began to break off analysis with me. He did not want to be tied down to set analytic times. He seemed in exploring the register of his sexual wishes partly to be trying for another way to find himself. Whether or not I interpreted directly or in Ferro's wider field, he felt "pussy whipped" by me, as for example when I interpreted his vulnerability in his being gullible.

He began turning up late or cancelling sessions. I struggled to preserve the analytic work. I wondered if we were both going through the motions. I wondered anxiously if I was colluding and being unethical. I thought that this is how some adolescents leave home and perhaps this was his way of leaving me. I came to think of it as, in Winnicott's terms, claiming the sessions like an infant creating the breast, to be there under his control when he wanted it. He began a long-term caring, sexual relationship but continued not to attend many sessions. But we now could think of this in interpretation as for example when he left five minutes early he was simultaneously complying with the family wish that he should value his sessions and also being his authentic self. He was making them his own, and not his parents'. He had disowned his own aggression and it had not been available for use creatively. He could see that I could survive his aggression. As that emerged in the transference, he claimed it and could take back the projective identification of his own wishes for revenge and triumph, and give up the life-draining obsessionality and doubt. He could then use his aggression in the service of his creativity, smashing his obsessional and autistic defences and becoming more truly creative in his film directing which was recognised externally.

Nine months before he terminated analysis, he said that he enjoyed creative writing. He said that he was happier than he had ever been and that he had never said this before. He said he was determined to make the most of his life. One of his short films was screened commercially. He felt that he was "reaching for the stars—and beyond".

Conclusion

We have seen how the six-year-old girl used drawing to symbolise an integration that she could not yet put into words; she had felt that she had broken apart and in coming together was assembling herself adaptively, using parts of me. My older patient could finally dream her envy of the creativity and allow her daughter and me space; she used vivid images in dreams that turned a page foreshadowing a new creativity in relationships. The adolescent boy who had turned to obsessional defences and then to obsessionally critiquing films could only free his creativity when he had taken back and owned his aggression in the transference, to power his own creativity. With him, it is clear to see the progression onwards from more violent art forms barely containing the pain. Finally, with the artist, Joan Rodriquez, who used painting over thiry years to understand her depression and work her way out of it, from *Vinegar Woman* to fairy tales, hers was and is great art.

References

Grotstein, J. (1997). Klein's archaic Oedipus complex and its possible relationship to the myth of the labyrinth: Notes on the origin of courage. *Journal of Analytical Psychology, 42*: 585–611.

Leunig, M. (2013). Opening Dax exhibition, *Reverie*, 9.5.13.

Quinodoz, J. (1999). Dreams that turn over a page. *International Journal of Psycho-Analysis, 80*: 225–238.

Sugarman, A. (2009). Child versus adult psychoanalysis: Two processes or one? *International Journal of Psycho-Analysis, 90*: 1255–1276.

Winnicott, D. W. (1971). *Playing and Reality*. London: Tavistock.

CHAPTER NINE

A little girl's analysis

Tonia Cancrini and Luisa Cerqua

Introduction—Tonia Cancrini, supervisor

For several years, I supervised the case of Silvia, a ten-year-old girl in treatment with my colleague, Luisa Cerqua. Luisa handled the treatment with great passion and competence. It was a work of great interest for both of us as it enabled us to understand in depth the huge potential of a psychoanalytic intervention during childhood, if managed in a systematic and competent way. We were able to see clearly how a lively and profound creativity could develop both within the child and inside the analytic couple. This allowed the child to overcome very primitive anxieties and achieve adequate maturational growth. At the same time, we were able to come face-to-face with all the difficulties and enthusiasms that belong to the treatment of children, a treatment that is always rich in surprises and where the analyst is frequently extremely involved. We will try to share the experience of the first year that we hope you will find as enriching as it has been for us.

History and first session—Luisa Cerqua, analyst

I will focus on the first year of treatment, with three weekly sessions, of a ten-year-old girl, Silvia. She has two sisters, who are eight and six years old. She does well in school, but she is solitary and quiet. Tall and slim, with long brown plaits, braces and very big feet. She is clumsy, wearing a school uniform that is slightly small for her age and which makes her appear like a "big baby". She is very smart and subtle.

Her parents consult me because they are worried about Silvia's passiveness when confronted with choices; she conforms to her mother's wishes as if she was scared to express her own. She is not willing to mix with children her age because, she says, they tire her. She loves reading and hardly ever plays much, never with dolls but mainly with complex electronic games. In her father's family tradition many aspects of female creativity have never been considered important, whereas male intellectual and speculative traits have always been highly praised. It will therefore be very important, in the course of treatment, for the child to attain a feminine creativity that, as we will see, gains an increasing importance throughout the analytic relationship.

When she was eight years old Silvia suffered a serious domestic accident, when her mother was absent and she was at her grandparents' house together with her sisters. During a fight with her younger sister she broke a window and was fairly seriously injured by the glass.

Silvia's mother told me she was worried about her daughter's health. She was herself in therapy because of issues that seemed to be related to her femininity and her marital life. Silvia's father, often absent because of his work, studies tsunamis and seaquakes and is used to keeping his emotions to himself. I was struck by his habit of watching horror films with his "girls" during the evenings they spent together.

Soon after Silvia was born, her parents separated for a couple of months and after their reconciliation their two other daughters were born.

Silvia's mother appeared to be hyper-present in her daughters' lives whereas the father, elevated to an intellectual and dominating pedestal because of his intelligence, appeared distant. After the accident he was, however, more active and present in the life of the family. Silvia's mother (having had a psychotic father) confessed her difficulties when dealing with male figures, seen as dangerous and potentially violent.

The young patient was angry and confused by something that still had no name, in the need to escape from the "uniform" of the perfect child, by then clearly too tight for her. Our dialogue begins by confronting her relational difficulties at school and focusing on a teacher who does not understand her. "My teacher says that I'm not the good girl I used to be because I tease others and I fight with boys", she confided. The first session ended with an unexpected question: "Why do you think we have to die?" To my utmost surprise the child, who had apparently—as stated by her parents—"never played with a toy", immediately began to play. The first game contained, I believe, many of the issues that emerged during the first year of treatment.

She approaches the wooden three-storey playhouse, calling it the house of children, and places all the members of the family in it. She puts a child, alone, in a cradle in the attic, the mother downstairs with a baby in the double bed. The other children want to climb into bed as well, but there is no space for everyone and someone falls off the bed and cries. Silvia speaks for the characters through gritted teeth, as if she does not want me to understand what they are saying. The grandmother "grumbles and criticises", the grandfather "stands there looking dumb", the father "cares about his own business and reads"! Then everyone leaves the house and the baby falls from the mother's arms. Silvia immediately says that there is a hospital and that the mother will stay with the baby. She says that the children are in school, alone, since nobody went to pick them up. It is Christmas at home and everybody sits down at the table, but the adults begin to fight.

I ask: "Where are you?", she replies: "At the window looking at the view. The children all climb to the roof to watch the sky. They have biscuits!"

Important issues immediately emerge: abandonment, being forgotten, the lack of a maternal container who can nourish her, her illness as a way to have her mother all to herself, the absence of space for children who find themselves alone watching stars and eating biscuits. She continues the same game setting up a house on my desk. At the centre of the house she builds a kitchen stove with some kitchen utensils that the grandmother uses to cook food for everyone. Every session ends with a lunch. We spend months cooking together an extraordinary variety of dishes. I must say I enjoyed myself, surprised to be able to give shape to what she requested. I relived the atmosphere in which, during my own childhood, my uncle built a Christmas crib and moulded small houses, animals and food out of clay. An unforgettable game. After many years I rediscovered that same experience.

Before the Christmas break Silvia shows her anguish about the separation and the lack of psychoanalytic nourishment. The game of the house becomes the game of the dairy-farm, besieged by a gang of gunmen and Indians trying to steal milk.

Supervisor

As you can observe, the child immediately brings into the game her most primitive anguish, related to the loss of the good maternal nourishment that causes the child to be afraid of falling from her mother's arms, of no longer being protected and sustained, of lacking any sort of support, of being victim of the theft of another who has become hostile and an enemy. The internal world is populated with persecutory presences: the gunmen and Indians recall the birth of her two sisters, when the child would have felt excluded and jealous. But it is also related to a previous time, to the primary relationship with her mother. The feeling we have is that of a discontinuity in the primary relationship. So, at times, what prevailed was the absence of a maternal mind that was, possibly, too involved in her own problems and difficulties. And it is perhaps in this maternal absence that we discover the devaluation of feminine creativity, a creativity that would have had its essential function during the first phases of development, giving the child the security of nourishment and care. In supervision we focused on these primitive levels which they engaged the analyst in a very deep involvement that required an intense and compelling work of *rêverie*. In this kind of situation, in which the psychoanalyst is called to a strong emotional and affective involvement, supervision is extremely important because it helps to contain the emotional load by sharing the most intense emotions. This is, I believe, one of the main objectives of supervision: helping the containment of very intense emotions and *rêverie* which is necessary if treatment is to be an emotional relationship that primarily moves through transference and countertransference. When working with children this appears to be even more relevant because, on the one hand, they involve us in an intense emotional way and, on the other, they themselves live the psychoanalytic relationship very strongly. This is what we can observe in what follows: the total involvement of the child in the psychoanalytic relationship, and the resulting deep anxieties about the Christmas holidays.

Analyst

After resuming analysis in January, Silvia immediately expresses her rage. She says she is very angry with the children of her compound who stained her with shaving foam and showed her a condom, children bragging about "yucky stuff", and herself fighting with them. She tells me that in February there will be another interruption because of the midterm break. During the session I perceive her mood as different from usual. I myself feel a sense of heaviness and boredom.

Silvia begins the sessions by being laconic and vague, she does not know what to do, she asks me to decide and only opens up unwillingly. At times she is more lively and seems excited; her ears turn red. She draws two mountains with icy tops and says: "Maybe the ice will melt in spring, the sun struggles to come out as well". This is how she represents our situation.

My supervisor points out that I worry too much and reassure Silvia about her distressing experiences. She shows me how, by doing so, I risk cancelling out the disquieting aspects that she is beginning to bring into the session, stains that certainly appear to her as upsetting, of aggressiveness and sexuality.

It is in this delicate phase that the shared thought of supervision was precious. It created around Silvia a field of female emotional thought that sustained my own thought. A dialogue was created that helped me give shape to deep emotional experiences. It enabled me, during the sessions, to recover the value of precious feminine levels of development. Feminine attitudes that build and fix, and even the absence of these feminine aspects can help us understand what is missing in her development.

Supervisor

We can observe, at this point, the importance of the psychoanalytic relationship. The child experienced the feelings of abandonment and exclusion in an extremely intense way. She felt alone and tormented by a persecutory anguish; the caring and protective object had changed to a bad breast. It is important in this phase to work with transference in order to find a path to follow and not to leave her alone and to value the importance of the relationship. It is important to remain in contact, to understand these feelings, and not to fall into reassuring her, as this can make the child feel not understood and obstruct the access to profound anguish. What cannot be disregarded now is the work on transference, with which the analyst appears to have difficulty because of the intensity of emotions and the child's deep involvement. During supervision we focus on these aspects, as well as on the analyst's countertransference, because it appears that the analyst is defending herself from the strong requests that the child brings with the transference, and is somewhat surprised by their intensity. The supervision becomes a place where we can live together to metabolise the strong emotions and work on the *rêverie*. This enables the analyst to find in herself a feminine creativity that is essential for the child in order to be able to trust the relationship.

Analyst

After the Christmas holidays two more interruptions take place, the first for the midterm break (beginning of February) and the second one (two weeks later) because of a bad flu I caught. It is the end of February. During the week in which I am sick Silvia cannot sleep.

When she comes back she appears upset; I talk to her about being alone with new emotions and without therapy, but she seems to want to drop the subject and laconically plays messily with play dough. After my illness the games assume a different intensity that make my participation and my *rêverie* more difficult. I feel burdened, as if struggling to be Silvia's "live company". She starts playing with the house again, but she now moves the characters, the small furniture and the small utensils in a repetitive way. The desk is now filled with a myriad of little objects with which she sets up the game. The grandmother is always busy cooking. She continuously, unintentionally, knocks over the characters and the furniture, putting them back to place obsessively. Her being so clumsy strikes me. She appears to be "stuffing herself" with the game. I perceive a little tyranny and at the end of the sessions I feel tired. During our time together we continuously cook dishes with dough, to the point that Silvia says: "We have cooked and eaten so much together that it's like we're related now!"

She often mixes and remixes the dough in a messy way. There is silence. I notice she is not asking me to help, she is doing it by herself.

I tell her. Her mixtures are however too flaccid and do not hold, they "wither". It is the same feeling I have during the countertransference in this phase of the work. I feel flaccid, lacking vital energy. I feel "withered"!

She tells a dream, where a damaged mouth appears:

> A friend of my mother's had a small son whom they took to teach him things. I held him and he was horrible, so I stuffed him in a bag that could widen and shrivel depending on what you put into it. I heard him screaming in the bag, my mum opened it and picked up the baby. He was hurt! His jaw had moved and I hadn't noticed! Part of his mouth was all crooked, he was horrible and I was so worried! I was close to my grandmother's place and there was a strange hospital, like a train with wagons. It was dirty and ugly. The child underwent surgery and I was very sorry, I didn't know what to tell my mother. Later he came out of surgery and he looked fine. So I told him that his teeth were much better now, they were all crooked before but not anymore. I was worried I should tell his mother that I had put him in the bag. I didn't want him to get hurt!

She thinks and then adds: "The jaw of the child I dreamed was crooked!" She then tells me she is going to a new orthodontist and is obtaining results with her teeth that had never been obtained by the old female doctor. I point out that maybe the child in the bag is something that belongs to her, something that she had wanted to put away and is now emerging. It was hurt in the mouth and had, therefore, problems eating and talking. But now it had protested, it came out of the bag and it is here with us, ready to be cured. Playing and eating together, I gradually managed to find a way to access the mind through the dream. The dream enabled us to come closer to a very deep anguish but in spite of (or maybe because of) it I feel a countertransference difficulty to proceeding towards a deeper and more lively way of being with her.

Supervisor

Our thought goes to the deep feeling of the child who, in the moment of absence, comes in contact with the emptiness and with dead areas that are filled with very intense persecutory anguish. In the moment in which she does not feel contained in the analyst's mind, the emptiness is filled with persecution, so that the child defends herself with obsessiveness. The game that allows a repetitive and monotonous pattern takes the place of thought and impedes true emotional contact. In her countertransference the analyst perceives this, even if she cannot give it meaning yet. This shows us that the level of anguish is too high to be tolerated. The problem on which we focus during supervision is how to give space to this anguish in a dimension that can be tolerable both for the child and the analyst. In fact the child, even though able to represent deep feelings and strong anxieties in her dream, brings with her a part of herself that is hidden in a bag and that must be fully reached.

On the other hand, in treatment, Silvia is showing needs that are primitive and her affective investment is huge. She shows her need of good nourishment and is asking the analyst for it. But, in order to do this, she needs to keep her aggressiveness separated and this remains for the moment outside the treatment. The collusion with the psychoanalyst on this is easy. We then slowly come to realise how important it is for rage to be taken into the psychoanalytic relationship. This is why it becomes fundamental to live and understand these needs and emotions within the transference as well as the attack on and the devaluation of the feminine world. Only after having understood this, and having opened the way to the gaining of trust and a revaluation of good nourishment, was the child able to feel what was missing in the relationship with her mother. It is now possible for her to seek in the relationship with the analyst what she could not find in the relationship with her mother.

The treatment is good "ecological" food taken from her grandmother's orchard for her. It is different from the disgusting school canteen. However, for it to be appreciated and for it to become good nourishment, it is important for her to overcome her mistrust of the feminine object (the female doctor who does not cure). It is fundamental at this point to interpret the negative transference in order to overcome the mistrust of the possibility of the analyst curing her. The child must therefore surpass the fear of a doctor who cannot cure her well enough, the fear that the only way is to go to the hospital, a place that is dirty and unpleasant and that she does not like. The doctor who can cure is male and the feminine character is therefore devalued. This fear must be communicated in a more profound way in order for it to be overcome. There appears to be a great difficulty to trust, to be able to come in contact with a feminine figure who is able to help her. What plays an important role here is the bad primary relationship, where there is a mother who was unable to help with a continuous and constant presence.

Analyst

I feel it is therefore important to deal with the cue about the uncaring female doctor. Silvia fears that I might be unable to come close and cure the parts of her that must be fixed. She stages, when playing with the house, the rich world she wants to live in, rich in presence and comfort, but also the interior fear of being empty and damaged in that part of herself that must put her in contact with life: the mouth. She has, inside her, a world of monsters, horror films, delirious family members, accidents. I become the mother-analyst of this child who is so full of scary things. What she had shown me at the beginning was the desire for a tidy home. In that same house a snake appears. She calls it "serpentè" ("serpente" being snake and "separè", a partition wall) made out of play dough that she built to separate the internal spaces of the house, a disquieting border that slithers like a snake.

In her house story there is something that makes her feel out of place, just like the snake. All this refers to her precocious childhood where the parental couple had many problems and was not therefore able to represent a point of stability and security. I think that the rage and suffering made her feel like the child in her dream with the crooked jaw. Silvia feels she has to pass by the hospital, that she has to touch things that are painful and disquieting. She fears that I might be unable to help her, but also hopes that slowly the trust needed for the teeth to go back into place can be acquired. The difficulty is to find an object that is other and that can give her the nourishment she needs, not just a servile and oppressed object that appears to satisfy her but is then unable to provide real nourishment. This will be a very complex problem that will require a great amount of attention. This is when the summer arrives.

The first summer interruption is dramatic. Silvia stops eating and loses weight to a point where she almost eliminates her feminine body. In the phase before the interruption she had drawn a lot and filled sheets and sheets of paper with tangles of colours obtained by using more felt-tip pens with one hand. She represents, in this way, the tangle of emotions that scare her, that in the analytic language we call the "big bundle", or "Gapico", a green and orange play dough puppet, ugly and squat, "but not evil". Gapico was the acrostic of jealousy, love, fear, rage and hate. She then drew networks of liquid glue that she poured directly on the sheets and waited for them to dry. They looked like labyrinths. She coloured them in, meticulously obtaining results that were similar to monochromatic windows; she worked greedily to use all the time and all the material she had. In the penultimate session before the summer break, while colouring, she told a dream.

"I change class in school. I am alone in a class of people I don't know. For a moment I feel happy because my mother tells me that now the children will say: 'Look, here's Silvia! Why is she with us?' But there is also Viola who is envious because she did not change class. She remained with the old class and tries to shoot me. So I reach a guard who takes me in his arms, but Viola continues shooting."

After a pause she adds: "That shooting is like strong hate; it's strong, so strong that it becomes a shot".

I tell her that Viola shoots because she is angry about how she was left out of the class. I suggest that maybe she is angry as well, considering that in two days she would not be there because of the summer holidays. She too was taken in someone's arms and held but has to leave now. She, therefore, feels put aside and excluded, in the same way Viola was with the class. I tell her that she is right, when hate is strong it can be like a shot and it can even kill. It is scary to feel so full of hate. Silvia listens to the interpretation of her dream and immediately remembers another one from the night before.

"There was a kitten that jumped down a terrace and died. It's one that was recently born. It wanted to climb down from the terrace where we keep them so the dog doesn't eat them, following its mother's path. But the jump is too high for it. So it falls and dies."

I tell her that the kitten that follows his mother looks just like her. We have travelled together and now it is time to say goodbye; she feels alone and she is afraid that she might lose herself, afraid she might fall like the kitten. The same thing had occurred during the Easter holidays. Now the break is longer, but we will be back in September.

In the following session, the last one, she uses tempera. She concentrates on her painting for the whole session, so as to complete the job before we separate. She creates coloured spheres that look like planets on a blue background. They evoke the deepness of astral space. The image of the falling kitten appears in my mind, together with that of

Viola-Silvia who feels so excluded and angry that she shoots, of Silvia locked outside the balcony during the serious domestic accident. I tell her about the fear of being forgotten and of losing herself, of dying like the kitten in the dream. A little like she had felt on the day of the accident.

That experience now comes back to her mind. She rethinks it and finally tells me about it. She says that during a fight her little sister had locked her out on the balcony. She wanted to return inside, so she broke the glass and hurt herself. I tell her that I am sure she had felt very alone and angry, and that she must have been frightened.

"I broke the glass without realising what was happening!"—she states with emphasis—"I only saw darkness! I didn't understand anything and thought they'd forget me there, outside, on the balcony! That they'd leave me there forever!" Then she adds a strong comment: "… and luckily the glass at the top didn't fall! Do you know that if it had fallen on my neck it could have killed me?"

At the end of the session Silvia appears to be happy about her painting and relieved. We say goodbye to each other and I feel quite calm.

After the summer I find a message on the answering machine informing me of a dramatic emergency. During the holiday Silvia had almost stopped eating, she had lost a lot of weight. They had been worried and had tried to contact me but, not being able to find me, had gone to a hospital. I realised that, though having seen her anguish of loss I was not able to grasp their full drama. Tolerating and thinking them had perhaps been traumatic for me too. Confronting that had implied a very complex and slow elaboration that enabled focusing on the total investment of the patient in the analyst and on the anguish of losing herself and dying without the treatment.

Conclusion—Supervisor

We repeatedly asked ourselves why, in spite of the very precise interpretations regarding separation and death anguish, themes that were also present in Silvia's dreams, such dramatic feelings arose during the summer. What struck us was that even though the psychoanalyst had understood many aspects and worked thoroughly on the separation, and even though the child appeared to have reached deep levels of maturation regarding abandonment, such as to bring to the session dreams that represented those deep anxieties and strong feelings, the absence of the psychoanalyst had nevertheless caused a catastrophe. We reasoned that the child could not probably maintain the same capacity of representation and comprehension without the analyst-container and had found herself overwhelmed by her emotions, of suffering and rage, fear and hate, and had not been able to do anything other than enact the catastrophe she felt inside. And this acting, on the other hand, would have enabled the analyst to comprehend in depth the pain and the anger that Silvia had experienced. At times, acting can be an important form of communication that renders explicit what risks remaining hidden. In this way the summer episode enabled the analyst to feel in herself this moment of fear and catastrophe and be able to gradually find the way to confront feelings that are so primitive and archaic.

On the other hand, we think an important point is that it was fundamental to reach this deep wound in order to be able to proceed further. Silvia probably needed the analyst to physically touch this feeling, not only through her stories. Once more, just as in other emotionally compelling moments, we could confront the total investment of the young patient towards the analyst through the supervision, where the solidity of a psychoanalytic couple allowed with the most dramatic moments to be faced. The analyst and the little patient were able to live and deeply understand the tragedy of separation and abandonment. This experience that has been very meaningful, vital, and creative for us is what we hoped, in writing about it, to share.

CHAPTER TEN

A psychoanalyst in the labour room: the birth of emotions

Laura Tognoli Pasquali

Some time ago I was invited to a gynaecology congress to talk about birth. I very much wanted to accept the invitation but I was afraid of feeling out of place.

With slight hesitation and needing to find courage, I found a theme that fascinates me greatly and that involves a particular aspect of birth: the birth of emotions. Feeling more at ease in my territory, I managed to enter the theatre of birth, where life begins: the labour room.

When you step onto the crowded stage of birth with your own knowledge and tools but also anxiety, admiration, desire to participate and astounded curiosity, you feel a kind of reverential fear that becomes bewilderment, commotion, astonishment.

The body dominates the birth scene and you have to be extremely careful not to disturb those who dedicate themselves to controlling the heart beat, driving away the ghost of death, helping a head overcome the painful journey through the channel of birth, embracing a baby who comes from another world, helping gasping newborns fill their lungs with their first breath.

If someone brings the heavy burden of emotions into that magical world where life begins with he runs the strong risk of being considered an intruder because the work pressure placed on whoever works in a labour room is huge and the requests from all directions are endless. So, over there, while obstetricians were intent on making the delivery as safe as possible, it occurred to me that there was a strong possibility of being escorted to the exit and asked not to disturb. Furthermore, it would be the least that could happen to me as the pressure of emotions present at the moment of birth is so intense and the primitive forces at work in the labour room so many, that it is normal that the delivery experts make every effort to defend, negate, stay away from them and above all negate the fact that these emotions with their strong, primitive power may affect their efficiency, may affect their actions and have a significant influence on the events of birth.

However, if the door open to the desire of helping the birth of emotions, the labour room could be the meeting point between the mind and the body, a place where medicine can delve into areas that physiology cannot explore and attempt to enter the realm of the mind, which is feelings, conflicts, fears, anxieties belonging to a human being who is body as well as mind. Emotions are the integrating force between mind and body and, if recognised, can contribute to the birth of what we define as a living individual.

If the delivery experts have invited me—and surely this could not have been possible when many years ago I was studying medicine— I cannot but come to the conclusion that there is a great desire within obstetricians to give birth to a new obstetric science that holds the idea of a body as well as of a soul and that there is a great desire to work towards integration and growth both personally and professionally. This can be done only by entering at long last that dichotomy within medicine between mind and body which had greatly damaging results for doctors and their patients.

Immediately, I would like to challenge some common fallacies. When one talks about the birth of emotions, our mind immediately connects to the tenderness of a mother, the love of a child, the concern of a helping hand, a father who is moved … it connects to those inner motions of love and life that once experienced make one feel good and generous, those feelings that give strength and hope and evoke images of parents who have loved us and were happy to have given us life. Of course these are the emotions we would all want to see blossoming in ourselves and the people who surround us in every situation, especially where there is a relationship that implies dependence and that therefore makes us feel more fragile.

It would be great if it was like this, if these were the only feelings. It would be great, but it would be untrue. It is propaganda, which has a huge fascination for all of us, but it resembles a video full of beautiful children born effortlessly, without any danger, very healthy and full of life.

The emotions we need the courage to bring to life in the labour room, the emotions that will allow the capacity to take the care for a mother and her child to emerge, can be very violent and the more dangerous the more remote they are from conscience. They are dangerous because they act as foreign bodies. They do not seem to belong to us and they unchain, on a psychological level, a whole array of defence mechanisms that have the duty to eliminate them. The result can be that of discomfort or disturbed behaviour or even a physical sickness when the reaction is local: an acute inflammation bound to end once the mysterious pathogenic agent consumes itself.

They can also provoke chronic diseases in the individuals (the so-called essential illnesses) or disturbing reactions at an institutional level that, far from finding a natural solution, need somebody able to recognise them and have the strength to face them. If ignored they become more and more virulent creating inside the institution a dangerously pathological environment.

I am thinking of certain types of work organisations based on the complete negation of the basic mother and child needs, of certain behaviours that sprout on an individual level and then tend to spread pell-mell from one operator to the other. These patterns of behaviour, whose root is unconscious, are unfortunately quite frequent in the labour room and seem to be dictated by a desire to humiliate and control mother by taking her place, negating her existence, acting on her behalf as though she were unable to understand or take any action. They result in the staff totally controlling the delivery with the weight of the enormous superiority of their technical competence and the power that derives from it. Generally the baby too is taken away from mother and "medically" controlled by "proper experts". These and other pathologies, unfortunately not so rare in the labour room, if taken back to their prehistory, seem to originate from a tormented envy for the great riches of mother's body and from an appalling fear of the absolute dependence from a woman of "huge power" that every human being, man or woman, has experienced at the origin of his/her life.

Competition, selfishness, fears, resentment linked to faraway experiences that have left in us a shambles of anxiety are easily evoked by the delivery events but immediately sent back to the unconscious realm. It is not easy to give birth to them. They stay dangerously hidden, like live wires: until you touch them nothing happens but if somebody does put their hand on them, they receive an electric shock they will remember forever.

Negation is the biggest obstacle that prevents the emergency of an affect. Negation is one of the many defence mechanisms that are needed to keep anxiety at ease.

Not seeing what is actually there is a very common mental operation, extremely effective to guarantee a state of psychological tranquillity. Unfortunately it does not have the power to change reality. It changes only its perception. The result is a contraction of the perceptive field and, in the final analysis, of intellectual ability. Negation makes us feel stronger but also more rigid, full of suspicions, anchored to what we already know, scared of all that is new.

So even a feeling needs obstetric attention to be aided at birth. Socrates said this a long time ago before politicians got rid of him as he represented a very dangerous individual. Dangerous because he used to teach how to search for the answers to the problems of life, not through official science but within one's personal thoughts and emotions. As did his midwife mother with babies, he used to help thoughts come to life, freed from the resistances provoked by misconceptions and from the omnipotent conviction of already knowing everything.

Allow me now to introduce a dream. Dreams are my most important work tool, my ultrasound, the window which allows me to glance at that newborn that all of us, male or female, teenage or elderly, bring within oneself during the most varied happenings of their life.

The images translated into words might not be as lively or immediate as those transmitted through a lens looking at a physical situation but I will, however, try to transmit the dream scenario and give a meaning to it.

The dreamer unfortunately is not a midwife who could have brought us directly in contact with the anxieties of the labour room. We have to be satisfied with the dream of a psychiatrist, who is also a kind of midwife, as, at the time of the dream, she is helping to give sense to the life of a very confused patient, full of anguish, who hides considerable aggression behind apparent docility.

In the dream she finds herself running away desperately, she does not know what from but she is certain that the danger is mortal. She runs anxiously to her grandmother's house, who lets her into the house with her usual warmth. So it is with great astonishment that once she sits down to tell her grandmother of her great escape, she sees what she recognises to be the object of her fear: her patient. She looks at him anguished and realises that his captivating smile has transformed itself in a scary sneer, in the smirk of a killer.

She wakes up terrorised.

On an unconscious level, the psychiatrist was escaping from the hidden aggression of her patient, having closed the doors of her mind to the anxiety of death that he had placed inside her. She had not recognised her fear and had actually substituted it with a feeling of fondness for her patient who was so needy and so deprived. The dream finds its way through the mechanism of negation forcing the psychiatrist not to run away from the perception of danger. Being more anxious, more scared and naturally more careful, she asks for help to face the communication of her patient's aggression. From his side the patient perceiving that a door has been opened in his psychiatrist's mind, feels more contained and can now communicate a violence that before he was at risk of acting out.

The professional risk a psychiatrist runs is to be subjected to great damage or even to be killed during the therapeutical effort to give birth to a thought. On the other hand the risk the midwife runs is to cause damage or even to kill a life going through the great effort of being born.

It is essential that both are very much in contact with their anxieties, that they learn to look at them seriously, that they never negate them, that they never hide them behind omnipotent behaviours. It is important that they are in contact with their limits and do not feel small if they feel the need to be helped. This help can be given to the obstetrician from the childbearing woman and to the psychiatrist from his patient: these are their best collaborators as long as they are truly received and listened to.

Going back to the dream, the person who has helped the psychiatrist in this work is not the mother, a "strong" rigid woman who would never have opened the door to someone with a mental illness and would never have dreamed of asking for help. It is the grandmother of her childhood, a fragile and smiling old lady, curious, slightly bungling (somewhat like me), who gives her granddaughter the ability to face and to represent in a dream the anxiety of death that the patient puts in her. If we stop to think and observe the dream attentively, we discover that within it something extraordinary has happened: physical stimuli and subliminal afferent signs coming from the different senses have been collected together to form comprehensible images full of emotional meaning. In the dream field, sensory elements of physical nature have been subjected to a transformation, they have become elements of the mind that can be used for knowledge. As a consequence of this miraculous transformation from the body to the mind, of this astonishing passage, something that seems very much like birth happens: a feeling that was not there before—fear—takes shape, becomes thinkable. It is brought to life at a mental level and will have an inevitable impact on reality.

Our mind is a factory continuously producing emotions that are born from the senses. Sensory experiences that, if not negated, if offered a space to be heard, become emotional experiences that we are affected by, inner motions that leave a mark inside, an internal change that already preludes and implies a growth. Around these internal motions, these first mental elements, thoughts which are more and more complex organise themselves. Thoughts leading to actions or to other thoughts.

But in order to initiate the process, it is necessary to accomplish that first passage that finds its way from the sphere of sensations to that of emotions, from the body to the mind. Adults already have in their psychological baggage all the necessary functions to make this step, it has been done so many times that they do not even remember how difficult it was to do it originally. The first step is taken by the newborn with his mother. The first emotion comes to life there, in that newborn couple that manages to transform the taste of milk into a sense of goodness. Good and bad, two words of oral flavour that will have a great future!

And with regards to words, in Italian the verbs "to be born" ("nascere") and "to know" ("conoscere") have the same root. Conoscere comes from Latin: "cum nascere": to be born together … an antique profound meaning that time and human distraction have blurred. However it is a concept which is very clear to the ones who take care of a woman becoming a mother. During pregnancy mothers are subject to many physical and psychological changes which make them naturally able to be born with their child. In particular they develop considerable capacity for identification becoming so totally identified with their babies that can give them the mental function which allows a physical stimulus to become a psychological representation, can lend babies their mind until they will develop one increasingly capable of working on its own.

I remember the thousand-year-old controversy between empirical materialism that affirmed the absolute priority of the senses: "Nihil est in intellectu quod prius non fuerit in sensu", to which idealists replied: "Nisi intellectus ipse". Psychoanalysis is now able to give the answer. The first intellect is in the mother who by containing and elaborating her baby's first sensorial stimuli transforms them into meaningful emotions ready to symbolise.

From this birth, knowledge begins. On this birth is based the possibility to understand the reality of the other while strongly maintaining one's own identity. Through this birth a harmonious relationship between mind and body will be established. This birth will be the internal model that each one of us will shape in the most varied ways to establish our own relations with the world of others.

It is unbelievable how this essential function which a mother can do at her best only if supported and helped by a father who stands by her is universally negated and often even impeded. It is often said about a newborn that "he's so small he only needs to eat and sleep" or "she cries to reinforce her lungs". It is as if together with milk, the child would not take in all those warm, round, and soft things, with that particular scent accompanied by that particular rhythm and position. As if crying was not an anguished communication of discomfort with which, through mother's understanding, the first bond will be created: I cry because I am hungry, because I am cold, because I am wet. So from a crying baby stems out a baby with a shadow, an idea of an identity: that of a baby who is hungry, cold and wet.

Whoever has the will and courage to see the intensity of the wordless exchange that happens between a mother and a baby in the first few days of life should then do the impossible to allow this emotional relationship to start, in the peculiar and unique way each mother and baby couple will invent, without being interfered with.

Even if I am within my psychoanalytic consulting room, I believe I care continually for mothers, fathers, and their newborn babies. In this sense I feel very close to the professionals who have the privilege to be present on the scene of birth. As they do, I too try to help a man, a woman, and their baby to being born in a strong bond of reciprocal respect and mutual help into a new life and into a newborn identity of great emotional value: being mother and father of the same baby. As a midwife of emotions, I will be in the shadows, far away from the scene of birth, but I will never give up reiterating how essential this primal beginning of life is to the process of growth and integration.

As members of society, we should all try to make our contribution and demand from the law and our institutions that they have appropriate structures and rules to protect and respect and give all possible help to mothers, fathers, and their babies during these beginnings of life.

Trying to integrate the body's elements with those of the mind, the male with the female, technology with nature, seems to be an obvious operation. Doing what should be done seems so simple and easy. Nobody appears to be against it. Yet there are many powerful forces that operate against.

They know it well, as they live it daily, those people who courageously try to remove pregnancy and labour and postpartum from the aseptic and solitary atmosphere of the hospital, to create a facilitating space for the growth of a mother, a father, and a child: the three characters on whom we put our hopes into for a better future.

To them, I want to express my deepest esteem and admiration.

CHAPTER ELEVEN

Generativity and creativity: dialogue between an obstetrician and a psychoanalyst

Sandra Morano and Anna Maria Risso

SANDRA: For some time now, my experience in obstetrics has led me to reflect on female creativity and generativity. Can creativity in women be identified with generativity? For women, giving birth has always meant being responsible for separating from the child they have conceived and given birth to, whilst, at the same time, not abandoning them, but nourishing and staying with them, sharing and promoting their development and carrying them forever in their minds. This would surely be the easiest portrayal and the most immediate creativity of women, since it is inherent to female expertise. Women, though, and regardless of their ability to procreate, have always claimed a creativity which has nothing to do with reproduction. Many of them, whether or not they have experienced childbirth, have expressed creative talent, producing both literary and pictorial works of art, and participating in projects or in battles which enhance their ability to formulate and achieve the most varied objectives.

> Children, like books, are journeys inside ourselves, in which our bodies, our minds and our souls change direction, and move towards the centre of existence. (Allende, 1994/2001, p. 284)

For others, in smaller numbers, this ability has been used in place of having children, and this has not prevented even those women who have not given birth from experiencing and deeply understanding the sense of giving birth. They have communicated this sense to us through narrative, if they are writers, through vision, if painters, and through emotion, if poets. Are these two different abilities to be placed in juxtaposition? Paradoxically, we know very little about how women view their creativity ... Is it possible to generate without being a mother? We can give birth to works of art which we feel to be our own creatures ... we can feel labour pains when we have something in our mind which is straining to get out, just as if it were in our belly. Is the body still part of this other kind of creation? And how true is it that the body no longer has much to do with procreative creativity? Today, when we know almost everything about the mechanisms involved in giving birth, it would seem that women feel distanced from their bodies, or rather from the "natural" process of childbirth. They seem to be wary of following a path which has been perfected over millions of years when, paradoxically, with our increased knowledge, they should feel more in control than ever before. The statistical evidence of this mistrust is well documented, at least in Italy, if we can judge by the number of caesarian sections (the Italians have the second largest number in the world). The reasons why this is so are less obvious, but the most commonly accepted is to do with the pain of labour.

ANNA: In answer to Sandra's question whether we can identify generativity with creativity or rather, whether generativity can be creative and creativity generative, I would reply that the key is labour. The work of giving birth seems to me fundamental, regardless of whether the outcome is a baby or, as Sandra says, a book, a painting or a poem. This work inevitably requires the need to separate from whoever or whatever has grown inside us. So here looms large the inescapable experience which since the dawn of time has essentially defined human beings' tragic destiny, which has made us grow and evolve, but has also inexorably limited us: separation. Separation is painful, hard, even dramatic. Babies knows very well that at the moment of birth they will be catapulted into a world of much stronger and more overwhelming smells, noises, and lights than any experienced before. They have to give themselves up to the force of gravity and experience a previously unknown sense of heaviness, losing the abilities acquired in the womb and being forced to struggle to reconquer them, whilst moving forward to acquire all the new skills which, with the help of the people around them, will allow them to survive.

SANDRA: So can women's refusal of labour be explained only as a fear of physical pain? Or are we not perhaps speaking about a different fear, masquerading as fear of physical pain, which prevents women from fully experiencing the joy of liberation/ revelation of what they are carrying inside themselves?

ANNA: I think we are speaking about women's fear of living or reliving the overwhelming experience of childbirth, bringing as it does not only life but also death: the mother may die, the baby may die, but what always dies is the unique experience of having another human being inside yourself, of not feeling alone, an experience which is never to be repeated except through another pregnancy ...

SANDRA: But why do we identify this supreme expression of creativity above all *with* pain and *in* pain? In the Bible, the pain of childbirth is portrayed as a special form of knowledge granted to women, not as a punishment, but almost as a privilege ... privilege in the sense of creation, generation, which, very far from springing from numbness (Adam's rib), requires the senses in every fibre of the body to be activated ... As Loewnthal writes:

To man, the Lord announces hard work and sweat, but not labour. Only women are granted pain which is flesh and spirit together, the pangs of birth and indefinable melancholy. This biblical insult to women has given them a perception of themselves and of the world in which the inner and the outer meet, and the skin blends with the innermost fibres. God has spoken to her: "You will suffer both here and there; do not struggle to distinguish one pain from another." (Loewnthal, 2005, p. 19)

I believe there is a recent cultural move to equate labour only with pain, which distances women from this ancient wisdom, devaluing the creative aspect of birth and the force of being connected—a force which is explosive, generating and to be tamed, a scream to be stifled, imagination to be curbed. It would seem to suggest to women something like: you cannot do this on your own, you need to participate less and be more dependent. It is useless for you to try to conserve your strength, you are up against pointless suffering. But why should the suffering of childbirth, alone among all suffering, be stigmatised in this way, when it is a matter of a few hours, a mere instant in the arc of a lifetime?

ANNA: If women agree to live through those few hours, that instant, together with their baby, the experience becomes a precious treasure for them both; the child, who in order to survive physically and mentally desperately needs help, can find this help first and foremost in the person who is sharing the experience and is not afraid to relive it in order to understand it and give it a shared meaning. So we are back to speaking of mothers, of women who, as Sandra warns us, are more and more inclined to avoid this journey, or at the very least to demand assistance, tempted as they are by the seductive offers of technology. Women are promised childbirth without pain, without labour, where the natural course of events is bridled, coerced, unexpectedly medicalised, impoverished, and deprived of its overwhelming emotional power, anaesthetised and silenced.

SANDRA: The senses are denied, familiar tastes and smells are prohibited, the surroundings impersonal and aseptic; there are no sounds, but noises, no discreet silence but outsiders, who chance (or work shifts) makes unwitting spectators of the most intimate displays and ancient feelings, regressions, emotions, stories of families forming and consolidating.

Right from the moment I crossed the hospital threshold I lost my sense of identity to become a nameless patient, a number. I was undressed, given an open-backed robe and taken to an isolated place where I was subjected to various additional humiliations, and then I was left on my own. Once in a while someone examined between my legs, my body was transformed into a single, painful, palpitating cavern; I spent one day, one night and most of the following day in that laborious task, worn out and scared to death, until finally they announced that my liberation was at hand and I was taken into another room. Lying on a metal bed, my bones crushed, and blinded by the lights, I gave myself up to suffering. Nothing depended on me anymore; the baby flailed around to get out and my hips opened to help her, without any intervention on my part. Everything I had learned from manuals and pre-natal courses was useless. There comes a moment when the journey, once begun, cannot be interrupted, we run towards a frontier, we go through a mysterious door and wake up on the other side in a different life. The baby enters the world and the mother enters a new state of consciousness, neither of them will ever be the same again. (Allende, 1994/2001, p. 284)

To what extent has this scenario, still very much the norm in most maternity wards, succeeded in interfering with procreation? If we think of all the paintings and frescoes which have portrayed birth over the centuries, those scenes of everyday life, frozen in time to reach out to us and enrich our sense of identity and history, we cannot help thinking that the elimination of disease and epidemics is not sufficient to justify the destruction of symbols and the abandonment of ethics and aesthetics in procreation. How can creativity endure in these conditions? Or, perhaps what we should be asking is how women have managed to preserve their strength and faith in their own creative abilities, allowing life on our planet to flourish, in these conditions. In the 70s Adrienne Rich wrote:

What amazes us, what can give us great hope and faith in a future where the lives of women and children will be restored and re-woven by female hands, is how much of ourselves we have succeeded in preserving for our children, despite the destructive environment of institutions: tenderness, passion, faith in our own instincts, the emergence of a courage we didn't know we possessed, the constant care of another human being and full awareness of how precious life is. (Rich, 1976/1977, p. 283)

With these words, at the end of her digression on motherhood observed through the great transformations of the twentieth century, Rich recalls two fundamental concepts: generativity as an act of creation, disrupted by the interference of a scientific vision of the world, or rather by the conflictual implications of its intrusion into childbirth; and hope/faith in the "lives of women and children, restored and re-woven by female hands". Today, and notwithstanding everything, we can say that generative power is still intact: we see it emerge even in the face of diagnoses of unexplained infertility, or in countries devastated by war, famine, and destruction.

ANNA: So women need help to preserve and protect this unique and special ability, and to continue to be curious and willing to experience it. Is it women who can help other women? I was thinking of Melanie Klein (1921/1978) who speaks about the thirst for knowledge as a driving force for emotional development, and Bion (1962/1972) who speaks about containment, describing how a lack of maternal containment can in various ways impede an individual's chance of fully realising their emotive-affective potential. Is this once again woman as "contained" and "containing" who can light up with creativity?

SANDRA: What the twentieth century perhaps jeopardised is the expression of an analogous creativity in medical treatment. The drastic increase in anonymity in hospital care has to some extent damaged the potential of scientific progress towards improvement. It is true that with better drugs and greater efficiency women's and children's lives have been saved, but childbirth has been reduced to the very opposite of creativity, governed as it is by dehumanising rules which necessitate drastic modifications in procedure. It has effectively consigned birth to the medical sphere, with obstetrics being taught and learned in exactly the same way as any other physical or psychological pathology. Reproductive medicine and foetal medicine today are undeniably pushing the frontiers of progress in the treatment of infertility, the discovery and early treatment, where possible, of foetal pathologies *in utero*. We would however question whether it should inform and restrict the expression of creativity in the entire female population. Paradoxically, this very progress has led to women becoming more dependent, more information has led to more insecurity, and the weight of progress has disempowered women.

ANNA: I am thinking of a baby girl, born with the anxiety of losing her sense of self and with the perception of an open cavity, out of which internal contents can flow and external dangers enter. The female anatomy clearly does not in itself constitute an obstacle to evolution but it can very easily become a mental space lodging huge anxieties which stand in the way of evolution (Micati, 1988). I am also thinking of a woman exposed to experiences which imply certain risks for herself and her children, a women who therefore, once more, and inevitably, is afraid. And so we have a woman who is forced to face something she fears so much that she tries to diminish it, thus diminishing herself, since she cannot help feeling afraid. By trying to minimise her own personal experiences she risks also diminishing the psychological qualities which develop out of it, for example the awareness that any creative enterprise implies risk. Therefore, here we are yet again back to the concept of coming into contact with loss, separation, and death (Conte, 2011).

SANDRA: So what about the caregivers? The obstetrician or midwife in whom Rich (1976/1977) placed so much hope and faith to be able to restore women's and children's lives? Where is the creativity or the freedom in caring for her peers, whose abilities she knows and yet whom she might have to treat by denying these very abilities? Thirty years ago Rich expressed a wish, which could be defined today as a gender wish, counting first and foremost on women's ability to drive forward a vision of helping in which they could express themselves with ease: strength, but with empathy, characteristics and requirements common to male as well as female caregivers who have attempted to change things, starting with physical surroundings. One such is the obstetric surgeon (Leboyer, 1977), famous for having dimmed the blinding lights and softened voices, which was a sort of violence against mother and baby in hospitals, in an attempt to create a continuum between the muffled cocoon of the mother's womb and the first moments of autonomous life in the outside world.

He was a visionary, who taught piety and humanity on the journey towards separation.

ANNA: I think you are suggesting that an opening and some comfort might be derived from imagining a couple who open up to a third person to introduce new opportunities for containment and communication, someone ready to take on part of the distress and primordial fears, and guarantee the free flow of feelings (Fornari, 1981). A father who can find space in his mind for the mother's feelings of fallibility and her hatred for the baby who makes her experience such feelings; space for the midwife who takes on the feelings of hatred towards the mother who, by bringing us into the world as females, has forced us to experience this condition; and, finally, space for the obstetrician who is prepared to share the mortal risks of birth and life. I like your definition of Leboyer as "visionary"; it makes me think again of Bion and his "reverie" (Bion, 1962/1970). I like to think of his dimming the lights and lowering voices as an expression of that receptivity, acceptance and gift of meaning which seem to me to be intrinsic in creativity. Generativity and creativity: generativity which becomes creative, and creativity which can be generative. I believe this may be possible in a situation of internal and external communication, which is as open as possible to understanding and containment and where the internal and external presence of a third party can guarantee human tolerability, bringing with it creative solutions, modifications, and changes. Here I inevitably think of your precious work, Sandra, which, with the creation of the Maternity Centre at San Martino Hospital in Genoa, has given a psychological home to mothers, father, newborn babies and their brothers and sisters, as well as to their family ties, their emotions and their feelings.

I would have liked to re-read what I wrote on leaving the Centre with baby Irene, but this notebook was begun much later. In any case, even without re-reading those lines, I have carried the feeling inside myself every day since. And on the several occasions that I've happened to walk by, I've always felt my heartbeat quicken at the wonderful indelible memories. And I always dreamed of being

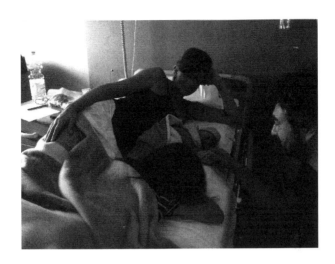

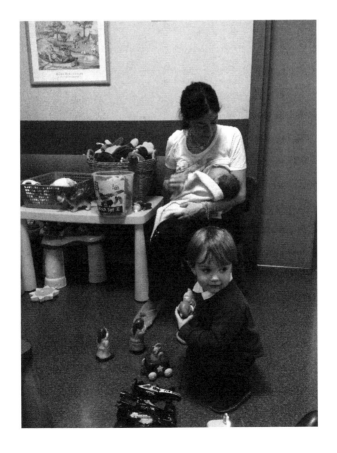

Figures. Mothers, fathers and babies born in the first Alongside Birth Centre in Italy in S. Martino Hospital, Genova. (Pictures property of Sandra Morano)

> able to relive the same joy for another child. And so it is today, as I write in this pink room where my son, Dario, sleeps peacefully. I'm back here after three and a half years and have found the same sense of familiarity, the same warmth, the exact same emotions … A feeling of home, together with my new baby. My husband and Irene, who were here with us, left a short while ago. There's a sense of family in the hospital, a medical institute which transmits feelings of warmth, midwives who are always ready to give you advice or a friendly word. Isn't this a precious gift to all mothers? (A testimonial from Sara who became a mother in our Birth Centre)

SANDRA: The maternity centre mentioned here, situated since 2001 in the obstetrics unit of San Martino Hospital in Genoa, is the first of its kind in Italy. Its aim is to create a dimension of familiarity, intimacy, and discreet assistance around the institutional safety of childbirth. The primary assistant is the midwife, with medical care during labour and birth, including specialist midwives, neonatologists and anaesthetists, being close at hand if needed, but in another part of the hospital. Continuity of care, a pleasant, colourful, and familiar environment, greater privacy, access to non-invasive methods of pain control (the use of water, the chance to move around and try out more comfortable positions, massage), the chance to have the father and other children present throughout the day—all of these are important elements in favour of women in labour, and can have a positive influence on the outcome. This kind of assistance cannot be provided in a traditional maternity unit, limited as it is by hospital regulations and routines (staff shifts, visiting hours, mealtimes etc.). The obstetrician, Michel Odent, founder of one of the first *homely* maternity centres in Pithiviers (France), writes:

> Traditional maternity wards are more and more regulated by a series of rules imposed by the medical directors to impose precise orders on working methods in order to respond to any situation. Home Maternity Centres, on the other hand, are essentially ruled not by orders but by managerial directives which can be elaborated patiently and tacitly from within the team as testimony to their homogeneity. Home maternity centres are changing and developing centres. (Odent, 1981, p. 67)

Beginning from actual spaces, symbolic of the restrictions of liberty, which are also mental spaces open to modifications and contamination, the creativity of generations can move forward once more.

References

Allende, I. (1994). *Paula*. Feltrinelli: Milano, 2001.

Bion, W. R. (1962). *Apprendere dall'esperienza*. Roma: Armando, 1972.

Bion, W. R. (1962). Una teoria del pensiero. In: *Analisi Degli Schizofrenici e Metodo Psicoanalitico* (pp. 167–182). Roma: Armando, 1970.

Bion, W. R. (1965). *Trasformazioni*. Roma: Armando, 1973.

Conte, M. P. (2011). *La fantasia dell'utero gravido come organizzatore nell'inconscio femminile*. Paper presented at the Psychoanalytical Centre of Genoa.

Fornari, F. (1981). *Il Codice Vivente*. Torino: Boringhieri.

Klein, M. (1921). Los viluppo di un bambino. In: *Scritti, 1921–1959* (pp. 17–33). Torino: Boringhieri, 1978.

Leboyer, F. (1977). *Per una Nascita Senza Violenza*. Milano: Garzanti.

Loewnthal, E. (2005). *Eva e le Altre. Letture Bibliche al Femminile*. Milano: Bompiani Overlook.

Micati, L. (1988). Female sexuality: Some observations on the forces that hinder its development and on their resolution. *Rivista di Psicoanalisi*, 34: 10–48.

Odent, M. (1981). *Nascita dell'uomo Ecologico*. Como: RED Editions/Publishing Studio (Agel).

Rich, A. (1976). *Nato di Donna*. Milano: Garzanti, 1977.

CHAPTER TWELVE

Dreaming about pregnancy when it is not there: two clinical cases

Anna Barlocco

Very often, creativity and procreation are compared, like a sort of psychic pregnancy of the creator. Famous women writers have compared their creative experience to the perception of their own mortality and transience. Margaret Atwood (2002) has spoken about writing as a negotiating with shadows; Flannery O'Connor (1961, 1969) considered writing as getting into the devil's territory without the fear of getting dusty.

But in procreation as in analysis and, generally, in the creative process, when some purpose becomes compelling—be it a baby, symptom disappearance, an artistic production—something gets stuck and stops flowing.

The yearning and concrete need is put forward and disturbs the mysterious process dealing with the threshold between life and death, as with what happens in a couple between a man and a woman, or in an analytic couple: something needing to be lived and enjoyed before one may even worry about producing it. If this does not happen, the couple is paradoxically robbed of its specific creative capacity.

Lately, in my work in hospital as a psychiatrist, I have started cooperating with the Mother and Child Department, playing different roles with patients showing psychic disorders in pregnancy and in postpartum. I work as a consultant, in the obstetrics and gynaecology ward, in the clinic, for less serious cases, and in the psychiatric department for the more serious ones. In the latter situation we try to keep, or at least to restore, as soon as possible, the contact between mother and child, with daily meetings in the presence of a nurse. If possible, without running risks, we prefer to choose a day hospital regime, instead of the ward, by organising a network with the family and/or other supporting people, in order not to leave the patient alone with her child. The day hospital is a place a mother can come to every day, either with her child or on her own, and return home later, for the rest of the day.

At the same time, as a psychoanalyst, in my own consulting room, I meet people who would get on with their lives while in therapy, getting married, having children, getting pregnant, giving birth and coming back to analysis. When this is the case, we can see better and deeper, as the long, protected times of the setting enable us to ascertain what is really important, when we succeed. We try to keep in mind the same findings in less confortable situations and under more pressure.

Recently, two patients who were in analytic treatment with me, a man and a woman, showed in different ways, serious reproductive difficulties. This made me think how deeply wounded one may be, when the longing for a baby is frustrated and everything becomes so difficult and about how this wound breaks in someone's life, by revealing, as a precipitate, primitive structures and constellations: emerging fragilities and relationships.

I have written about both cases, each with its own brief notes, foregoing a more detailed description, but focusing on a sequence of vignettes from our analytic work. I therefore especially favoured, in my choice images and actual dreams, dreams and images representing what was happening in true life. Presenting both a man and a woman would also allow us to see the same problem in both sexes. I was curious to see how gender difference emotionally affects the different way of living in one's own body a very similar experience. This reminds me of a beautiful sentence of Antonin Artaud: "Du corps par le corps avec le corps depuis le corps et jusqu'au corps" ("Of the body, through the body, with the body, from the body, and unto the body").

G and the artificial insemination

G is a thirty five-year-old man, an only child, with a family history background affected by a problematic relationship with his father, whom

G felt as a violent, never satisfied, and humiliating parent, and an affectionate mother, although aloof, dull and dominated by the father, and who never protected him enough. He has a degree and is working in a psychiatric institution; he is an attractive man, for whose equilibrium competitive and extreme sports have also played an important role in his life.

He was married two years ago and had been in analytic therapy for two and a half years, when he had a check up in order to detect couple fertility, while his wife, who would really love to have a child, does not seem to have any problem. G, who seems to be pushed by her wishes, discovers unexpectedly he suffers from oligospermia. They therefore make up their minds to follow an artificial insemination path.

Beginning the path: first lacking a roof on one's head and, later on, finding a funny hat

He starts the session by complaining that there is no longer any spontaneity, his life is a continuous race from morning till evening, everything has a timetable, an aim, it is done on purpose, and this makes him feel as if he could not breathe. He then tells me about the artificial insemination proceedings and says:

> Sometimes I get the impression that I am leaving a vanishing trail, in my running. The trail … reminds me of the vanishing spermatozoa and I fear they'll get lost. In my second spermiogram they were even less than in my first, and soon there might be none available for new attempts. I dreamt I was in a house, but the house had no roof. My wife and myself were inside, but we were also outside. I was making love to her, but suddenly I noticed there was somebody else; it was strange and also very embarrassing.

Something, normally as private and intimate as love making, is not so any more. He lacks a roof: with his wife they find themselves outside. Lovemaking is not private anymore, concerning them as a couple, but there is somebody else watching and this is odd and embarrassing.

From the inside something is carried out of the body: an egg from her, a sperm cell from him. The two cells will meet only outside; it will happen outside in a test tube, not in a place protected by the warm uterus walls. Only at the end will the embryo in fact get implanted.

One feels unroofed; one might lose one's head.

Something, which used to be spontaneous, is not so any more: now it has a timetable, an aim, it is done on purpose. All of this should create life, but on the contrary it cancels it and there is no air in this frantic running, where not only sperm cells get lost in their wake.

He remembers an episode:

> "I had to masturbate, in order to collect sperm. In the room there was a pornographic magazine. To me it seemed a dreary way of making a baby. Eventually I noted a funny cap, somebody had left it there. For some reasons this made me laugh and set me in a good mood".

A funny cap with a peak: at last something to help him protecting his head and protect his eyes from this blinding artificial light.

A cap to save him from the absence of a roof, to help him avoid this mechanical, impersonal, pornographic situation and to put him back in contact with something more human.

Who knows if my words as well, have played the funny little cap role.

The first try is a failure and the implant does not succeed.

A very long silence, oppressive, and tense, which, somehow, I endure with him or I try, with no success, to interrupt.

He tells me he is sorry he cannot speak to me.

Silence.

He feels blocked.

Silence.

"What's inside stays inside. I have images, thoughts. But I discard them all".

I try to say something. But I feel impotent.

"They keep turning inside me. I don't know how to let them out".

Silence.

"I would like, but I can't do it. I am completely blocked inside."

He wants to show me, trying to make me feel here today, how he feels when his waiting has no answer, when something from him cannot meet something from me. It is frustrating, one waits and waits and nothing happens.

His images, his thoughts cannot meet my images, my thoughts, in order to create something new. He is sorry, but he feels impotent, blocked, he is sterile.

He keeps me waiting and he waits; a ruthless superego sets up this waiting time, making him feel that what is happening is his fault. He is with a father saying, "you must", but he does not know how to do it. He would really like to do it; he has a huge desire to do it. He is not up to it, he is dried up, and nothing comes out of him.

In the transference, nobody cares for him, nobody comforts him, and nobody tells him, "If you don't succeed, it doesn't matter".

Something powerful and violent prevents him from crying, from letting off steam, from getting somebody to comfort him.

He exhales deeply, slowly, and than he says: "It's true, this thing makes something else become concrete, something that was there before".

The echography and the "traffic jam"

While he was coming to my study, he met a pregnant friend with her first child by the hand. They talked and she told him of a common friend expecting a baby, thanks to artificial insemination. What a laugh! In his job he even had to study the problem of unwanted pregnancies!

Everything seems to play the same tune, one cannot think of anything else.

It seems too much, having to enquire about unwanted pregnancies, and also studying with me his desire to give birth and what is preventing him from realising it.

> At the Centre for Artificial Insemination, for the first time, they have told something to my wife too. While doing the echography, the doctor said, as if it weren't important, that her ovaries seemed "somewhat lazy." Then we went out. As we were crossing the city, in order to get home, thanks to a demonstration, we got into a traffic jam and we were stuck. My wife was excessively angry, because of the traffic jam, she was furious. On the opposite, I kept calm. I definitely cannot think about a child, I have the insemination too much in mind and this feeling of being responsible, being the cause of this disgrace. I feel ashamed, but I felt relieved at the doctor's words. There is something wrong with my wife too.

This "traffic jam" is the real image of what is happening: everything concerning having a baby gets into a traffic jam, from which nothing can be borne.

The traffic jam is the clash between wishing and not wishing: my wife should be fertile in order to have a baby, but she should be non fertile too, in order to share the responsibility of its not coming.

Between happiness for the friend who succeeded and getting stuck in the envy for her and for all those cursed fertile women.

So everything slows down and becomes lazy, like my wife's ovaries, and meanwhile the child is lost, because one cannot think about him.

Waiting

He has odd feelings, often in half sleep, but also when he is awake. He cannot remember dreams, or sequences. Broken thoughts. Confusion. He says:

> There is this parallel life, eating up everything, and you don't even know when it will end. We had to wait for my wife's menstruation, in order to fix the ovary stimulation and it was late. I cannot sit for a varicocele treatment, as it could be bad for the sperm cells and I had a pain in my testis for a few days. It is what you might call impotence in all its meanings, either concrete or not. I was used to challenges, either with myself or with other people. Now no more matches, as this might also cause damages. Now I feel the fragility of my whole life, breaking up on me.

He is fragile compared to this thing, bigger than him; he gets broken up and turned into pieces by it. It used to be a heroic competition between him and others and he feels ruled instead of being a ruler.

Everything is reduced to waiting for menstruations, with his wife reduced to menstruation, uterus, ovaries while he has become testis, spermatozoa, both of them becoming partial objects.

Strange feelings, "beta elements", broken up things, they cannot dream and the world is belittled. One may loose the overall view.

He becomes a testicle, which lately hurts; this feeling of being so partial, so reduced into concrete partial objects, is starting to hurt.

While gathering egg cells and sperm cells, one needs to play the betrothed

This morning they have been at the centre, where he went with his wife in order to collect her egg cells and his sperm cells.

We don't know whether there will be sperm cells. They told me that, if it were not the case, they'd use the frozen ones from the previous samples. This is really stressful for me. Last time they found three sperm cells, the previous time six, the first time five. What a misery! The poverty, the impotence, the mystery of ignoring why I am so faulty. I ask myself whether my wife and I will stick together in case of failure. It will be easier for me to give in, because I can't bear to deny her this possibility. My wife is down-to-earth, she says that a child, one way or the other, will be there. She has suggested an artificial insemination by donor, if we fail this time. I don't want it, it would seem to grow the child she had with another man, I can't stand it, and it overcomes me. I would rather adopt a child. But she doesn't agree, she wants a baby, by all means. Last night she went to sleep, while we were watching a film together, and I felt bad. I keep forgetting my dreams, I feel as if I had a huge injection of pragmatism and everyday routine. I feel my wife takes me for granted and there is a part of me very angry which doesn't want to fit with the rest, and sometimes it makes me doubt about everything. When this happens I'd like to push a button in order to make everything disappear. Wife, child, everything. To be on my own, stop. I have become more detached. I am giving up things I used to care for. Walking out of the centre, we went for a walk. We went in a bar near the seaside and my wife sat on the furthest chair from me, although the one near me was free. I got really angry and told her: "Did you ever have a fiancée? Don't you know how to behave?"

There is a mind black out and this is no good. There is not any more fantasy, no more love for what one is doing. Even his life has become a partial object, because it lacks affection. He does not want to agree with this expected daily behaviour.

His wife is not helping him, she fell asleep watching a film he did not want to watch on his own, and he does not like this. His relation with me in the transference is similar to how he feels at the moment with his partner, and similar to the poor and dreary relationship he has with his sperm cells.

Together we have to watch the film he is running. He wants me to talk about it, to make him take part in a richer mental life, because a child is not only made with ova and spermatozoa, but also by talking about it and longing for it.

He is asking for a closer relationship, in order to avoid identification with somebody who either crushes or is crushed, with a father who crushed him, while he was disappearing. He also needs to stop thinking about problems from the point of view of competition, as he is now imagining the artificial insemination by donor. He wants me closer and if we succeed, maybe he will succeed too in being nearer his emotions and his partner.

He needs help to go back to taking part in life, to be able to live his thoughts and emotions, to have a fiancée once more: to be able to feel his wife's love again as it was in the past, when this "traffic jam" was not yet there.

Getting near the second attempt

"Last night I dreamt about something I can't remember. I don't feel like seeing friends, I always feel slightly apart. Nearness lasts just for a moment. A boat leaving the shore, while nobody knows where it's going. A misfortune. All of this is my burden, my responsibility. I am at its mercy, I have no power, no control, it really isn't right."

He remembers: "I am in the waiting room, when they take my wife to the implant. I am waiting all by myself. Finally she is back. She is stunned, weakened. I feel like looking after her and I go and get food". He also remembers:

> I am working and my wife calls me on the phone, she is bleeding; it went wrong and she is on her own.
>
> This time it will be different; I want to be with her. I asked for a week off at the time the implant will take place. How will it end, this time? Anger. You'll have a child; you'll never have it. Great hope, great sigh of relief or despair. My whole life is blocked. Our couple exists, but there is a negative space where everything piles up. A heavy and chaotic pile, pulling everything down into it. An absence, pulling life down into it. The couple needs protection; there is a need to protect each other, so that things might flow easily. If I think that something might go wrong this time, like every other time, the image I get is a horrible scattering.
>
> Silence.
>
> Now I remember the dream I had last night. I am waiting for my wife. But it is not possible, because she is dead.

We are back into a traffic jam.

He is waiting for his wife, who is not expecting a child. He wants most of all his wife. He is waiting for her, he is waiting but she will die with no child, with no child, she does not feel alive. He cannot keep her alive, he is responsible and he feels the burden. The mother will die if the child won't come, the mother is suffering.

He would like to take care of her, to be there. He feels he is hurting her. There should be a need to protect each other, but the only way of looking after her, seems to be giving her this child.

He needs help to solve this heavy and chaotic burden, to change this indigestible thing, this concrete thing in a thought, a mutual love, a really intimate relationship, so that things might flow, run smoothly naturally. A safe nest for conception, built together by husband and wife.

If, on the opposite, one does everything "in vitro" and if everybody has to carry his burden on his own, one dries up and things do not flow anymore. If one seeks control, a race, and also if one wants with all his means, then something will get shut. If it fails, then there is only the horrible scattering left.

There again, if you do not succeed, there is death. If the child does not come, there is nothing left, not even their couple and he fears that his wife is dead, that she will not be there for him anymore.

A new failure but in some way there is a happy ending

He starts the session by recalling a dream he had the night before.

> I am in my village, crossing a square which in real life looks onto the sea, but in my dream it leads to a mall. I go in. I look at the shops, enquire about prices, and ask information. There is another person with me, an older man. Then, suddenly, I am in a hospital ward. A voice says, speaking about me: he is a psychiatric patient who is trying to be promoted. I think: how odd, it looks like one of those films with a final dramatic turn of events. It was all fake. I thought it was a mall and on the other hand ... I was astonished, even amused.

Only later he tells me that the previous week it was a failure: it was possible to try only three times because there were only three sperm cells alive, two from the fresh sample and one from defrosting the previous ones.

The following day he has been told that every attempt had failed.

> Yesterday we talked to the gynaecologist and the biologist, in order to check the actual situation: the frozen egg cells are in great number, so that my wife won't have to endure hormone stimulation again. I am relieved because it was a practice I felt bad about. In a few months we'll be having a third try with sperm cells from a fresh sample. Meanwhile I was told that my spermatozoa were few, but of good quality. Yesterday the biologist said that for sperm cells to be defined as "good quality", only four percent of them have to be of good quality. Can you imagine four percent of three!!! They added that these four out of one hundred (of three) could reach the target either at the first or at the hundredth time. I will have to see an andrologue to plan hormone stimulation. My mood, after this talk: I was ..."shattered"! I then took a day off to spend with my wife and we talked about what was happening to us individually and as a couple. She told me that she wanted my child, adopted or not adopted, but with me. I told her that I couldn't stand the idea of a donor. If I were on my own, we would already have made up our minds about adoption. As she feels it so badly, I'll try again, even if I feel very bad about the whole business: all the stress, the testis pain as I have to delay the operation, giving up sports, matches, drinking wine in the evenings. We were happy together. Having talked this way, after our session, made me relax. At the end we fell asleep, hugging each other, on the beach.

He then goes back to his dream.

> Looking around shops in my village is something familiar, nice; the mall reminds me of the fertilisation centre. I thought it would be enough to go there, make up my mind, and ask for a child in order to get it. But no, it was an illusion. Even the ward has to deal with fertilisation; I am a patient there. "Psychiatric" makes me think about my job, where I am moving up. Thursday night, after the news that everything had failed, I went to see my parents. I told them and also thanked them for supporting me in the most difficult

times of my life. They have been near me. They have changed and I did the same. You would have never expected me to say such things, in the worst time of my life, would you, doctor? Me, who never wants to be seen sick, me not trusting anybody, me not want-ing to reveal myself. I felt I was growing up in this critical moment. I know this is due to all the work we did together and I felt like telling you. Even if it failed, I feel better, because this time we dealt with it together.

Forming a couple with me helped him to find his wife again.

He is not trying to buy a child any more, but he can think about it with her.

With him, now, there is an older man, telling him it is a psychiatric patient's, a fool's idea, imagining becoming a fake father, with no men-tal space to "behave like fiancées". Not feeling loved and thinking to be able to love a child. He has been promoted.

Now the child belongs to both parents, it is not only hers by a donor, or only his "adopted" one. Spaces become wider: there is a square open-ing on the sea front and a beach where one might go to sleep, even find peace.

There will be more attempts, they might succeed or fail, but there will be no more scattering. He will not feel any longer that he has lost everything forever, dead husband next to a dead wife.

Being two together, they may face many trials.

E: pregnancy, abortion, and longing

E is a thirty-six-year-old woman, who has a degree and works in a nurs-ing home. Her mother was very young when unwillingly she became pregnant with her by accident. She married the father, who had to start working, giving up university studies, which he very much cared for. E was a premature baby, born in a high-risk delivery, so that she spent her first month in an incubator. Her parents' marriage failed very soon afterwards, with serious quarrels, and she grew up mainly with her grandmother, whom she loved very much.

Her mother married another man and had two children with him. When E was a teenager, there was an episode of sexual harassment between her stepfather and herself, and she was very disappointed with her mother who, when she was told about it, refused to leave her husband.

She tells me how she spent her childhood waiting for meetings with her own father, who was a very busy man, ambitious and successful. She felt sure she was very different from the daughter he would have appreciated and felt paralysed by his critical gaze, feeling clumsy and unable to live up to his expectations. Her father had a few relationships with women whom E got to know and whom, sometimes, she even came to like. Finally he remarried the last one, who was the same age as his daughter.

E had some very problematic relationships, becoming involved with partners who were already part of a couple. In these relationships, she sometimes got trapped against her will, because she did not know how to end them. She has been in analysis for five years and has been living with her partner over a year and a half. She has always been afraid of pregnancy and childbirth and had fantasies about adopting, but a few months ago with her partner, they decided to have a baby.

A cave full of cobwebs

She comes in my study and tells me she had the test, she is pregnant. She tells me about her partner's and her astonished faces, when the test pink line appeared, as well as the emotion about the echography: at first the embryo could not be found and she worried it could have stayed behind in the oviduct. She was then very happy to see it in its place, in the uterus. He is six weeks old and she saw his heart beating.

She tells me about one of her dreams: "I was going down a dark cave, there were cobwebs which normally scare me, but I managed to keep calm and to get out. In my opinion six hours had passed, while for the other people, outside the cave, only half an hour had elapsed." She associates: one of her colleagues likes going into caves, he says it is relaxing; going through those narrow tunnels helps him think, while she feels anguished in such enclosed spaces. Her colleague tried to kiss her, but with no effort she prevented him. She likes being with her partner and would have disliked betraying him. Since she knows about her pregnancy, she pays attention to her tummy; she tries to picture what it looks like. She thinks she should change something, she will have to slow down and she fears that the rest of the world will not wait for her.

The six hours of her dream are like six weeks in true life: she knew it from the test only half an hour ago, but it was already there six weeks ago!

There is an adult herself, who is looking with the gynaecologist and myself, at the echography, and who has known it only for half an hour. And there is another herself, identified with this child, who has known it for six weeks.

So now she is a pregnant woman and she is astonished.

It is in its place in her uterus, it didn't stop in the oviducts, so this changes her identity and her rhythms. There is not just the baby in the cave-uterus, but herself identified with the baby. She is rather afraid about her need to slow down, to change her life and rhythm, and she is afraid the world, meanwhile, will not wait for her in this delay.

There are cobwebs where there is a risk to become entangled, for example to remain entangled in an old way she does not feel her own any more; she has no wish to be kissed by her colleague and she succeeded in avoiding it. Now there is another way of being three and she tries to figure it out.

The miscarriage

She had a spontaneous miscarriage. She told me this in a calm way, with a phone call in which she said she would not be able to come to the session on that day. In the following session, she seems wanting to get rid of the fact, set it aside as soon as possible, in order to get on. I feel as if she were warning me, as if she were saying: do not ever think of speaking about this! I think I must know how to walk on thin ice: to hold onto the tragic aspect, not denying it, but, at the same time, not trying to hunt her down.

Monsters, dragons, and confetti

She arrives at my place out of breath and she tells me about a series of dreams, one after the other, she dreamt since her last session.

> I dreamt a young dragon with two heads, whom I felt like killing.
> But there was also another dream in which I saw a beautiful baby.

Then a flash: I had to sit for my high school diploma, but I didn't want to do it any more. The last one: my friend Monica shows her drawings in a museum to a painter: I am jealous because of her creativity and I am thinking: her drawings are no good!

She associates:

When the gynaecologist told me the baby hadn't grown, I remembered my fear of getting hideous, because of a huge tummy. It's nature who gets rid of embryos with serious deformities, the gynaecologist said. Abortion means to get rid of new things as well.
Silence.
I recall a child who never plays, he just draws monsters. Once he tore in small pieces the sheet of paper on which he had drawn some monsters, and then made them fly like confetti with the fan. When I was amused by his playful invention, the child did not believe me.

Many dreams, many signals, many voices speaking all at the same time. One has to listen to all of them; one has to be near the ambivalence, the unrestrained après coup. The child is not there anymore and she is asking herself whether his killing is not her fault, because of her wanting and not wanting it. We are not talking about a symbolic destructivity, it is not a game. She really felt this experience in her body: creating a monster and tearing it apart.

She is also bringing on the analytic scene a more creative self, "her friend, Monica".

Of such a creative person she feels envious, in her internal museum. What she is doing is enviable and therefore ugly. She becomes critical of her own creativity and she may be asking herself how critical can she become of other people's creativity. Also: I am envious of my friend Monica and this is no good. No good. Dangerous. Maybe homicidal, as well. So she asks herself: was I the killer?

She does not want me to believe her, when she says she can only produce monsters, in order to tear them apart, increasing her anguish of having killed, and pinning her down to her faults.

She hopes I could be a painter who could encourage her to draw, who could trust her to pass her final examination, even when she is not feeling like sitting for it.

And after all that, I should appreciate the seductive appeal of an airy game, while sharing her wish to rise again and blow away confetti with a fan. Sending away her terrible experience, feeling free. We cannot trust entirely the manic defence, but its lightness helps to endure the pain.

It is nature which, as the wind blows dead leaves, brushes away what failed to live and starts a new cycle.

Merciless policewomen and fingers touching softly

She tells me about a dream:

> I am overtaking on the emergency lane and the police notice me. A pursuit follows. I escape, first in my car, and later, by running. I reach a house, asking the owners to help me hide. I keep running away in different rooms, with the policewomen after me; they are on me, they keep coming. At last I manage to hide in a cocktail cabinet, where I feel safe. The police enter the room. The owner is going to open the cocktail cabinet. I then touch his fingers lightly, so that he knows I am there. Finally, the policewomen don't find me. They have tortured the house inhabitants, to make them confess, and now they are changing clothes, right in the room I am hiding in. Meanwhile they are talking and it seems that the policewomen have also been in jail and became policewomen only later on. So it can't be very serious, I think, if one can be first one thing and then the other. I feel relieved.

She associates:

> The cocktail cabinet in my dream looked like the one in my grandmother's house, a place where I felt safe. My grandmother was strong; she has been my real mother. My mother was a fragile mother. A baby mother.

Abortion was an emergency and the emergency lane means you may stop. She would like on the opposite to be able to overtake, to cope with the emergency.

I feel confused, and again on thin ice: how do you stop somebody without making him feel a victim of persecution? She is afraid of stopping in order to look at her fears and her ambivalence and feels the frenzy of persecution.

If I now stop her, I am the sadist policewoman who will not let her use the emergency lane, when she feels like it. If she makes a mistake, she cannot get away with it: the cruel policewomen, inside her, want to catch her and attack her.

She also thinks that policewomen are on the right side, because you are not supposed to overtake on the emergency lane and to be in collusion is not a real help. Therefore, if I do not stop her, I am the imprisoned policewoman, who cannot do her job.

It would be better if somebody could stop her. He should tell her, nicely: stop and think a while, let us look at this experience together. One may want to and not want to. To escape forward immediately, breaking up the experience in small bits and pieces, in order to place it in the electric fan, does not mean to be safe. One should find a way of reaching even the most painful voice, saying: if you do not look at the monsters, the child will not believe they exist.

Getting in touch with one of my experiences, which is very similar to her own, helps me to move on this thin thread, through an unconscious contact: it is true that one can be "one thing first and then the other", first to have an abortion and then to give birth to a baby, first being a fragile mother, much too young, and then a strong mother-grandmother, who can hold her in her grief, while telling her: come and stay with me a while, safe in my old cocktail cabinet, keeping quiet. Do not torture yourself and torture those who want to help you. We shall drink together a small glass of that herbal drink made with lemon verbena … You will take heart and you will be able to start again.

The image of E, pursued, hiding in the cocktail cabinet/safe shelter/mother-grandmother. Fingers touching softly. A sign caught by somebody, who, even under torture, does not betray.

Who is the character played by E in the cocktail cabinet/safe hide/strong mother-grandmother?

Is it her inside me, is it the two of us together?

Is it not a sort of prefiguration/identification with a new child who, this time will be safe from every attack inside her, as she has now become a strong mother-grandmother and a safe hide.

"Of the body, through the body, with the body, from the body, and unto the body."

For this image as complex and "polysemantic", I cannot think of any other word except the following: touching.

The flight from the window

She puts in an envelope the pregnancy test, the one and only echography and the rosary beads left by somebody on her parked car, during the days she was expecting. She had found the rosary beads and associated them to the child, like an omen, and therefore kept them.

Life signals of that mysterious being who lived inside her such a short time.

> A short time, but I already had a name, Giovanni. This name was his own name, so that yesterday I was thinking that, if I ever have another child, it wouldn't have any sense to call him the same name. I think of it in terms of the soul. Even the echography image: she found the right word, *mysterious*, it looks as if it came from space.

Silence.

> I recall something that has nothing to do with it. A young girl I have met only once and who then jumped from her home window. Now she is in hospital and her mother had to take time off her job. She will have to go in a sheltered flat, right near here, next to her.

I think this is pertinent: Giovanni has flown, as well, from his home window, his uterus-home. She is also a mother in waiting: waiting is useful to her in order to think about him.

One has to enter a sheltered flat next to me, to linger in a hospital, in order to cure broken bones. I am thinking: a hospital/sheltered flat/ cocktail cabinet.

Let us look together at all those things she wants to stow, in all of them there is something to do with her soul. It looks as if there was something magic in the rosary beads appearance, as it deals with life, but also with death.

She is gathering in an envelope, which contains them all, everything dealing with Giovanni, in order to start anew with another child who will have another name.

A pregnant lorry with a big tummy and spiteful sprites

She dreams about: "Two lorries are parking: I watch and admire them. We had just been with my husband in a room, which didn't belong to us. Then the owner arrived and we succeeded in persuading him we were no thieves: he kept our purse and we had to work hard to have my husband's driving licence back."

She associates lorries and pregnant women's big tummies: she met two of them with huge tummies. The driving licence is used for driving; it is the driving licence parents need. She would like another pregnancy, but her husband is worried.

They had been in a house belonging to other people, but this does not mean that they are thieves. If she looks at other women tummies, it is not because she envies them, she does not want to steal. She is looking and admiring them, to see how it is, how one does it, how they do it. One must be convinced just like one has to be convinced that, even though the parents' driving licence has been held up for the moment, working hard, one may succeed in getting it back at the end.

There are two lorries and two are the pregnant women in the association: they are two, he and herself- and also myself and she!—due to have this pregnancy: if he is too worried, if the fear of repeating the traumatic experience is too great, there will not be any driving licence and without it, you cannot go anywhere.

The lorries can park; stop, and start again, find their place as parents.

In the same session, another dream:

> There is a sort of sprite flying around me. I think: it's a nice sprite, but she is also vicious. She does things out of spite, she is spiteful. I remember that today, while I was coming to your place, I felt something coming down on me. I moved away, thinking it was an insect. It was a small white pigeon feather, a nice looking small feather.
>
> Watching the small feather fly, I noticed the church door, normally closed, but open on that day. I felt like going in: I liked the church, I had never been in, and it was so silent inside. I found myself praying Jesus to send me a child. I saw that inside the church there was a piece of Lourdes grotto. I felt fine, I was at peace.

Lourdes is the place where incurable sick people would go looking for hope and asking to be healed, and she hears a voice telling her that a miracle is needed to overcome this fact. That sprite turns around her, she is mean and spiteful. It is her miscarried child who first deceived her and then left her empty handed. With an empty tummy, she is a useless lorry, which is not carrying anything any more.

It has a benign look, this sprite-white feather, leading her to a place where she can find some silence and some peace. It seems to tell her: now stop, let it be. It reminds you of the white little feather left behind in the air, by a stork, which presently flew away.

Waiting

Many months follow, many dreams follow and ambivalent associations showing longing and fear. It is really very difficult to avoid the trap of a claustrophilic situation. Time is petrified and squashed. Crushed by this unnatural attention to the biological cycle scan: every delay, a hope, every menstruation a disappointment.

I note how often twin couples appear, as if this time the ambivalence were felt even inside the body. It is like being pregnant with two twins and one of them dies, while the other survives. Sometimes she is the twin who survives.

Her dead twin sometimes is herself: an unwanted and miscarried self. One day she remembers her mother saying about her birth: "Eventually, your father and myself, we decided to keep you".

Many dreams, so many that I cannot remember some of them, and others we let go and fly away.

Maybe having dreamt them and shared them is sometimes enough to have an internal representation, even with no interpretation on our side.

Sometimes looking at certain images, as condensed and creative as dreams can give us, we may think: what else is there to say? Do we really have to say something else? Why?

We happen to feel poor in spirit trying, with our psychoanalytic language, to run after something, which seems sometimes to have a superior quality, either pictorial or poetic.

But even so …

What I definitely remember is her wish to leave for Africa.

> I was leaving for Africa, with my car, on my own. My mother was rather worried and I told her not to worry. She then smiled, made a gesture with her head forward and told me: go ahead. I was eating something with my husband and he was telling me to be careful.

We said goodbye and I left. Then I saw a girl in a car: the girl was coloured and pregnant with a round tummy and a nice looking round face and she seemed happy and the girl, it was me.

Shortly after this dream, while I was starting to think about this chapter and while the pregnancy, which I felt as mine, was also starting.

E is pregnant again

The happy end has been overpowering.

At the end of Wednesday evening session, when we talked about other topics, she tells me that the usual, frequent delay is longer this time: she could have had her test in the morning, but she preferred to wait for the following day, in order to be able to tell her husband straight away, as he left home this morning earlier than her. Maybe she was also thinking of me, as on Thursday her session is early in the morning.

The morning after, when I open the door, I realise my eyes are in contact with hers, hoping to discover the pink crescent, meaning positivity on the pregnancy test. She notices it and lowers her eyes, with a chuckle. I saw her. She tells me about two dreams, she dreamt in the night:

I watch the sea in the night, the water is very still. On the water you can see the reflection of two moons, I look at the sky expecting to see two moons, but in the sky there is only one. I woke up worried at the thought that it could be twins. This morning after having seen the positive test, I thought they weren't twins, but one of them was the dead child, the other this new one. I went back to sleep and I had another dream of which only an image is left of a chubby, lovely, coloured baby with the small folds of the skin little babies have.

She remembers the coloured pregnant mother, round and chubby of her previous dream: now she is the coloured mother and the baby is her baby. The sensation was of great calm.

The baby is mulatto, the mother is coloured and I think that, maybe, that child is also our child.

I do not tell her, though. If I did, I would feel clumsy and intrusive.

There are no more cobwebs in the cave this time and it seems to me that there is nothing else to say in order not to spoil the special neatness and clairvoyance of these dreams she had while she had not yet had a test, although her body already knew it.

But even so ....

Conclusion

A few more sentences in order to give a fuller explanation. I chose to speak mainly about dreams. Dreaming with the two patients about pregnancy and what was preventing it, living together their frightening anguish, their excessive hopes, their unlimited sadness, brought about an analytic nearness which, I think, gave me an access into the most creative area of their personality, free from the sterile dominance of superego requests. I think that one of the most important therapeutic factors of analysis is the experience of a true closeness in a couple, where you may feel as one with another person, as a result of its evocative and magic climate. I believe that it is only in this climate that a non intellectualised insight may occur, with the true power of helping people live their life in a fuller, richer, and freer way.

References

Artaud, A. (1947). Suppots et suppliciations. In: *Oeuvres Complètes*, XIV. Paris: Gallimard, 1978.

Atwood, M. (2002). *Negotiating with the Dead: A Writer on Writing*. Cambridge: Cambridge University Press.

O'Connor, F. (1961). *Letters of Flannery O'Connor*. S. Fitzgerald (Ed.). New York: Farrar, Straus & Giroux. 1979.

O'Connor, F. (1969). *Mystery and Manners*. S. & R. Fitzgerald (Eds.). New York: Farrar, Straus & Giroux.

CHAPTER THIRTEEN

A particular kind of sterility

Jones De Luca

"Mental sterility" may be viewed as generated by obsessive and violent symptoms which arise as a horde of primitive (wild) thoughts preventing fertilisation. In the presence of a desire to have a child, analytic work highlights how the obsessive ideas serve the "task" of exploring different aspects of the equipment required for motherhood.

Most children are born by chance. It is not easy to make the decision to bring someone into the world, so chance helps us (Sergio Bordi, personal communication). Fifty years have passed since Marie Langer stated, in her *Maternidad y sexo*, that the social changes in progress would lead women to encounter increasingly greater difficulties in what is considered women's first creativity: menstruation, conception, fertility, and breastfeeding (Langer, 1951, p. 28). Increasingly we have the opportunity to closely investigate these issues in a clinical setting. In the case I present here I focus on one specific aspect: the anguish caused by the possibility of conceiving a child, and its consequences.

Maria

Maria consulted me when she started developing unexpected feelings of hatred and repulsion towards a close friend who had become pregnant. Maria thought: "That will never be me." She was very surprised by her own reaction because she had always wanted a child. Everything about her seemed to indicate this: her maternal instinct, her sweet, almost infantile facial features, her hair styled in a soft bob and her light-coloured blouses with embroidered collars.

She reported vague obsessive symptoms which she was keeping under control by periodically taking medication. However, in her opinion, medication was preventing her from becoming pregnant, and achieving what had always been her greatest desire. However, when she was well and did not need medicine, other types of obstacles came up. For instance, on one occasion, her husband had major economic commitments, so they had to postpone their plan to have a child (Goretti Regazzoni, 2012, p. 1157); another time, an antibiotic taken for toothache meant having to wait. Sometimes there was an absence of sexual intercourse for as long as several months. When I asked her the reason for these long periods of abstinence, her reaction was one of irritation and surprise. She maintained that it was normal, and said she never expected such a question: what did this have to do with her issues? She was a college graduate, was very intelligent, had a prominent position at work, but it was as if she was not connecting sex with the birth of a child; on this topic she seemed very naïve.

Paraphrasing Freud, we might imagine that her libido had not yet developed to a sufficient degree to be able to integrate and utilise the identifications necessary for a pregnancy (Bordi, Muscetta & Princivalle, 1976, pp. 243–294). I proposed that we conduct an analysis or rather, an intensive therapy of three sessions a week, explaining that a certain frequency was necessary to address such an important issue (in her environment one session a week was considered "analysis").

She pondered the idea and then asked me to start right away, informing me that she had decided she would not take any kind of medication. This was quite risky, as she had virtually always been on medication. As pharmacological discoveries have relieved patients from mental pain, the psychoanalytic method—three or four sessions a week—may feel less sensible and prudent than the therapeutic recommendations found in the expert consensus guidelines. In Maria's case avoiding drugs was perceived as unusual and significant by both the patient and the analyst.

We also decided on a face-to-face position: the patient did not want to lie down on the couch, and I, too, preferred to have her facing me. After only a few weeks—when being listened to in an analytic relationship made her feel that she could entertain the idea of getting pregnant—all hell broke loose. This sweet, submissive young woman soon turned into a sort of fury who was capable of thinking anything. Everything was called into question, and fierce obsessive ideas generated doubts about everything.

It all started when a stranger treated her to a cup of coffee at a cafe across from the office where she had a high-ranking job. Once at the beginning of the analysis when she was not able to think reflectively, she insinuated that the man might follow and then rape her, leaving her pregnant with the child of a stranger. She was no longer able to stay at home alone (the man might break in), and her anguish was extreme, and since we could not rely on medication, we had to try very actively to understand where these thoughts were coming from. She asked me: What does this all mean?

I asked for her associations, asked her what the "coffee" man made her think of, perhaps he reminded her of something? I asked her what she had felt at the time and explained to her that it had to be something important if it provoked such frightening consequences. She remembered that she had felt light and beautiful, the man was young and smiling. Basically he resembled her husband, and so by following her associative connections, we could see that the stranger who threatened her with pregnancy was none other than her husband, whose undiscovered aspects frightened her.

Her husband

This man, who up to that point had been considered a gentle and reliable partner, is now scrutinised mercilessly. Obsessive ideas concerning him or associated to him had begun to torment her.

PATIENT: Ugly things come to my mind; I look at my husband and I think I could hurt him, get a knife and …

ANALYST: These thoughts are really painful and scary, but also interesting for us. Let's try and see what they mean.

We watch how these "absurd" thoughts are growing and what they mean: the patient is anxious and curious at the same time.

P: But what does this mean? I'm afraid I'll kill him!
A: Saying that you'll kill him is a bit of an exaggeration and an extreme thought, but perhaps—again exaggerating—is it possible that your husband, who loves you, did something to deserve these thoughts ... When did you start thinking of the knife?

She tells me it happened during a time when she felt serene. He was happy because of his new work project and enthusiastic about his next work trip. This trip would have taken him far away, and could have been the first of many. So I ask her what this might mean to her. Is she thinking of a future child? If her husband starts travelling, she might have misgivings about his reliability. We then discover that, hidden deep inside her, heavy accusations are lodged against him. At one point she says, in a frenzy:

P: He is selfish; he has postponed the decision to have a child when I asked to have one, because he was involved in other financial investments; he is somewhat insensitive, and will me leave alone with the child once I become a mother.
A: You are very angry ... Perhaps you didn't know?
P: I have never realised that I had such critical thoughts about my husband.
A: There might be reasons to expect him not to be considerate of your problems? He doesn't know how bad you feel.
P: Yes, there are: he sees me as independent.
A: And it has been difficult for him to guess your needs, hidden as they were behind an adult efficient woman but in this difficult time he will have to become more aware of your fragility.

In her obsessive production, however, Maria "knew" that her husband's absence—that it, his failure to invest his resources in her, rather than in his job—would have endangered the child. The child component of her psychic organisation—which a pregnancy would awaken from the long sleep in which she had cast it in favour of parts of herself better able to perform skills—would also be endangered.

A: You are afraid of what is going to happen once you become a mother.
P: I'm afraid I'll hurt someone … not only my husband.

Currently, the task of supporting the mother in the family is mainly delegated to the child's father, who becomes the focus of the narcissistic investment the woman needs in order to face such a difficult task (De Luca, 2007). The couple relationship also becomes the main battlefield for a wide range of feelings—anguish, identifications, projections, and projective identifications—that the birth of a new life reconnects in our earliest memories, as we search for the gestures others used when taking care of us as children. (Where have the mothers-in-law gone? And the sisters-in-law and the other witches with whom we could share unbearable split-off parts?)

Maria has good reasons. Through her obsessive productions, she begins to explore the conditions she would find herself in if she became a mother. In the transference, my support during pregnancy is immediately questioned. She comes to sessions feeling desperate because of the anguish she feels, and looks at me hard with wide eyes like a child full of reproach. As if I could not face her stare and was afraid of her, I ask:

A: How are you?
P: Very bad since last night.
A: So just after the session!
P: Yes!

She had not slept all night, her thoughts had begun to trouble her immediately after the previous session and had not stopped since.

A: What has happened? These sessions really bring trouble?

She raises a smile which seems to mean "You've finally noticed!", and then says in a very serious tone:

P: After our session I thought of knives again, and other things, too. I thought that I no longer love my husband and something terrible was going to happen. I thought bad things about you, too.
A: I must have got you very upset.

I thought: "She's going to say that 'I have to separate from my husband'".

P: This is what makes me mad at you, doctor! How can I separate? Now he has to leave and I'll be alone. I'm so scared! The thought of that man at the coffee shop breaking in during the night haunts me. Then I thought that perhaps I wrote a note while I was at work. I wrote ugly things about myself—very ugly. This note might have ended up between some documents. Now everybody will read it and know how sick I am.

A: So perhaps I seem quite irresponsible to you. It looks like I can't understand your anguish and, on top of that, I seem to give you dangerous ideas, like leaving your husband.

I say that she must have been very concerned about the path taken with me, who, like the stranger at the café, had unleashed so many terrible thoughts inside her. Then, on a lighter note, I speak of the danger one runs by offering a cup of coffee ... I think that these accusations bring us back to the lack of responsibility by those who should provide care, and I say:

A: It is as if you were a child in the hands of irresponsible parents.

The idea of the note shows the extent of her feeling that her anguish might not be contained inside her mind or within the sessions, but invade her workplace and cause serious problems. I ask myself how and where I am making room for her persecutory anxieties. I wonder if I should push her to take medication, or inform her doctor or family members. Would she be able to go to work feeling so persecuted?

A: You feel very lonely and scared. Your husband is thinking of his trip, and perhaps this causes you to "no longer love him", since he is going away.

This is the last session in the week. The date of her husband's departure is still far off, while I will be away from the following day. The reference to the analytic relationship is made gently, without focusing too much on the transference:

A: So, maybe you fear that I won't be very reliable either ...

Now the challenge is in the transference: could things be different than in the past? The problem of being alone when I am away becomes predominant. Weekends are hell. The struggle against the thoughts that her mind presents to her is brutal. She comes to our Monday sessions worn out by weekends during which she has to telephone me several times, without being able to sleep, without being able to go out, subject as she is to terrible threats concerning what she might do: threats that, within the four walls of her own house, take on an almost real dimension. She is very considerate and it bothers her considerably having to call me, but the phone calls, in which we continue to search for the meaning of these thoughts, are able to calm her down. The work goes on constantly.

Her phone calls put me in touch with the destructive attack against her parents, re-experienced in the transference. I accompany her as she examines the frightening ideas that force her to telephone me: ideas against herself, myself, and our work. I think that all accusations have to be investigated because she is defending her future child and the child she had been in the past.

During sessions, she starts to discuss what I say, she contradicts me, and sometimes even challenges me: so, in the meantime, the unfolding—in the transference—of a relationship that possibly features a moderate degree of conflict gives her a sense that a couple does not necessarily have to "always get along" by ignoring difficulties. She starts to feel that seeing herself in such a "bad" light is more tolerable, while her rage, which sterilises everything, could melt away.

Two mothers

However, as soon as the obstacle of the relationship with her husband was overcome, and once she obtained his full cooperation for their shared project, she in turn became the one called into question.

> When women were faced with the possibility of achieving their conscious desires of motherhood, they were so anxious that they lost, at least temporarily, their fertility: from all this we can assume again that the conflict with motherhood had influenced the choice of the husband, as well as afterwards it had disrupted the ability to conceive or carry a pregnancy to term. (Langer, 1951, p. 223 translated for this edition)

Obsessive ideas featuring the most varied and fierce content abruptly started to appear as Maria approached ovulation: this time, however, her ideas revolved around the theme of possibly harming her child.

Reaching the core

Even though she did not seem to be aware of her fertile days, these ideas came punctually and were "well-informed". (This has been explored by female psychoanalysts since the 1930s; see, among others, the research by Benedek, 1960/1979, on the deep perception of the time of ovulation through dreams during analysis). Every month they prevented Maria from being sexually approached exactly on the days that were favourable to a pregnancy.

With regard to these same ideas, she maintained that she had harmed (or had the potential to harm) her closest friends' children, whom she saw on a regular basis. These children adored her and everybody thought she was very friendly and good with them. Friends and relatives gladly entrusted her with their newborns and toddlers. However, as her obsessive symptoms grew out of control, she had to limit these situations.

Two Marias existed. One represented the idealised and perfect image of the "good mother", the other was a fierce and harmful woman who could by no means be integrated: the "bad mother". The integration of the "bad mother" is an issue often brought to psychoanalysts. In the 1950s, Marie Langer proposed the study of a "modern myth" of the "bad" mother: a babysitter who roasts the child she is watching while the young parents are out to dinner. I would add that one reason why this tale met with such popular success is related to the new family structure that was emerging in those years: in order to devise a vehicle for the "bad mother", a female stranger had to be used in the "myth", thus stressing the fact that parents were not getting any help from their family. In another variant, in the judgment of Solomon, the maternal figure is split in two: a murderous mother who could accept the killing of her child, and a "good" mother who would give up her son as long as he can stay alive (Bordi, Muscetta & Princivalle, 1976). Other myths refer to the myth of Medea.

> ... their female counterparts exert an equal fascination and suggest
> that the Medea myth as recounted by Euripides can be invoked

to elucidate a central unconscious fantasy found to underlie the psychogenic frigidity and sterility of several of her female patients. (Leuzinger-Bohleber, 2001, p. 323)

I have researched this topic for many years (De Luca, 2007) and noticed several times that, when faced with the perception of violent or aggressive impulses towards their children, many mothers abandoned their maternal role in favour of more suitable figures. The child was suddenly entrusted to others, and sometimes this relinquishment and the consequent abandonment of the child had had a devastating effect.

After these observations I started to extend these considerations to my patients who were childless, and I wondered if their lives had not been organised in such a way as to prevent pregnancy. What was to be avoided at all costs was the birth of a "bad mother". I began to recognise a "contraceptive" method in these promiscuous lifestyle choices, in unsuccessful love affairs. This was a helpful insight for patients, confirming my hypothesis with good therapeutic results.

Returning to Maria

Every month Maria experienced her menstruation with deep depression—as if it was possible for a child to be conceived miraculously, regardless of any biological law. She said: "It must be premenstrual syndrome" (Benedek, 1960).

In obsessive thinking, the content repressed is faithfully preserved and reported in the obsessive idea (Navarro, 2004). Consequently, on every occasion, we were able to reconstruct the meaning of her ideation and track down the underlying fears connected to the dread that traumatic childhood experiences would recur. Furthermore, on every occasion, through the new transference experience, these past experiences took on a new meaning and the dreaded thoughts quickly cleared up.

She did not seem able to understand how someone could soothe someone else's anguish, and was dubious about the possibilities offered by analysis. At times she seemed to reproduce an almost identical session, or a thread of thoughts we had explored together; the same anxieties were violent as if the same experience had to be repeated one or more times, then she changed subject. I found myself repeating again and again the experience of letting a violent, destructive discharge arrive and then Maria finding containment in the attentive listening of an psychoanalyst who was not too frightened. Sometimes I was under the impression that she would go back to the place of her anguish just to see if the remedy would work again. I told myself, "She is quickly learning how to deal with an anguished child."

On every occasion, she bravely decided to carry on: without medication she wanted to stretch herself and see what her mind was able to produce, despite the anguish and pain caused in recalling her unhappy childhood. The hope was that of a recovery. In the past, she had never experienced anything like this mental hell, with the exception of an episode when she was a teenager, which was immediately resolved by a pharmacological intervention. Overall, her equilibrium had been good and only the actual attempt to start a pregnancy caused it to collapse. (Would she have become "sick" had she not wanted a child?). Anguish had surfaced only briefly, like the tip of a rock at low tide. The "bad mother" had been sighted, then she was concealed again. However the perception that sailing those waters would be extremely dangerous was acute. Was she right? Had we asked her neighbours, colleagues, and closest friends, they would all have said that it was impossible that Maria would not be an excellent mother. By this point, however, she and I had taken into consideration that her misgivings might be valid.

She grew up with a mother suffering a deep depression, whose absence was perceived almost as cynical, and who left her at the mercy of a jealous and paranoid father who was liable to say anything about her. She had laboriously established a truth about herself, which refuted her father's accusations—a truth based on her reliability at school and later at work—but the underlying ground was unstable. When she was a teenager, her father followed her, recorded her phone calls, and locked her up in the house for days.

Maria was responsible and generous. However, even if these traits had been demonstrated in many instances, they were not rooted in a vision of herself shared by her parents at important times of her growth. Moreover, the enormous rage she had to control and remove from her consciousness—as it would have been extremely dangerous in her relationship with her father—served as fertile ground for the doubts about her "goodness". For this new task—being a mother—she could not count on the experience of growing up with a mother she could identify with, because her mother lost in a state of constant depression had always rejected her.

The therapeutic process progressed very quickly; we started shortly after Christmas, and while the first few months of the year were characterised by strong obsessive productions, even before Easter we explored her ability to be a mother with such a difficult past, and she was already experiencing moments when she was able to control the course of her thoughts. Six months since the beginning of the analysis she was quite well with calm periods becoming longer. She told me proudly the explanations that she had been able to give herself to stop the horrific chain of obsessive thoughts and asked me to confirm. Was she good? Did I agree with her interpretations? Meanwhile, she kept looking sideways at the window to see if despite the summer heat that was coming I had taken care to properly close the windows: who knows who might be out there. The persecution was just outside the window, still lurking.

Our summer separation was experienced with great fear, and she needed me to promise that we would stay in contact. I decided to use Skype. This variation of the setting anticipated, in Maria's imagination, the moment when she, after birth, imagined herself alone and far from everyone, locked up in her home; in the same way she, as a teenager, had been closed off from the world with her only contact being the persecutory figures represented by her parents. This had happened during an incident in which she was seen by her father with a boy. During my vacation, the computer with its backlit screen, where she could see me, could have been—in her imagination at that time—the only channel of contact with a persecution-free world.

So we kept in contact via Skype while I was traveling. They were not sessions as such, but were modeled on the pattern of our phone calls. At first they lasted quite a while. She needed to become comfortable with the medium and reassured about my "survival". By the end, just a few minutes were enough for her to see me, be listened to, and reassured of my presence beside her. She had only had the empty eyes of her mother for mirroring, and had never been "seen". Being able to see me was important to her in the same way our face-to-face therapy had been important.

When she heard I had returned from overseas, she calmed down completely. When we resumed our sessions, she was quite well and her thoughts were not persecuting her. At this point, she was approaching the idea of having sexual intercourse and had an enjoyable time during short vacations with her husband. At the beginning of autumn she was completely engrossed by the discovery of a new physical intimacy and soon after she realised she was pregnant.

This brought an outbreak of obsessive thoughts and she felt completely foreign to the idea of a child. She considered herself cold and cruel, unable to love a baby. In the course of the second month, she had a miscarriage (this was a little over one year into the analysis) which she reacted to as if she had damaged the baby by her delayed acceptance of the baby.

The use of a pregnancy test, which permits the immediate detection of pregnancy, also means that the child is immediately a reality, without leaving any time for the imagination to come to grips with a child who is not yet so "real". Consequently, the conflicting emotions that would normally be elicited by delayed menstruation immediately become a battlefield where it comes to the life or death of a real child (Goretti Regazzoni, 2012, p. 1157).

After this experience, her fear was that of being tormented by the obsessive idea of pregnancy and having to begin the long journey of being unable to have children. At that point she decided she would not deliberately seek to become pregnant again and let chance (nature?) take its course.

She recovered very quickly and became pregnant again, almost unexpectedly, after a very short time. The pregnancy passed almost without enthusiasm, with vague fears and slight obsessive symptoms: it almost seemed as though she could not abandon herself to the joy of having a baby, except for short lapses (a functional split recurred). She only went to the gynaecologist at the end of the third month, almost as if she were keeping a secret, and her medical checkups were limited. The summer holidays arrived shortly before her delivery, and this time did not reveal any particular separation difficulties: the patient felt that I was close.

In the last few months, she spontaneously used the couch.

Childbirth and postpartum

At this point a delicate issue arose: what to do after giving birth? Maria thought that the most important thing was being able to stay close to the child. In addition, her analysis had already achieved its goal: having a baby. She imagined that I would be at her complete disposal without establishing a return to analysis after delivery.

The patient had repeatedly had the opportunity to join me when needed (as in the first vacation), had considered my closeness "good enough", and our connection was very strong. We had worked hard in order for her to feel able to "make it" and to trust in her own abilities. Her relationship with me was now very different from the initial one marked by the suspicious intrusiveness of her father with his continuous raids at her home as a young bride. I felt quietly confident. She felt distant those times when she anxiously asked (and I asked myself) who would be close to her if she had negative thoughts alone with her baby. Even then I preferred not to make decisions and move with caution: I preferred to leave the question in the background, without taking any position on the next step, but remaining available to the patient and her needs.

The delivery went smoothly in early autumn. In the first few weeks, she rang me occasionally, to update me: the girl was beautiful, the nursing was going well and she often held the baby in her arms. There were no other problems. She never felt the need to call me, even though she knew she could at any time.

She called before Christmas as she wanted to come by for a visit and show me her little girl (who was three months old). Two years had passed since the beginning of our work.

While she was in my office with her baby, I observed excellent contact between them and, despite an abruptness of movement like that of a person who had to learn something as an adult that should be innate, I could tell she was very capable. The baby fell asleep in her arms and she sat contemplating her (looking like a Virgin in a fifteenth-century painting).

Maria said, "I spend a lot of time like this, holding her in my arms. Everybody says I shouldn't, but then I remember you said I should do what I feel is right; and in the Far East they pick up children a lot. So I think that too little time has passed since she was in my belly." She was very well, in fact they were both well.

Six months later

When her child is six months old, she calls me. She is fine, she has not had any negative thoughts, but she would like to come and see me. During our conversation, she talks about exclusive breastfeeding and the thought of how she will manage when she has to go back to work, possibly in three months time, as her child will have to eat baby food then. Her mother has been very close to her and has also helped her feel good.

Discussion

Maria had not certainly grown up with a "usable mother", and perhaps there were no places inside her where she could find gestures and useful ways to take care of a child of her own. As we know, an adequate identification with the mother is essential in becoming a mother (Deutsch, 1944; Pines, 1982; Zalusky, 2000). This had threatened her chance of becoming a mother.

When her anguish was most trying, when she—so respectful and shy—became overpowering and tyrannical, and felt the need to call me because her thoughts were intolerable, I would tell myself, "Fortunately, she is not dealing with a child. How would she manage otherwise?" And immediately, I wondered if this was not exactly what Maria was trying to make me understand: how could she manage with a child? Being on medication was not perceived as safe terrain for bringing up a child. She needed to feel me constantly close to her, in order to refute whatever was inside her that was continuously turning me into an indifferent and sarcastic mother. Together we had to demonstrate that her father—whose accusations were clearly echoed in her obsessive ideas—was in the wrong. If she had been expecting a child at that time, would she have been able to continue her pregnancy?

An important part of her maintained that she should not have children. This was undoubtedly due to her damaged internal objects, so that identification was impossible. But it was also due to her perception of a state of pain that for her was inherent in being a child, whereby children were also loathsome because of their vulnerability towards the "bad mother" that she herself might become. It was a vicious circle. Who would help her?

Every time a problem arises concerning the expectation of a pregnancy it is not only the mother who is involved, but also all those people with whom she has relationships (Bordi, Muscetta & Princivalle, 1976).

Through her obsessive ideas, Maria had assessed her husband, her parents, and then her parents-in-law. The result of this evaluation led her to think that she could not expect any help at all in her task.

Often, in Western civilisation the nature of the family structure poses serious problems of isolation for young mothers, making it difficult to nurse children, as well as distributing both aggressive impulses and complex emotions among several people and alternatives. These young women are the daughters of the generation that first experienced the consequences of the break-up of the extended family network, and their mothers brought them up in solitude. In solitude, they had to contain the "good" and the "bad", and very often they did not have anybody to help them (not even materially) take care of their offspring. Then the desire to get rid of the children (even if only briefly) when facing the hostile feelings that they arouse, as Winnicott reminds us, could not be experienced guiltlessly.

As Langer pointed out as early as in the middle of the twentieth century, this type of social organisation increases the difficulties related to motherhood. In Maria's case, the effective state of her objects was not encouraging. Nobody could have actually provided her with valid assistance. I had given her credit for her symptoms.

At this juncture, we might consider that the "sterility" resulting from these states is not only related to a situation in which women, prosecuted by the attacks (possibly justified) launched against their mothers, cannot take their place as mothers themselves. This sterility is also the fruit of their identification with the child: they are unable to make another person experience what they have gone through.

> I was driven by the experience of many women who—now more often than in the past—are able to clearly state that they do not want to have children. I wondered about the price they pay, psychically, for this experience in terms of their sense of guilt, lack, partiality, and much more. This decision is often heavily penalised by the collective. Only rarely, instead, do people highlight that these women—being aware of their shortcomings or limits, and often with a great deal of pain—prefer to protect their unborn child from themselves. (Neri, 2010, p. 5 translated for this edition)

It was Maria's motherly disposition that made her feel that giving birth to an unhappy child would mean granting herself her own demise. We might say that, as if following a "selfish gene"—which certainly does not care about the health of the phenotype, but rather checks out all possible conditions of continuity and wellness for the transmission of a specific genetic pool—Maria felt that she was unable to guarantee a motherly environment that allowed for the development of a child. Taking this hypothesis into account as part of my work enabled me to start approaching Maria from her "protective" side.

She felt helpless and alone as when she was a child. Being an adult required that she excluded her evolutionary and creative child component, which she perceived as a threat to the structured part of herself. In the transference, instead, her early dependence emerged: an element that is fundamental to be a sufficiently good mother. Maria came to analysis and asked for help. Meeting this vital part of herself should have been perceived as being born again. On the other hand, in the countertransference, I sometimes found myself perceiving the patient's criticism and devaluation as an inadequate mother.

In the analysis, she did her best to ask for help with all the anguish and urgency that she needed to express, but at the same time this could lead to a verdict against her as a potential mother. She perceived her dependence as something that weakened her and put her in the hands of someone cruel, who would despise her and confirm her inadequacy. The verdict would be that she had to remain sterile. Stubborn and courageous, she tried to combat this verdict, while, at the same time, she was gathering newer and newer "evidence" of her guilt, in order to put my "blessing" to the test.

It was difficult for me not to abandon this battlefield. So I "enacted" the part my patient assigned me: I accepted being "irresponsible" and "imprudent", even "cruel" at times: in other words, a "terrible mother". In this way, integrating the "bad mother", and experiencing active containment at the same time, the patient could move out of the persecutory climate she was living in, come to know and accept the "violence" in her she feared so much, and make room for her fertility.

Acknowledgement

I would like to express my gratitude to Oriana Bonan and Silvia Currò for their assistance in drafting the English version of this text.

References

Allison, G. H. (1997). Motherhood, motherliness, and psychogenic infertility. *Psychoanalytic Quarterly, 66*, 1: 1–17.

Benedek, T. (1960). L'organiszazione della pulsione riproduttiva. In: L. Baruffi, (Ed.), *Il desiderio di maternità* (pp. 214–242). Turin: Boringhieri, 1979.

Bordi, S., Muscetta, S. & Princivalle, M. (1976). Contributions to the panel "L'aborto come vissuto nella realtà psichica e nel mondo esterno" (Presented at the III SPI National Meeting, Venice). *Rivista di Psicoanalisi, 22*: 243–294.

De Luca, J. (2007). Associazioni sul mito di Medea. *Rivista di Psicoanalisi, 53*: 1033–1054.

Deutsch, H. (1944). *Psychology of Women.* New York: Grune & Stratton.

Goretti Regazzoni, G. (2012). On procreating today. *International Journal of Psychoanalysis, 93*: 1153–1173.

Langer, M. (1951). *Matenidad y Sexo. Estudio psicoanalítico y psicosomático.* Barcelona: Paidos. Italian edition: *Maternità e Sesso.* Turin: Loescher (1981).

Lansky, M. R. (2005). The impossibility of forgiveness: Shame fantasies as instigators of vengefulness in Euripides' Medea. *Journal of the American Psychoanalytic Association, 53*: 437–464.

Leuzinger-Bohleber, M. (2001). The 'Medea Fantasy': An unconscious determinant of psychogenic sterility. *International Journal of Psycho-Analysis, 82*: 323–345.

Moccia, G. (2006). Le memorie identificatorie nell'organizzazione del transfert (Presented at the XIII SPI National Meeting, Siena, 2006). In: A. Nicolò, (2007). *Attualità del transfert. Articolazioni, varietà cliniche, evoluzioni.* Milan: Franco Angeli.

Navarro, J. B. (2004). *Neurosis Obsesiva: Teoría Y Clínica.* Buenos Aires: Lugar.

Neri, N. (2010). Introduzione. In: N. Neri & C. Rogora (Eds.), *Quaderni di psicoterapia infantile.* Vol. 59: *Desideri di maternità* (pp. 5–12). Rome: Borla.

Pines, D. (1982). The relevance of early psychic development to pregnancy and abortion. *International Journal of Psycho-Analysis, 63*: 311–319.

Pines, D. (1990). Emotional aspects of infertility and its remedies. *International Journal of Psycho-Analysis, 71*: 561–568.

Winnicott, D. W. (1975). L'odio nel controtransfert. In: D. W. Winnicott, *Dalla pediatria alla psicoanalisi* (pp. 234–245). Florence: Martinelli.

Zalusky, S. (2000). Infertility in the age of technology. *Journal of the American Psychoanalytic Association, 48*: 1541–1562.

Web resources

The New England Journal of Medicine. (1997). *Expert Consensus Guidelines.* Available at www.psychguides.com/gl-treatment_of_obsessive-compulsive_disorder.html. Accessed 22 June 2013.

CHAPTER FOURTEEN

Discussion of "A particular kind of sterility" by Jones de Luca

Ester Palerm Mari

Jones de Lucas presents us with a case in which the problem of physical sterility in a patient with intense obsessive symptoms is paramount. In an effort to understand what underlies the symptomatology she also shows us the moments in the treatment when the symptoms become more prominent. I will concentrate my reflections on some aspects related to the patient's request for help such as the parental figures, identity, ego weakness, and some technical considerations; I will then comment on the extended family, the nuclear family and the importance of unconscious phantasy and conclude with some additional considerations.

The request for help

The patient's request for help is motivated by her feelings of hatred for her friend who is pregnant, as well as by her desire to discontinue the medication she was taking, as she blames it for her lack of fertility. Consequently, I wonder if her request for help is really guided by her wish to understand her internal world better, or rather only to become pregnant.

Since, coinciding with her accepting the analysis she is offered, the patient simultaneously decides to stop taking her medication, could this decision be seen as an enactment aimed at using the analysis as a substitute for the medication and with the consequent phantasy of becoming pregnant? Often in fact, and above all at the beginning of an analysis, the aims of patient and analyst do not always coincide. It is in the process of the analytic work that the request for analysis is clarified and readjusted.

When the motivation to begin analytic treatment is limited to concrete aims, the patient tends to project those aims into the analyst who must then focus her attention on them. In Maria's case it was her obsessive symptoms and her wish to become pregnant. In cases like these the risk of making such concrete aims the final objective of the analysis is present, and if these aims are, in fact achieved, to consider them the confirmation of the success of the treatment. Consequently and in my view, it is not the presence or absence of symptoms, or pregnancy in the case of Maria, that determine analytic work but rather the broad understanding of the internal world of the patient. In this sense it would be important to recall what Bion (1967) said about working in the analytic session "without memory or desire" with free floating attention in order to facilitate non-focalised listening, unbiased by prior knowledge or judgments made *a priori*, to achieve, in this way, a greater understanding of the dynamics of the patient-analyst relationship. It is in this manner that analytic work will allow us to have an understanding not only of symbolic meanings, but also of the different subtleties related to how the patient uses his mind, and in this case, and speaking about Maria, how she will affect her analyst's mind. As regards Maria the analyst becomes aware of her mental sterility that causes the obsessive control we observe in her.

Considerations regarding parental figures

The analyst shows us how the patient communicates her internal experiences dominated by primitive functioning and defense mechanisms. Her internal objects appear to be damaged and identification processes seem likewise affected. Not only is the figure of the mother deteriorated, but also the father figure and indeed the parental couple. Psychoanalytic literature emphasises the importance of having internalised a "good parental couple" that presupposes love and a mutual appreciation in order to be able to achieve adult mental functioning. So, to be capable of the maternal function multiple identifications are required: identifications with each parent, with the needs of the baby, and with the creative parental couple that involves the image of a containing father in the mind of the mother. That is to say, the absence of a sufficiently containing paternal figure interferes with the mother's adaptation to the needs of the baby, resulting in a deficient regulation of the symbiosis between mother and baby.

Likewise, the absence of a loving bond between the parents causes a failure in the integration and internalisation of the parental couple. This failure becomes an obstacle to the integration of masculine and feminine as well as to loving and hating aspects. This has direct consequences on the development of the baby's identity and promotes an early oedipal conflict with sado-masochistic characteristics that makes the transition to triangulation difficult.

Feldman (2009) on the other hand relates oedipal phantasies to thought processes. He says,

> The phantasy of the oedipal couple is closely related to the way in which the patient is able to use his mind to create links between his thoughts and feelings, and to tolerate the anxieties that result from such links. If the anxieties associated with the phantasy of the parental couple are too great, then there will be a corresponding interference with the capacity for making connections between elements in the patient's mind. (Feldman, 2009, p. 125)

When the parents' relationship is attacked, probably due to poor maternal holding or to the baby's jealousy or envy, then destructive attacks predominate and the understanding and learning from experience are affected. Britton (1989) maintains that tolerance in accepting the parental relationship allows the child to put himself in the place of a third person: that of the non-participating observer. He says,

> The primal family triangle provides the child with two links connecting him separately with each parent and confronts him with the bond between them which excludes him. If the link between the parents perceived in love and hate can be tolerated in the child's mind, it provides him with a prototype for an object relationship of a third kind in which he is a witness and

not a participant. A third position then comes into existence from which object relationships can be observed. Given this, we can also envisage being observed. This provides us with a capacity for seeing ourselves in interaction with others and for entertaining another point of view whilst retaining our own, for reflecting on ourselves whilst being ourselves. This is a capacity we hope to find in ourselves and in our patients in analysis. (Britton, 1989, p. 87)

For this reason, the difficulty in tolerating the parents' relationship has affected Maria's capacity to adopt an observing attitude. Despite her professional achievements, the difficulties she has in managing her internal world have affected her cognitive capacities. This allows us to understand the surprise and irritation the patient shows in initial meetings when the analyst asks about her long periods of sexual abstinence and she responds by saying that she would never have expected such a question, and that she did not understand how it related to her worries. The patient is unable to link this with her desire to become pregnant and the analyst shows us her mental sterility in full detail: "She did not link her sex life to the birth of a child".

All of these factors account for the foundations of Maria's identity being so profoundly affected. We see a cynical, absent mother, a paranoid father, and the total lack of a creative parental figure. In addition to this, Maria denies the parental relationship. She does not link sexuality with the birth of a baby. Her bond with her father, with her mother, and with the parental couple, along with the attacks made on the parental relationship have negatively interfered in the establishment of her psyche and with her sense of identity. The parents' limitations in containing the projections in a more tolerant way gave greater relevance to the aggressive aspects than to the loving ones. Dominated by her love and hate, her relationships are subjugated by these two feelings. That is why, when faced with the uncertainty, frustration, or the absence of an ideal object, the relationship is transformed into a persecutory one. In these conditions she defends herself from the introjection of an object that does not generate in her a sense of well-being, and she projects all of her bad feelings. Her analyst thus speaks to us about her "two mothers"—one that she imagines her friends see—a good mother—and the other being the bad feeling she carries within which create difficulties in her identity. At the same time the difficulty she has in integrating and linking her feelings keeps her ego fragile.

All of this makes technical considerations necessary to understand the analytic work.

Identity, ego weakness, and technical considerations

In order to have a sense of one's own identity the internal world must necessarily have been developed and differentiated from the external one, and the ego from those of others. The more difficulties the patient encounters in integration and recognition of the internal world, the more she will encounter in life and in analytic work.

The patient's request for help appears to be embraced by her infantile and omnipotent aspects, with no awareness of the internal fears that she experiences. She projects her fears and incompetence in figures and situations in her environment. Her desire to have a baby obeys a narcissistic desire rather than a longing to share such a project with someone. In that line of thinking, discontinuing her medication was, it seems, a one-sided decision without taking into account how this decision would be seen by her analyst. Would the analyst agree with this decision or feel ignored in her analytic function? I question the meaning of this decision and how it was understood in the analysis.

Only a few weeks after the analysis began, although projected in an external situation, analytic work was experienced as violating her, and danger is represented in the persecutory experience of spawning unknown and/or strange things. The analyst's considerations regarding whether analysis was the treatment of choice for this patient are unknown to us.

It is obvious that analytic commitment requires that the analyst live with uncertainty and the anxiety that change awakens. In order to sustain it the analyst needs to call on their container-contained function (Bion, 1962). It is, however, not only necessary when patient and analyst are in the session, but also when they separate. Both parts need to have their own Bionian function, and it is probably because of this that the analyst prefers being face-to-face with the patient when the latter had a weak ego, little ability to contain, and shows a fear of accentuating regressive tendencies with the use of the couch.

In my opinion the care the analyst uses when speaking to the patient, intervening cautiously as she does, may be the expression of her countertransference in the face of the patient's weak ego. On other occasions I believe that the analyst offers herself as an auxiliary ego to attenuate the patient's fears. Sometimes she uses a technological medium to contain the patient during periods of separation. She appears to realise that the patient is fearful of having more understanding and acquiring more insight into her problems. The patient wants to have a baby-analysis without going through the uncertainty that change awakens or the complexities inherent for her of tolerating moments when there is no understanding of her internal world. I believe that if the analyst insists excessively on helping her achieve insight when she cannot tolerate it then she runs the risk that her interpretations are perceived as intrusive or, if she can face them, she will be fearful of a persecutory disintegration or unbearable suffering. If, to the contrary the analyst adopts an excessively permissive or passive attitude, the aims of analytic work will be limited and the changes superficial rather than structural.

The complexity in approaching these patients with diverse levels of functioning manifests in the technical difficulties and in the impact made in the countertransference. When a very primitive type of functioning predominates, then the need for containment and feeling understood prevails over the patient being able to understand herself. The analyst accompanies the patient with interpretations that Steiner (1993, p. 135), in his chapter on technical problems in psychoanalysis, calls "analyst-centred interpretations" which means that the analyst accepts the patient's projection onto the figure of the analyst without showing him that he is mistaken in his projection, but rather keeps what was projected until the patient can face it himself. The other type of interpretation that Steiner talks about is the "patient-centred interpretation" where the analyst interprets what the patient does, thinks, or desires in general along with the associated anxiety; these two types of interpretations may also be combined.

In the clinical material presented we can see when the analyst wants to highlight how the patient's internal world can be seen in the relationship between analyst and patient, that is to say in the here-and-now. In consequence her interpretations are centered around Maria in order to understand her. The analyst says, "you fear that I will not be very reliable ..."

Previous reflections on how the analyst makes contact with the patient's mind lead us to considerations regarding the role of the countertransference. Taken in broad terms, its function is to become aware of the patient's projections, how we are being affected by these projections, and what kind of reactions they awaken in us. The patient does not know how to speak about feelings. Her life is invaded by fear. She is unable to examine her own mind.

Only the analysis of the countertransference aids us in retaining a creative view, integrating the analyst's and the patient's contribution, as well as the relationship they create in each session. It does not only function in the sense of containing projections, but also in the same process of working through it helps the patient to understand her own mind. It is therefore necessary to understand not only what is being said to us but also how that is being done. How we may be stimulated or, conversely, paralysed. Understanding how changes in the setting are experienced, why and what repercussions they have in the analytic relationship, what aspects have been modified: the image of an accessible analyst or a submissive one.

Hence it is important to assess not only what we know and the changes brought about, but also the process that was used. In that sense Maria shows a greater understanding of her symptoms but I wonder how she went about acquiring more insight. If she gained the greater insight she shows through historical reconstruction there is a risk of intellectualisation. It may also represent a way she has of protecting the analyst from her fear of harming her. I consider therefore that a certain amount of analytic work should be done in the present and in relation to the analyst in order to explore the validity of the patient's conflicts in the present. Linking together past and present promotes the patient's capacity to question how she participates in what goes on in her life. With this I am stressing the importance of the aim of psychoanalysis as that of increasing the patient's ability to be introspective and to help the patient to introject the analytic function and thus have an ever greater ability to develop her own personal attributes and resources.

It is evident that all of this work cannot be done in the session. Part of it is done outside of the session when the analyst may reflect on what has taken place and explore his or her own work with a creative eye.

Extended families, nuclear families, and the importance of unconscious phantasy

The analyst reflects upon the differences between families in which the unit is extended, encompassing different generations, and the new families which tend to be much more limited to the nuclear unit where there is less availability to project the intense emotions that child-raising arouses.

The extended family affords more models of identification, and a greater possibility of projecting painful and split off aspects into different people in the home environment. This model can serve as a support in moments of great emotional intensity such as at the birth of a first child. It affords time for one to work though and identify oneself with the new situation. Nevertheless, without making less of the advantages, when changes and the anxiety they stir up cannot be worked through, there is a risk of becoming trapped in a paranoid-schizoid type of functioning.

In the end it is the internal family, created by each of us that constitutes true analytic work. It seems to me that we can reach an understanding of the trauma or traumas suffered by the patient, but analytic work must also reveal the unconscious phantasies and the feelings that different situations have awakened in the patient, and what keeps the patient stuck on these traumatic aspects.

I agree with the analyst about the girl child's need to identify with her mother in order to be able to gain access to maternity. However, the internal mother must be sufficiently repaired in order for the new mother to be able to carry out the maternal nurturing functions. Working through and tolerating one's own mother's shortcomings is, for that very reason, a necessity. Resentment and rage towards the mother must decrease. The mother as an ideal object must be given up. Only if this occurs can an image of the mother—both in the aspects we accept and those that we reject—be internalised. Only if this happens can we understand her shortcomings and her competence. Identifying with this mother opens up for us a path to a containing maternity, with the ability to observe, think, analyse, and take on responsibilities.

When Maria was able to become a mother she felt incapable of containing all of the changes that pregnancy and maternity involve. Without an internal mother it was only with great difficulty that she could establish contact with her baby and was, because of this, unable to enjoy her pregnancy. It was only towards the end of the third trimester of pregnancy that she was able to see a gynaecologist as if it was only through external reality that she could become aware of her baby. It was also in these last months that the patient used the couch, but we do not know the reasons that led her to that. Nor can we be sure about the way that affected the analytic relationship. It was only at the birth of the baby that Maria and her mother could become close. My hypothesis is that Maria was then able to recognise the help of the analyst and cease rejecting her infantile needy part and begin to accept it. On the other hand she began to feel more sure of herself when she had to make decisions although she needed the analyst to reinforce her decision. In that way she was able to sustain her desire to hold her daughter in her arms despite the lack of support from other people, as she herself expressed with the following words: "I remember you said I should do what I feel is right".

Final considerations

With the risk that is involved in discussing clinical material on the basis of necessarily limited information about a psychoanalytic treatment, and lacking a session that might have provided more details regarding the patient-analyst relationship I will nevertheless make some comments about the consolidation of therapeutic achievement.

Raising a child requires not only a containing attitude in the parental figures, but also a continuous adaptation that promotes the experience of growth and separation that maturation requires. The mother needs an internal dialogue to contain the baby's anxieties and her own anxieties arising from the relationship with her baby.

This creative process can become encumbered by excessive or insufficient attachment. In the first situation the mother can take care of her baby, but, at the same time, project into the infant her own needy parts. In that situation mother and baby run the risk of becoming trapped in a narcissistic identification that impedes the baby's separation from mother because the mother needs this identification to maintain her own sense of identity. The second situation would be that of premature detachment when the baby has not yet been able to internalise the containing role of the mother's mental apparatus in benefit of his/her own mind.

Perhaps Maria rushed into motherhood, but it is also true that at times without a "nudge" growth does not occur. Maria found herself present in her analyst's mind in a different way than she had been in all other relationships. What she experienced was an analyst who was seeking to understand her, and this may have made it possible for her to continue the analytic work that has allowed her to observe herself, think and explore her own mind to gain in self-understanding and growth.

I would like to thank Jones de Luca for enabling me, with her rich material, to contribute with these reflections.

References

Bion, W. R. (1967). Notes on memory and desire. *Psycho-Analytic forum, 2:* 271–280. Reprinted in: E. Bott Spillius (Ed.), *Melanie Klein Today Volume 2 Mainly Practice* (pp. 17–21). London: Routledge, 1988.

Britton, R. (1989). The missing link: Parental sexuality in the Oedipus complex. In: R. Britton, M. Feldman & E. O'Shaughnessy (Eds.), *The Oedipus Complex Today: Clinical Implications* (pp. 83–101). London: Karnac.

Feldman, M. (2009). The Oedipus complex: manifestations in the inner world and the therapeutic situation. In: *Doubt, Conviction and the Analytic Process.* London: Routledge. Also in: R. Britton, M. Feldman & E. O'Shaughnessy (Eds.), *The Oedipus Complex Today: Clinical Implications* (pp. 103–128). London: Karnac.

Steiner, J. (1993). Problems of psychoanalytic technique: patient-centred and analyst-centred interpretations. In: *Psychic retreats: pathological organizations in psychotic, neurotic and borderline patients* (pp. 131–145). London: Routledge.

CHAPTER FIFTEEN

"With you I can bleat my heart out"*— older women in psychoanalytic practice

Christiane Schrader

The chapter's title came from one of my female patients. She belongs to the generation of those women described by Margarete Mitscherlich-Nielsen (1987 [1985]), with a hint of irony that was frequently misunderstood, as "peaceable". She depicted women eager to keep the peace, having grown up in a patriarchal society, intimidated and drilled for subservience or suffering from traumatisation. They were inhibited in their self-assertion and strength of aggression, often with massive repercussions on their creativity. Her concept of the "peaceable woman" was based on her psychoanalytic work with women who today constitute old and elderly patients. Her psychodynamic findings provide the starting point of a case study that exemplifies the steps that a sixty-nine-year-old patient took out of a restrictive peaceable position that is still possible at this age. Before discussing Mitscherlich-Nielsen's contributions to understanding my female patients and in particular Mrs F. (whose details have been de-identified) I will comment on ageing in women today and the role of creativity for resisting and coping with ageing.

---

*In the German language the term for a goat's bleating ("meckern") is used idiomatically to express complaints from women in an aggressive tone.

Ageing today

Demographic development in Western industrial nations has led to continually increasing life expectancy and a rising proportion of the elderly in the overall population; in Germany this already amounts to over twenty-five per cent. There is no generally accepted definition of what constitutes old age since it depends on the criteria used. For centuries in many cultures any individual was regarded as old when they were constitutionally unable to care for themselves. In our culture gerontology pinpoints old age at sixty or sixty-five, when retirement from employment is often considered the transition phase into old age. Even for psychoanalysts the "empty couch" (Junkers, 2013; Quinodoz, 2013) is nowadays no longer a taboo topic. The stage of ageing is no mere appendix to the phase of adult life characterised by decline in proximity to mortality as postulated by previous deficit theories. The biological, psychological, and social processes of ageing and this phase within the life cycle have undergone change and we now assume that changes, compensation, development, and deterioration constitute a mutually interdependent process. Today's phase of old age covers on average one quarter of a lifetime since statistically the current life expectancy of a sixty-year-old woman is approximately twenty-four years, that of a sixty-year-old man twenty years. The ultimate phase is thus on average longer than childhood and adolescence together.

Along with the prolonged life span the period of different generations living together is extended. Never before have children's parents survived for so long, and never before with such long phases of grandparentage and great-grandparentage. The average duration of marriage has doubled in the last hundred years, as has the duration of healthcare for the aged and ill, especially in cases of dementia with its impact not merely for months but for years. On account of civilisation's achievements, the deficits and impositions of old age, including dying and death, have been largely postponed to ultimate old age—so that our life cycles reflect years that have been "won". This has influenced our images and theories of age and ageing—but also our personal experience, our plans for life, and our identity that require reappraisal in later life. Transition into old age may concur with liberation from disagreeable professional or family duties and evoke new vitality, or may disrupt compensation channels and release fears. This transition to old age confronts the victim with irrevocable and increasing losses, with dying and death, and poses final challenges to generativity, spirituality, and transcendence. The body plays a prominent role in the ageing process, becoming the "organiser" of psychological development in older age demanding care and acknowledgement of physical limits (Heuft, Kruse & Radebold, 2006). "My body and I, we seem to need half an hour longer every morning" was Mrs D.'s compassionate comment on this development. The body's status is no longer the silent agent or perpetrator of our activities and emotions as in youth and middle age. Yet it is still constantly alert, for instance, to regulate resisted affect as psychosomatic affect equivalents; it remains the "container" of protective and traumatic "embodied memories", introjections and impulses that may be aimed against the body-self and body. It may assume the role of "final companion". Its changes compel confrontation with narcissistic (shame) conflicts and the increasing dependency of old age. Older people live in a multitude of intra- and intergenerational relationships with a vast scope of possibilities for satisfaction and support, and potential for conflict. Comprehension between generations who speak different languages may not be taken for granted. Historical and political influences have moulded personalities and biographies that can suffer traumatic cracks or ruptures as a consequence of sickness or deficiencies through age. Not only can serious illnesses have traumatic results, older traumas can be re-actualised. This holds true for both victims of Nazi persecution and the subsequent second generation who were themselves confronted as children with trauma, or exposed to it transgenerationally. Other victims of World War II catastrophes and its aftermath were then children or adolescents and now belong to the aged (Radebold, 1992).

Liberation from social roles opens a space for complex identifications including bisexual tendencies which may encourage creative impulses. In age there is a so-called gender shift: women become more active, autonomous and independent—after retiring from work men often become more passive and withdrawn. Gender roles and societally determined images of old age that also influence identity development are currently undergoing radical change. On the one hand traditionally restrictive stereotypes of age are being shattered, on the other hand new idealistic images of destructive potential are appearing for example, "forever young".

The phase of old age is highly dynamic with a multitude of inner and external changes and the necessity of coming to terms with these developmental tasks. Variations of human individuality are the focus of the analytic process. Here the largest inter- and intra-individual differences are to be found. Older people have acquired broader experience of life, conflict management, affect differentiation and regulation, as well as other ego functions. Simultaneously ageing generates conflict potential for example, where impairments of physical mobility, vision, hearing, or cognitive functioning have become inevitable, there may be considerable tension within the personality. Creative potential for reconciling the losses and conflicts of ageing is thus a significant aid and desideratum both individually and collectively.

> Creativity of the aged is not restricted to art production, but signifies the intelligent use of faculties provided in the course of evolution such as medical science, technology or social networks. The majority of the elderly develop new ideas and skills, an *everyday creativity*, in order to compensate for handicaps (italics added). (Luft, 2013, p. 599)

Today we no longer share forty-two-year-old Freud's scepticism about the analysis of over fifty-year-olds, which has long presented a stumbling block for research and clinical practice. Not only did Freud revise this attitude later on, the success of psychoanalysis and psychotherapy for resolving psychological and physical illnesses, conflicts, traumas and developmental tasks has been proven. Mitscherlich-Nielsen (2010) turned Freud's point that the sheer mass of information must complicate analysis of the aged inside out by clarifying that the richer life experience of the older person would always offer possibilities for understanding.

Women's ageing

The processes of ageing occur asymmetrically and asynchronously for men and women in biological, psychological, and social respects. Biologically menopause ends women's reproductive capacity, but not that of men. The former reduction of female potency and creativity to motherhood automatically implied debasement of women around the climacterium. The ensuing projection of old age, even of dying, onto the female body and the woman is legendary and richly documented, for example in literary works, of which Thomas Mann's (1953) final story, *Die Betrogene* (*The Black Swan*), is an impressive example.

Since female potency and creativity have ceased to be restricted to motherhood, and menopause and old age are no longer synonymous and reduced to the status of inevitable losses, the psychoanalytic view has also changed. Menopause is no longer equivalent to a super-individual normative crisis. For the experience of crisis and conflict of this phase of life depend decisively on conscious and unconscious factors of womanliness, psychosexuality, and reproductivity that a woman has developed. Did she find an adequate partner? Did she want children? Were her wishes fulfilled and how? What identifications, internalised conflicts, and inner objects constitute her personality and her possibility to secure a good and creative bodyself, inner space, and good objects? With the consummate experience of old age Helene Deutsch (1975) pointed out that a woman's mind and her "complicated" emotional life assist her in calibrating unavoidable losses in menopause and subsequent phase of old age. Today we would prefer the term complexity of female emotional life when considering the diverse identifications of women and their bisexuality that mostly gain a new lease of life after menopause. I agree with Schlesinger-Kipp (2002) that the climacterium offers challenges and chances for inner and outer changes, essential processes of separation and mourning and the reworking of women's psychosexual identity. They are preparations and route-maps for old age. If unconscious conflicts that had previously been defended against were resolved with greater success, psychological energies would be liberated to enable a more intense experience of one's own identity and sexuality.

The female body is healthier, more functional. Women tend to take fewer risks, pay greater attention to precautionary prevention, live longer. Yet they suffer more from physical complaints (especially of the locomotor system), from psychological disturbances (especially depression), from functional bodily complaints and the loss of physical attractiveness. On the basis of their clinical experience Pines (1993) and Quinodoz (2009a) emphasise that body language in symptoms and the therapeutic relationship plays a more significant role for older than for younger patients. That corresponds to my experience. Physical complaints, their somatic and/or psychological causes linking with fears and insecurity, together with problems of treatment, require wider attention than with the young. It is essential to differentiate and understand bodily and psychological signals in the analysis and psychotherapy of the older person. Necessary physical treatments may require difficult negotiation through the potent but primarily apparatus-orientated medical jungle. No easy task for many older women. They must submit to receiving treatment from young professionals of their children's generation, surrender their primacy of experience or accept that their own regressive infantile wish to be cared for may not fulfil their expectations. On top of these rivalry and envy conflicts the accustomed role of the carer must be surrendered—a role that has often masked internalised self-renunciation and fear of helplessness well. Communication across the generations is far from being simple or straightforward. Frequently when new patients phone, I hear the words, "Just a few sessions, I'm sure I don't need much."

Older and old women who live in marriage or partnerships often remain alone on account of their different life expectancy. Since good partnerships tend to get better in time and difficult ones more frequently break up or divorce after the family phase is over, there are more women who live alone. They set up more intensive social networks than men, live with male or female partners, children, grandchildren, their own aged parents, relatives, friends, or colleagues opening up a wide range of satisfactions but with potential for conflict. The topic of social and/or existential loneliness crops up when losses increase as one gets older, or when fears and conflicts disturb the relationship. Deactivating such fears and conflicts through analytic insight is invaluable for the quality of life and creative potential of the old, where friendships are no longer merely superficial but deep or when family members who had long ago fallen out can be reunited. Later in life inner objects assume greater significance, and inner processes have greater priority when areas of activity become more limited; dependency increases again and inner representations of primary objects play a stronger role. After menopause a woman bears stronger similarity to her own mother than at any other period of the life cycle, both are now menopausal and latent inner conflicts gather fresh fuel, since the future is no longer infinite, and possibilities dwindle in which to resolve conflicts in the relationship. Although there was no change in her tempestuous attitude to her aged mother whom she looked after, yet Mrs M. (sixty-six) still attempted to gain her love. Mrs S. (sixty-seven) worried about becoming equally demanding in age as her own mother had become although she had originally been unobtrusive. Mrs F. (sixty-eight) discovered the extent to which her strict mother had become part of her too; she wanted to reject this but still understand both herself and her mother. Inevitable wounds and losses endured in age set aggression free that reactivate conflicts of ambivalence. On the other hand facing the proximity of death there is the wish for security of good, protective objects (the "good breast/mother", the divine father), and also for most women, the wish to die in the family circle.

Margarete Mitscherlich-Nielsen's revision of the psychoanalytic theory of femininity

Margarete Mitscherlich-Nielsen contributed to the forefront of feminist-inspired revision in Germany of Freud's femininity theory as the first psychoanalyst there to follow the ideas of feminism. She shared the critical vision of the women's liberation movement regarding the centuries-old patriarchal oppression and alienation of women and their unconscious identification with attributed inferiority, and she criticised Freud's concepts of phallic monism, the myth of vaginal orgasm and feminine masochism. Since then the developmental possibilities of postmenopausal women and their creative potential are no longer ascribed to phallic rivalry but are examined as genuine female possibilities. There are many women who have been embroiled in responsibility for children and family and their own professional, artistic, and other creative ambitions, who feel liberated at this stage. She also criticised the intimidating effect that these and other psychoanalytic theories had on women. The ideological implications of these concepts, as well as the theory of aggression and its inadequate gender differentiation, was presumed to have led to the discouragement of women for decades, that mostly went unobserved by women, and by male and female analysts. At the same time Mitscherlich-Nielsen postulated the psychoanalytic method as fundamentally emancipatory since it enabled the examination and transformation of societal double standards, individual mind blocks, taboos and inhibitions in order to open thinking space for creative attempts and action:

> To my mind it is extremely important that women be better understood in their individual psychological process of their upbringing and early and later experiences so that they are aided to acknowledge both themselves and their own desires. Hand in hand with the

development of feminism women's sexuality has been revalued, which together with psychoanalytical findings offers possibilites for women to take themselves seriously and encounter the so-called feminine ideals set up by men with a more critical view and distance. (Mitscherlich, 1978, p. 82)

In her 1985 book, *Die friedfertige Frau* (*The Peaceable Sex*, 1987) she discusses in depth the relationship of women and gender to aggression and hatred. She uncovers the subtle mechanisms of many women's passive aggression and sadistic impulses that are transformed into a self-punishing, masochistic reproach and victimised attitude while they unconsciously act out destructive tendencies such as devaluation and revenge. Totally without irony and with great fervour she pleads the case for introspection into one's own attitude of innocence and reproach, to overcome fear of one's own aggression, and learn to endure one's own guilt—instead of, in her succinct words, flight into "hope sickness" that she had observed in many women (Mitscherlich, 1990, p. 9). For this apparently peaceable syndrome of "hope sickness" conceals unconscious attacks aimed at the self, one's own body and inner and outer objects; it postpones and shifts activities of change to others. Instead of this she recommends that women face their putative weaknesses, such as emotional and loving capacities, responsibility, caring and reconciliatory tendencies and develop them for themselves as active and self-confident strengths, and also for societal discourse.

Mitscherlich-Nielsen urged many points that are now accepted as standard—but were especially inspiring for the understanding the psychodynamics of analytic work with older women: one example is that psychoanalysis did not take enough into account how significant the parents' norms, attitudes, values, and fantasies are for their children developing self-confidence or an inferiority complex. She emphasised the central role of unconscious identifications in general and especially for the transfer of gender-specific roles and their transgenerational tradition.

She laid stress on the imago role of the early all powerful mother for both genders. This infantile and never completely overcome dependency, that can mobilise hatred and tendencies to undermine and thus cause guilt, may lead to arrogant or tortuous "moral masochism" in either gender. She viewed this dynamic of dominance and dependence as a significant source of the male need to devalue women.

A girl's identifications with her mother are specifically marked by the persistent similarity to the mother, and as corollary, the greater mutual ambivalence. That is why so many women find it difficult to reach autonomy and independence. The fear of loss of love creates a stronger need for recognition and confirmation, conflicts of envy and the adoption of parental identifications and assignment of guilt. Anal-sadistic and sadomasochistic conflicts and dominance and submission may become even weightier and generate splits of idealisation and (secret) contempt in self and object representations. With her husband, Alexander Mitscherlich, she had helped to reestablish psychoanalysis in Germany after exile at the hands of the National Socialists and to open the door to examination of societal and political themes. She was an enthusiastic mediator of psychoanalysis in the public eye and an important figure of identification for us as young women and future analysts. She did not spare herself in transmitting her concepts and in contemporary cultural debates; even at the end of her life she retained her impressive intellectual alertness which enabled her to continue working and be creative.

Older women in psychoanalytic practice

When Freud (1905a) postulated the impossibility of analysis beyond the age of fifty, and fourteen years later Abraham (1919) contradicted him with his findings that it is not the patient's age that is decisive but the nature of the illness, this did not initiate further discussion. Today has seen the unfolding of structural change of the ageing process, unknown at that time. Psychoanalysis has changed to include patients of all ages. Papers in the *International Journal of Psycho-Analysis* (mainly in the seventies and eighties) which Junkers (2006) edited give some insight into this gradual development. Segal's pioneering work on the early "incomplete" analysis of a seventy three-year-old male patient (1958) led to the concept of the "midlife-crisis" where the irrevocable proximity of death looms (Jaques, 1965). The patients reported were mostly in their fifties and some in their early sixties. They all grasped at analysis as a "final chance" because the imminent end of a working life crowned with success that had absorbed and immersed them from old fears and traumas now confronted them with states of panic. Only Pollock (1982) had previously mentioned therapy cases with patients of over seventy. Pines (1993), Quinodoz (2009a), Radebold (1992), Radebold and Schweitzer (2001) and Alegiani (2012) report that educated women, often those with therapy or analytic experience recognise the opportunity of the years ahead to work through lifelong conflicts in analysis. They want to live a better life in their older years, to develop further mentally instead of making do with mere dreams or brooding over separation, loss, and dwindling skills.

But their number is exceeded by those who do not consider psychotherapy or even a few therapeutic sessions for their own sake, as they are unaccustomed to talk about themselves; their expressive skills are limited so that they initially need encouragement and feeling valued to be able to face their fears and inhibitions. Quinodoz emphasises the necessity for the analyst to appreciate and acknowledge the patient's inner riches and intrinsic value before the patient is able to do so.

From my clinical practice I can confirm this. For the past thirteen years I have been occupied with psychotherapy of ageing and research of the aged. At that time my oldest patient had been in her late fifties and turned sixty in the course of treatment. Since then I have seen approximately forty women over the age of sixty. They were born between 1927 and 1951 and aged between sixty and eighty years old. They belong to the generations whose biographies and developments were influenced by former authoritarian political systems and education, the horror of two world wars, the terror of National Socialism and its aftermath in their childhood and youth, as well as the transition to democracy. Eighteen came for low-frequency short- or long-term therapy; some came only for an initial interview, some profited from two or three sessions or sought some other form of help, some I referred to other colleagues. To this day there has been no patient suitable, motivated, or likely to have the motivation for high-frequency analysis.

Although the proportion, particularly of female patients, has slightly increased in recent times, older patients continue to be significantly under represented—in all clinical directions. The older female patient's perspective is marked by ignorance, prejudice, taboos and fears, aspects also to be found in analysts and psychotherapists. Transference and countertransference are also influenced by age, position in one's personal life and its conflicts; thus colleagues who are over fifty—and closer to themes and conflicts of ageing—find this work easier; they accept more older people in therapy or analysis. Younger colleagues sometimes make their first experiences with older and old patients as professional beginners in young adulthood. Although I recall fruitful sessions and treatment of "youngish old" in a psychosomatic clinic where I was first employed, I am still very much aware of the difficulty in the middle or end of one's twenties to work with older patients who might have been my parents from the perspective of age and who may still have been in the throes of considerable conflict with their children's process of individuation. Not all patients are prepared to accept rapid regression in their transference as Quinodoz reports. According to Radebold (1992), whose findings correspond to my own, this is the case only with very depressive and dependent elderly patients. Other patients question or test out younger therapists, either overtly or more subtly, entrain corroboration, claim inseparability or expectations towards or disappointments over their own children. Such "reversed transferences" (Radebold in Heuft, Kruse & Radebold, 2006) are far from easy to handle for therapists with little experience and to resolve in a therapeutic relationship. Where they are not recognised, they may contribute to therapeutic resignation or prevent the analytic therapy or analysis taking shape.

Both Quinodoz (2009a) and Coltart (1991) report a lack of temerity on account of possible inadequacy in the analysis of an older person. Insecurity about working with patients whose personal experience has not been experienced by the analyst sheds light on the innermost fears that the analyst's position might collide with a reversed counter-transference, for example a daughter position. It also illuminates the significance of life experience and generational position for the implicit theories (Sandler, 1985) with which we work.

Some observations from interviews and therapy

For the majority of my older female patients there are obvious traits of Mitscherlich-Nielsen's peaceable attitude. Why were they seeking help? Many came on account of consequences of changes and losses through somatic, somatopsychological, and psychosomatic illnesses and resultant conflicts. Mrs D. (seventy-five) was stricken with tinnitus and subsequent depression which exacerbated her troublesome dependency on her husband even more. Mrs S. (sixty-eight) suffered from Parkinsons and was also depressive. Her lifelong fear of her highly ambivalent relationship to her mother and becoming dependent became virulent once more.

Bodily relationships of mental disturbances are generally on the increase particularly in women and as age progresses whereby somatic and mental influences may overlap into "individual complex multi-morbidity"; the consequences for welfare "do not follow simple rules" (Heuft, Kruse & Radebold, 2006). This diplomatic statement calls attention to the fact that questions crop up in the analytic listening process that might be rarer with younger patients: Mrs B. had become depressive after a cancer operation and disappointment with her partner. She feared a relapse when a "lump in her throat" developed when avoiding conflicts that might end in leaving her partner. In her initial interview this remark gave me some hope of discovering the psychogenesis of her fears. But could I be certain? At that moment it was impossible to know if her cancer had flared up again and might be terminal. Not until later on and after investigation was it evident that the illness had not returned. Or—have physical factors been overlooked in an illness diagnosed as psychogenic? Mrs A. (sixty-three) suffered from postoperative cramps and pains that were initially diagnosed as psychological. She was really desperate, felt she was misunderstood, but did not dare to contradict the doctors openly. Finally it became clear there was iatrogenic injury that they had at first not wanted to pursue.

Mrs O. (seventy-five), formerly a medical doctor, developed problems of insomnia and stomach complaints when confronted with the life-threatening illness and imminent decease of her husband, fifteen years her senior, who "had always kept everything under control". Over and above contemporary ideals of education her childhood had been traumatic with losses in exile, flight, and the serious illness of a sibling with whom her mother had had to cope single-handed because her father had been drafted to the army. The extent to which she had been drilled to "keep calm and carry on" became evident in the initial interview in which she sat cramped up on the edge of her chair. Our patients permit us insight into their fears and their denial, claim tolerance for their insecurity and ignorance. One is increasingly confronted with probing into bodily and ageing influences that take over life, for example with the question if and to what extent a patient is suffering from dementia and/or depression (cf. Quinodoz, 2009a).

One frequent motive for seeking therapeutic help is the death of a husband or other close relative they are unable to mourn for or cope with: for Mrs H. (sixty-eight) "everything broke down" after her husband's death; in many respects he had been more a motherly object.

Mrs S. (sixty-five) could not get over her brother's suicide and feared her own depressive reactions behind which anxiety about her ageing and being left alone "as punishment" became apparent.

The resurgence of unresolved relationship conflicts with parents, partners, and other relatives now in need of care is a further reason to seek help. Mrs E. (sixty-five) came after coming up against her limits in caring for her aged mother. She struggled against the outbreak of uncontrollable rage and helplessness and felt a sporadic impulse towards suicide: "Something has got to happen. In the last few weeks I keep thinking about racing into the next concrete edifice and then it's all over." Her earlier relationship to her mother had been full of extreme conflicts and animosity. She had therefore turned to her dominant father with whom she was strongly identified. She had constantly upheld her defence against her unconscious identification with her now weak mother demanding care. On account of the care for her "little, old mother" and her own ageing she now came irrevocably into contact with this part of her self—but also with her own hatred and death wishes.

Acute or reactivated traumas play an important role in old age. Changes within the framework of the ageing process can also have traumatic effects. When the husband of Mrs D. (sixty-four) felt unable to endure his increasing weakness and illness he had committed suicide. Their marriage bore signs of sadomasochistic and dependence conflicts. After more then a year she was still suffering sleeplessness, inner agitation, and intrusive memories: "I can't get the images out of my mind."

Furthermore many of the elderly and old belong to those generations who suffered crushing experiences and traumatic wounds and losses through persecution, war, flight and expulsion that can be reactivated in old age. Mrs B. (sixty-eight) was suffering from extreme feeling of guilt, and after the onset of the Iraq war in the course of her psychotherapy, earlier traumas were reactivated and causing panic that she had experienced in bomb raids and attacks in her childhood. In the analytic work we not only uncovered that she had not felt secure with her timid and rather depressive mother. We also worked through the fears felt when her emaciated father returned from war imprisonment and her hopes were shattered that her depressive mother and the entire family would recover. At once, it was apparent she had had to support her parents. We were able to comprehend the guilt she had taken on and her unbroken loyalty to the post-war vow of silence prescribed by her father never to reveal that he had initially supported the Nazi regime. As a little girl she had emulated her parent's attitude. ("We were all enthusiastic.") She now felt shame and guilt, but was able to dissociate herself from her parents, and alleviate her feelings of guilt and widen her horizon in forming relationships.

For all my female patients, stimuli from outside have played a role. Most came through referral from medical doctors, psychologists in clinics or were encouraged by friends and relatives, particularly their own children. Their conscious expectation towards psychotherapy was limited or small. They wanted to overcome acute illnesses, alleviate or get rid of symptoms, find solutions for problems, live a better life again. To this end they expected advice from me or instructions. Only one had had previous therapy experience, another had been member of a self-help group.The ones who stayed in psychotherapy were those with extensive mental trauma and with whom it had been possible in the initial interview to develop a perceptible and significant interaction or scene enabling me to transmit with my words a feeling of being in touch and understanding that aroused their interest or their hope.

Mrs F.: "With you I can bleat my heart out"— an unwanted-wanted child

Mrs F. (sixty-eight) was a well groomed, casually dressed, and younger-looking woman who rapidly inspired both interest and sympathy with her friendly manner and her story. She had been referred by a neurologist and was suffering from painful discomfort in her legs causing her worry since she was reminded of a serious depression she had gone through thirty years earlier. With the help of medication, treatment in hospital and subsequent outpatient psychotherapy she had overcome this illness. Apart from that, her old panicky fears of being unable to fulfil the demands required of her had increased as she got older, so that she now felt tormented by chronic self-doubts and unable to make any decisions. She trembled, withdrew into herself and developed intestinal symptoms.

In a totally split-off way in her initial interview the patient mentioned that her male friend of long standing, a married man, had been diagnosed with cancer. At that time she saw no connection with her own complaints and was optimistic about his recovery, yet her account immediately caused me alarm, and I wondered if it was being left to me to feel the fatal threat while she disavowed her fear of loss and projected her threatening affects into her body. I saw here her unconscious motive for coming, but it took time for Mrs F. to feel this fear and comprehend these connections. After traumatic childhood experiences she had later sought a "better and more beautiful world" outside of her family. When I said this to her in our initial interview she was touched by this idea that was new to her but pictured a well-known feeling and desire. She repeatedly returned to this interpretation to exemplify what she wanted from me when she later faulted me for not saying enough and not giving her explanations as she claimed her former therapist had done. I gathered the impression I was supposed to help her to avert the threat she was experiencing of the collapse of her self and her good inner world that she had preserved. Later on she told me that her male friend, a successful and educated man, was her ideal "soulmate" partner, with whom she had been able to cast off fears of loss and personal failure, and experience a satisfying sexual relationship. She took pains to ascertain that she did not come too close to him where she might otherwise have had to fear his rejection and come up against unintegrated ambivalence and hate. He did in fact die a few weeks after therapy had begun.

The splitting of ambivalence and other sequelae of severe and cumulative traumatisation were apparent in her history. Mrs F. was the unplanned first-born child of her parents (with a sister five years younger) while her father was enlisted in the war and her mother and grandmother ran a farm. Her mother had terminated an earlier pregnancy with an abortion and also repeatedly attempted to abort this baby, but the patient remained and—according to the mother's narrative—she had wanted to keep her after her birth. In her second year she had been in daytime care with a foster family for several months. "I grew up afraid, that was the basic feeling throughout my life." She lived in terror of her mother's violent temper and beatings and feared losing her, if her mother ran away or threatened to kill herself and the children, which frequently occurred during the patient's prepuberty. In her first seven years security and the feeling that everything including herself were all right were provided by her maternal grandmother, a woman with backbone. After the war the family moved to her paternal family in a city, living in cramped conditions. There she endured an uncle's sexual abuse petting her genitalia. She did not, however, dare to tell anyone. She preferred her "quiet" father to whom she felt closer in character, whom she idealised and sought and found in her male friend. Her father had, however, been a "womaniser" whose temper could flare up and who could be mean. She described the marriage as sadomasochistic battle which ended in divorce. With a stepfather the pattern of sadomasochism and separation was repeated, reinforcing Mrs F.'s urge to support her mother. She was in constant fear of losing her mother ("Mama's little girl") and unable to feel or express the fury of her younger and more rebellious sister, but became the "quiet, darling girl attempting to please everybody else" and considering she would only be able to achieve her own wishes by indirect means. This was the dynamic structure unfolded in her transference.

After leaving school she was trained in hotel management. She got to know her husband there. His appearance, his apparent self-confidence and the vehemence with which he courted her were pleasant factors in his favour, plus the fact that he came from a "good family" in comparison to her own background. We understood that she had unconsciously been seeking a kind of replacement family with an ideal father (-in-law). On the conscious level she had hoped to make progress in her career and her life with her husband. When her wishes remained unfulfilled in her marriage, elements of destructive sadomasochistic conflict dynamics developed that had been split off. Because of her fears of loss of self, her guilt, and unintegrated ambivalence she was neither able to separate in her inner world, nor in reality, so that she developed a serious depression. In this period of sickness she had death wishes towards her mother and her husband, and fears of carrying them out. Her husband later left her; there was a divorce in the course of which her husband made strong and hurtful accusations. To my astonishment Mrs F. persistently clung to the idea that she still felt married to him.

Course of treatment

The dynamics of love and hate, of, you love me, you love me not ... was transmitted throughout the transference and countertransference relationship. Mrs F. repeatedly put me in the position of the "child" who is threatened with being left and aborted. Alhough I was convinced she was involved in the process and profiting, she contrived to impart the feeling that I must fight for the therapy, psychotherapy of one single session a week for a total of eighty sessions. On the conscious level she feared the recurrence of frightful depression, of old conflicts, that too much might be "stirred up". I think that she was unconsciously intimidated by the violence of her own drives and ambivalence and of potential dependency if she was under my control or feared undergoing severe punishment or traumatisation at my hands.

In the second interview she immediately demonstrated her enormous fear. As she had developed trust in her previous therapist because he had constructively held her rage towards her husband, she at once also tested me whether I would punish her if she were not cooperative. She muddled up her appointment, was fearful and was promptly convinced I would send her packing. Initially she tried to do everything properly for me, wanted me to return her favour and give her explanations and tips as her former therapist had done. Again and again she tested whether our therapeutic relationship was sustainable if she was not a "good girl", informing me when she had not really wanted to come or disliked coming on several days. She made these remarks with a quiet undertone of excuse—"I don't really like to mention this ..." Had I not expressly told her to speak absolutely openly about what was going through her mind, she would have been unable to utter these words. Holiday breaks and communicating them were especially tricky. She regularly developed somatic symptoms and when I asked a simple question about how she felt seemed almost persecuted, confused, and panic-stricken; she refused to utter a word. Separation and saying "no" to me as an apparently powerful opposite only seemed possible this way. Interpretation was not enough. Sitting opposite me she needed to make absolutely certain of her "no" to give her more security. Later on she took the offensive and said, "With you I can bleat my heart out ...", there was obviously a lot more power, pleasure and intensity involved— sometimes vehemence, sometimes a hint of twinkling flirtatiousness in which she sought my corroboration in spite of her grumbling tone.

Her friend's death was six months in the past when she first told me of her strong sexual desire. She was familiar with this sensation, was ashamed, yet still glad to be able to speak of it with me as a woman. I interpreted her feelings as longing for her friend, for his proximity, for sexual satisfaction and asked whether the intensity of her experience might also be evidence of her fury that she had been left by him.

Approximately midway in therapy and to my total surprise Mrs F. summed up her central relationship conflict in two dreams. With a smile she recounted the first dream: I dreamt I had to serve the Federal President. He was just sitting there. I handed him something and kept on saying, "Here you are, Mr Federal President." While saying this she nodded slightly. That was the way she had always felt in the company of others, even today it was still often the case. I pointed out the gap she experienced between herself and others, and we discussed various examples with her deceased friend. "And what about being here with me?" I asked. "Now you're talking", replied Mrs F. She saw that she did in fact want me to be "big and experienced", even if she might then feel small and inferior. "But you should never dominate or humiliate me. I haven't been aware of any such thing here but I always fear it." "That you might discover another side to me like with your mother, father, and husband?" I asked. The atmosphere of this dream work became pleasant and relaxed. In her dream Mrs F. had expressed a central relationship conflict that had repeatedly occupied us. "Why did I dream that dream?" had been her first question.

Before our next session she had had another dream: I saw a huge rhinoceros in front of me. It came running up to me and I ran away. There was nothing to be seen near nor far except a little wooden shed. I hid inside it, bolted the door. In the shed there was also a goat. I was afraid, but the rhino did not come in. My impression was of threat but also of great vividness. I thought of the "tomboy" she had been as a child, of her grumbling, of her insistent drives and affects and replied to her quesion, "You are dreaming the answer to our last session." Mrs F. rapidly discovered that she is not only the timid hidden goat bleating out its message. "I did wonder," she said with a smile, "if the rhino may have something to do with me too." She made the connection between her sexual desires but also her fury, the (phallic) horn and the death fantasies that she had felt towards her husband in her depression and her mother when she was in mortal fear of her knives. She acknowledged that deep within she feels capable of desires similar to the position of Federal President, of being able to dominate, to admit pleasure and fury and the capacity to pursue and attack, although she had mostly felt she was being pursued. We understood the rhinoceros as image of the child's split-off drive fusion and affective life at a time when it had been essential to defend her mother from her fury.

After these dreams it was possible for the first time to speak of her experience of the holiday interruptions.

PATIENT: When you ask me, I get the impression you don't want to let me go.

ANALYST: Then I would feel that longing, then I would feel the way
you did as a child towards your mother? You wouldn't be
able to move on?

PATIENT: Yes, something like that ... but I didn't want to go away
from my mother when I was a child ... but later on I wanted
to get away.

In the following holiday which she spent in the region she came from,
she had some slight somatic complaints for which no physical reason
could be found, but she granted herself "treatment" for the first time by
considering her mother and her relationship to her, her ambivalence,
pains and yearnings and also her mother's objectively difficult situation at that time.

There ensued a phase in therapy in which she overcame her inhibitions, and began to clear up her financial demands towards her
ex-husband. She also examined her fantasies about his supposed success or failure in comparison with her real life for she feared she had
come out of it badly on account of her illness. To demand what was due
to her initially caused her panicky fear of his punishment and revenge,
and massive guilt that we worked through. But finally he did consent
and she felt genuinely divorced from him for the first time. On the occasion of her seventieth birthday she expressed the wish for me or her
friends to arrange a wonderful celebration for her, and she would not
have to make any decisions on anything.

ANALYST: A kind of children's birthday party?

PATIENT: Yes perhaps, they didn't have them in those days.

Finally she took pleasure in arranging a nice celebration and confronted
her own rivalry and envy conflicts with her female friends who had
partly achieved more in their lives and to whom she had repeatedly felt
inferior. Here she rediscovered the rhinoceros: one of her friends always
gave her a little rhino serviette ring.

The relationships to her deceased friend and her mother were
repeated themes of our work. At the end Mrs F. remarked that one of
the most important results of therapy, possibly the most significant
for her, was her mental reconciliation with her mother. It was also
important that she herself still felt physically fit and healthy for her
age. That was doubtless her inheritance from her mother, for which she

was grateful. As by her dreams I was now surprised how directly the transformations of her mother imago influenced Mrs F.'s body self and body experience.

"It is the patient's whole life-history that is changed when a forgotten memory is reintegrated—and that memory is itself modified by being brought into the whole life-history ... In so doing, the analyst can help elderly people to play with their memories in order to reconstruct their own internal life-history" and "keep internally, in psychic reality what we lose in external reality ..." (Quinodoz, 2009b, pp. 777–778). Obviously it has only been possible to partially reconstruct Mrs F.'s inner story. The complexity of the threats and temptations of transference and countertransference and the sexual symbolism of the material could not be exhaustively dealt with in the framework of one hour a week psychotherapy. But the patient's internalised relationship to an overpowering object on which she felt too dependent to structure her desires and her fury, and with which she was also unconsciously identified, could be comprehended in the fundamental themes of her parting from her deceased friend, in transference and in the reconstruction of her relationship to her mother. I later heard that she felt greater confidence in her female friendships, set clearer limits, claimed her wishes with less anxiety and found a new friend in a language course with whom she developed a relationship of mutual trust.

The end of life looms up irrevocably in the second half of one's life and reveals the existential dynamics between Eros and Thanatos, between fear of death, self-abnegation, resignation and revolt, joy of life and clutching of "final chances", in analyses and in life, with the "radicality of age" (Mitscherlich-Nielsen, 2010) that need not fear the future. With increasing changes due to ageing, narcissistic (shame) conflicts and dependency conflicts are inevitable. The balance of envy or fury and gratitude plays a significant role for personal satisfaction and mental health. The timelessness of the unconscious, the pendulum swing between past, present, and future and memories of "better days" form the narcissistic shield that enables us to retain our young core although we have aged (Teising, 1998). "Defence of ageing and death are specific human creative acts so life is not petrified in spite of our awareness of death" (Luft, 2013, p. 599). Losses, narcissistic wounds, and imminent (self) hatred require mourning, liberation and "constructive resignation" (Jaques, 1965). Actualisation of ambivalence between love and hatred and the developmental tasks of new integration are the central conflicts of ageing. As Danielle Quinodoz writes, "Ageing is possibly the opportunity to discover how to love oneself and in general love better" (Quinodoz, 2009a, p. 13), in that a contribution towards reconstruction of an older person's inner history—however limited this may be—can be a source of genuine and mutual pleasure. To this end creativity in its many forms can also contribute.

Acknowledgement

This chapter has been translated by Carolyn Roether.

References

Abraham, K. (1919). Zur Prognose psychoanalytischer Behandlungen fortgeschrittenen Lebensalter. *Internationale Zeitschrift für Psychoanalyse, 6*: 113–117.

Alegiani, R. (2012). Analytische Psychotherapie im Alter—was den Prozess trägt. *Psyche, 66*: 145–168.

Coltart, N. E. (1991). The analysis of an elderly patient. *International Journal of Psycho-Analysis, 72*: 209–219.

Deutsch, H. (1973). *Confrontation with Myself.* New York: Norton & Comp. (1975) *Selbstkonfrontation.* München: Kindler.

Freud, S. (1905a). On psychotherapy. *S. E. 7*: 255–268. London: Hogarth.

Heuft, G., Kruse, A. & Radebold, H. (2006). *Lehrbuch der Gerontopsychosomatik und Alterspsychotherapie.* München: Reinhardt.

Jaques, E. (1965). Death and the midlife crisis. *International Journal of Psycho-Analysis, 46*: 502–514.

Junkers, G. (Ed.). (2006). Is it too late? Key papers on psychoanalysis and ageing. *International Journal of Psycho-Analysis Key Papers Series.* London: Karnac.

Junkers, G. (Ed.). (2013). *The Empty Couch.* London: Routledge.

Luft, H. (2013). Höheres Alter—Bedrängnisse und kreative Antworten. *Psyche—Zeitschrift für Psychoanalyse, 67*: 597–622.

Mann, T. (1954). *The Black Swan.* New York: Knopf.

Mitscherlich, M. (1978). *Das Ende der Vorbilder.* München: Piper.

Mitscherlich, M. (1985). *Die friedfertige Frau.* Frankfurt: Fischer. (1987, *The Peaceable Sex. On Aggression in Women and Men.* New York: Fromm International Publishing.)

Mitscherlich, M. (1990). *Die Mühsal der Emanzipation.* (*The Hardship of Emancipation*). Frankfurt: Fischer.

Mitscherlich, M. (2010). *Die Radikalität des Alters.* Frankfurt: Fischer.

Pines, D. (1993). *A Woman's unconscious Use of her Body*. London: Virago.

Pollock, G. (1982). On ageing and psychopathology-discussion of Dr Norman A. Cohen's paper "On loneliness and the ageing process". *International Journal of Psycho-Analysis, 63*: 275–281.

Quinodoz, D. (2009a). *Growing Old: A Journey of Self-Discovery*. London: Routlege.

Quinodoz, D. (2009b). Growing old: A psychoanalyst's point of view. *International Journal of Psycho-Analysis, 90*: 773–793.

Quinodoz, D. (2013). On: At what age should a psychoanalyst retire? *International Journal of Psycho-Analysis, 94*: 793–797.

Radebold, H. (1992). *Psychodynamik und Psychotherapie Älterer*. Berlin: Springer.

Radebold, H., & Schweitzer, R. (2001). *Der Mühselige Aufbruch*. München: Reinhardt.

Sandler, J. (1985). A Discussion of the various theories. In: *Models of the Mind: Their Relationships to Clinical Work*, (pp. 119–127). Madison, CT: International Universities Press.

Schlesinger-Kipp, G. (2002). Weibliche Entwicklung in den Wechseljahren. *Psyche, 56*: 2007–2030.

Segal, H. (1958). Fear of death—Notes on the analysis of an old man. *International Journal of Psycho-Analysis, 39*: 178–181.

Teising, M. (1998). Körperliche Realität und innere Wirklichkeit im Alter. In: M. Teising (Ed.), *Altern: Äußere Realität, innere Wirklichkeiten. Psychoanalytische Beiträge zum Prozess des Alterns* (pp. 125–139). Opladen: Westdeutscher Verlag.

PART III

CREATIVITY IN THE ARTS
AND LITERATURE

Using contents from a sewing box: some aspects of the artwork of Sonia Delaunay and Louise Bourgeois

Maria Grazia Vassallo Torrigiani

There is a bias that for centuries has weighed women down. The professor of English and Women's Studies, Susan Stanford Friedman, incisively formulated it in these terms: creation is the act of the mind that brings something new into existence, procreation is the act of the body that reproduces the species: a man conceives an idea in his brain, while a woman conceives a baby in her womb (Stanford Friedman, 1987). Culturally, physical and mental creativity have long been defined in terms of gender: procreation was considered the sole legitimate, satisfactory creative experience for women; mental, artistic, and intellectual creativity was instead the stuff of men.

Women who challenged this centuries-old bias were met with a whole series of internal and external obstacles: guilty feelings, rejection, contempt, and insinuations regarding their morality, mental health, and (even) womanhood. Venturing into circles reserved to men was viewed not only as a transgression, but also as an assumption or expression of masculine characteristics, such as self-confidence, ambition, determination, aggressiveness, and competitiveness that in a woman were perversions of-or at least counter to-the intimate essence of womanhood.

Today women have reached full awareness that they can indeed attain satisfaction and recognition in both creative circles, albeit still with greater difficulty than men. They know that they can "give birth with the body and with the mind", as in the title of the book of essays by Francesca Rigotti (2010), in which the Italian philosopher advances some intense ethical–philosophical reflections on the maternal and "maternal thought" from an anti-essentialist perspective. According to Rigotti, defining "maternal thought" as thought that stems from experiences unique to women, such as maternity, does not mean that the ethical values of caring for and nurturing others, on which such thought is based, reflects a presumed nature/essence inherent in the female body and mind. Such a view moreover equates female with maternal and thus risks confining women exclusively to the role of mother. The activities in which mothers are engaged—Rigotti maintains—stimulate certain faculties and give rise to certain styles of life and thought that can also be adopted despite the lack of direct experience (Rigotti, 2010). In psychoanalytic terms, we might say that the "maternal functions" of caring and nurturing may also be carried out by anyone who is not, has never been or can never biologically be a mother, man or woman as the case may be.

In psychoanalysis, many conceptualisations and lines of research have focused on the need to distinguish between "maternal" and "female." There is a "sexual feminine"—a phantasy of excess of drive—that, as Amalia Giuffrida (2001) points out, psychoanalysis has detached or concealed from the "maternal" and from the nurturing breast. However, there is an erotic breast as well, the connections with which must be identified; there is an *érotique maternel*, in which regard Hélèn Parat (1999) speaks of the impossibility of separating the nurturing breast from the erotic one, hence requiring an integration that all women must painstakingly work through.

The tension between mother and the mother who is a woman—and as such subject to needs and desires oriented towards other experiences—is also viewed in the light of other perspectives. For example, in the perspective that regards the maternal as the experience of, or drive towards, undiversified merger between the self and other that eliminates all boundaries. In such a perspective, the maternal is the basis for experiencing not only feelings of omnipotent completeness, but also an anxiety-provoking threat to identity, the risk of loss of autonomy and subjectivity. In this sense, the maternal represents a complex, conflictual psychic experience that calls for activating processes that enable times of both differentiation of the self and reunion with the other, in a rhythmic alternation of the two experiences.

In Rigotti's book, she takes up Stanford Friedman's work and shows how, despite the centuries-old gender-based subdivision between physical creation and mental creation, all our constructs of mental creative processes are nevertheless expressed through maternal metaphors, and based on the processes of physical generation: we speak of "a work pregnant with meaning", "the birth of a project", "the gestation of an idea", etc.

In their language research, George Lakoff and Mark Johnson come to the conclusion that the non-physical is nearly always conceptualised in terms of the physical, and that our conceptual metaphors are thus deeply rooted in human culture and physical, sensory, and emotional experience (Lakoff & Johnson, 1980). In a psychoanalytic perspective, such considerations on language should prompt us to reflect on just how much, on the psychic level, creative mental processes are unconsciously connected to bodily representations and sexual and procreative fantasies. I will return to this soon.

Mental creativity and the bisexual mind

If, as Freud stated, poets and artists have always enjoyed special insight into psychic reality that only subsequently psychoanalysis brought to light through its own methods, then allow me to recall the title of the well-known book by Virginia Woolf: *A Room of One's Own*. In much of this extended essay, the English writer addresses the relationship of women to artistic creation from the perspective of women's longstanding exclusion from the world of writing. She does so by introducing various fictional characters, amongst whom the imaginary sister of Shakespeare, who though endowed with the same passions and talents as her brother, is condemned to literary obscurity simply because she is a woman.

The expression "room of one's own" in the title has immediate, profound implications: how can a woman devote herself to her creative passions, if she cannot count on some personal space for autonomous, free thought and expression? If she is invariably relegated to a role that imprisons her in the home, or rather, only in some rooms of the home—the kitchen, the bedroom, the nursery—immersed in taking care of her loved ones and building the physical and emotional bonds that connect human beings and family generations? Another aspect that comes to mind when contemplating the expression "room of one's own" is the need of a differentiated mental space, that is, an inner place where to achieve the necessary psychic experience of separateness.

A very interesting passage appears in the book's final pages, where Woolf, almost absent-mindedly, reveals her belief that the artist's mind is androgynous:

> And I went on amateurishly to sketch a plan of the soul so that in each of us two powers preside, one male, one female; and in the man's brain the man predominates over the woman, and in the woman's brain the woman predominates over the man. If one is a man, still the woman part of the brain must have effect; and a woman also must have intercourse with the man in her. Coleridge perhaps meant this when he said that a great mind is androgynous. It is when this fusion takes place that the mind is fully fertilized and uses all its facilities. (Woolf, 1928, pp. 113–114)

From her words, it is clear that Woolf does not regard the "androgynous mind" that gives life to artistic creation as androgynous in the sense of asexual: the differences between the male and the female are not negated, but rather the two sexes cohabit in the mind, they are in a state of tension one with the other.

The psychoanalytic literature contains many contributions that explore the link between creativity and bisexuality (in the sense of the bisexual functioning of the mind). I will limit myself to a few brief remarks on this. For example, Joyce McDougall writes:

> It has always seemed to me that the pleasure experienced in intellectual and artistic achievements is redundant with considerable narcissistic and homosexual fantasy since, in such production, everyone is both man and woman at the same time. Our intellectual and artistic creations are, in a sense, parthenogenetically created children. Furthermore, clinical experience has taught me that conflicts over either of the two poles of homosexual libido: that is the wish to take over the mother's creative power as well as the father's fertile penis, may create serious inhibition or even total sterility in the capacity to put forth symbolic children. In a sense, all creative acts

may be conceptualised as a fusion of the masculine and feminine elements in our psychic structure. (McDougall, 1993, p. 75)

In this view, the creative act is associated with phantasies regarding the psychosexual organisation of bodily representation; hence the risk that it be perceived unconsciously as a narcissistic, omnipotent, destructive attack on the parental objects, as a threat to their generativity, which involves the risk of punishment and retaliation. Janine Chasseguet-Smirgel theorises a "specific sense of female guilt", which she links to the workings of the instinctual sadistic-anal component of psychosexual development. Faced with the intrinsically female desire to incorporate the paternal penis, women would find it more difficult to integrate the aggressive component, thereby prompting repression and counter-investment, which hinder creative accomplishment in anything that might take on an unconscious phallic meaning (Chasseguet-Smirgel, 1984). And on the other hand, in some psychic configurations the creative act itself involves the risk of becoming infiltrated by or tending towards a perverse, omnipotent solution that denies limits and differences, as Chasseguet-Smirgel (1984) has illustrated in *Creativity and Perversion*. But I am not going to go further into this aspect.

Nowadays, as we have largely overcome gender stereotypes, there is widespread recognition of the importance of psychic bisexuality in the intra- and interpsychic equilibrium of each and every individual, that is, when it is based on a healthy process of cross identification with the parents of both sexes. Through such identification processes, each individual can take on the characteristics of the opposite sex, make them his or her own by interiorising the traits and qualities of both parents and of the significant objects of both sexes.

In the theoretical perspective that stresses above all the differences in the development of the two sexes with regard to the primary object, in American circles Jessica Benjamin attributes great importance to a daughter's identification with her pre-oedipal father. The object relationship with the pre-oedipal mother—who is obviously of the same sex—would, for the girl, be marked mostly by difficulty in differentiating herself from the mother in order to achieve autonomy. In this perspective, the pre-oedipal father, who represents an object for identification and expression of subjectivity and freedom, helps the daughter work through the process of differentiation from her mother (Benjamin, 1995).

Fausta Ferraro, in two papers published in 2001 and 2003 on the creativity and bisexual disposition of the mind, sets out a precise, thorough outline of the concept of bisexuality. She relates Freud's views to Winnicott's, and delves into the theoretical construction of psychic bisexuality not only as the result of cross identifications with both parents, but also as an aspect of the self. Ferraro shows how Winnicott's conceptualisations with regard to elements of the "pure feminine" and the "pure masculine" contribute to further distance bisexuality from the biological, and replace the dialectic of active and passive with the notions of being and doing. This enables us to consider masculinity and femininity as precocious constitutive aspects of mental life, both of which are present in every infant's primary object relationship with the mother, and construe them in terms of the ever-present tension between aspiring to fusion, and the vital need for separateness. In Ferraro's words:

> The so-called male element has to do with the establishment of an active relationship or the undoing of a passive relationship, the pure female element is related to the breast (or mother) in the sense of the child becoming the breast (or mother), and the object is the subject. The male element does, while the female element is. (Ferraro, 2001, p. 489)

While, in a certain sense, Winnicott's use of the terms being and doing refers mostly to the content of an experience, Shmuel Erlich instead uses them with regard to experiential modes. That is, he considers them to be not only psychic contents, but also proposes regarding them as structural dimensions inherent in the processing and the giving form to experience in the dimension of separateness/fusion between subject and object. Erlich considers being and doing parallel, contemporary modes, both present and interactive from the very start, and the same sensorial input can be processed in two distinct experiential modes. Moreover, infant research also confirms that since birth children are endowed with both modes of experience: there exists an innate capacity to differentiate between self and object, just as there is a capacity to indiscriminately merge with the object. Erlich does not consider the modes of being and doing as intrinsically related to gender. He maintains that they cross the boundaries of gender and are subject to selective reinforcement, especially by cultural factors, which can act to prioritise and value one way, while repressing or devaluing the other. In any event, feminine and masculine are to be understood as psychic characteristics present in both women and men: they are mental functions or stances in continuous, dynamic oscillation (Erlich, 2003).

From the "sewing box" to art

Art is a way of communicating one's own personal experience of oneself and the world in symbolic forms. It is an expressive practice that gives voice to experiences and emotions through a great variety of means, materials, forms, structures, and colours. The expressive techniques, contents, and languages utilised are determined by internal and external, individual and historical-cultural factors, some known and others unknown to the artists themselves.

If the mind that creates art is androgynous—or bisexual—it is nonetheless embodied in a sexual body, in the body of a man or a woman marked by both an individual and a collective history that is instead not androgynous. Furthermore, as mentioned earlier, the female body "embodies" the psychic tension between the maternal and erotic, and it bears the vestiges of a history of subjection to and exclusion from the male world (including the world of art).

Indeed, in the visual arts, for centuries women's bodies have traditionally been "objects" on display, objects that were idealised or, in any event, modelled according to the male view. When women began to express themselves, they tried to communicate what it meant to be a woman and to live in a woman's body, in the sense of a place in which the self is experienced and defined. Very generally speaking, women artists have more often taken personal, often autobiographical inspirations for their works. They have demonstrated greater interest in exploring the themes of the body, sensoriality, emotions, and the more gender-related aspects, strongly investing such topics with their own awareness. Since the 1960s women's presence in the art scene has grown considerably, and women were largely responsible for the push to ground artistic enquiry in bodily experience, contributing to making it a contemporary trend by now followed by male and female artists alike.

Women artists have not only taken up the symbolism of the male language and universe, and have proven themselves able to master it, but have moreover explored new ways to linguistically symbolise their own experience as women, experience that is symmetrical rather than complementary to men's.

The visual arts have long been dominated by a hierarchy of languages and expressive means: the rich, "high" language of painting, sculpture and architecture was contrasted with the poor, "low" language that found expression through what we would generally define as crafts, or "applied art", a kind of Class B art. For instance, weaving, sewing, embroidery have always been considered female activities *par excellence*, expressions of the know-how that mothers pass on to their daughters. They constituted a precious endowment involving the domestic virtue of caring for the body, and satisfying its needs for protection, warmth, comfort, and wellbeing. We might even say that they represented a sort of symbolic extension of the female-maternal function.

Nowadays there are no hierarchies in the materials used for artistic expression and women, through their creative quests, have broadened the range of the technical-expressive possibilities for the whole of contemporary art, introducing practices and materials originally relegated to the private, domestic universe of the female. It seems to me that all this testifies to the possibility of eliminating gender stereotypes and prejudices by highlighting the fertility and enrichment produced not only by an exchange of practices and knowledge between men and women, but also—within the same individual—by the fertile dynamic interconnection between the masculine and feminine aspects that intertwine and take form through artistic creation as well.

I shall offer for your consideration some examples of the creations of two artists who are quite distant in both style and expressive power. Despite their differences, I believe the works of both allow for a reading seeking to trace the echoes of an artistic language originating in the female-maternal regions of the mind, not so much in the works' content, as in the expressive language and the materials used.

In the title of this paper I refer to the "sewing box". This image relates to a traditional, painstaking female duty: to creatively and imaginatively fashion—using needle, threads, and assorted pieces of fabric-cloth and covers that act as "containers" for the body, that serve as interfaces between the internal and external, almost a second skin to protect and afford feelings of comfort and pleasure.

Symbolically we can think of the psychic skin of the mental container, which the mother weaves for her child with her own *rêverie*, the psychic skin that gives cohesion to the self. Moreover, due to their tactile qualities, cloth and fabric evoke a form of knowledge grounded in the sensoriality of touch, of contact, as in the profound, carnal intimacy of one body with another.

Sonia Delaunay

Sonia Delaunay conducted her artistic research in close collaboration with her husband, the orphic-abstract painter Robert Delaunay. They were among the young avant-garde artists living in Paris in the early part of last century. Sonia and Robert Delaunay's art consciously aimed at an optimistic celebration of the essence of modern life—speed and movement—and did so through the dynamics of colour, working on the rhythmic interplay of dissonances and harmonies. They called it "Simultaneity": contrasting colours mix in the observer's eye, and when observed adjacently, the colours will influence each other. Robert was interested in colour theories and engaged in discussions and debates on art theory. As for Sonia, she wrote that her research was not so much grounded on abstract or theoretical analysis, as on her own sensitivity and the liberty to play freely with colour.

Jacques Damase, one of the most eminent experts on Sonia Delaunay's work, maintains that she "offered abstract painting a formula, of which, regretfully, it did not take advantage. (She united) the rigour of simple geometric forms with an inner life and poetry which emanates from the richness of the colour, the musicality of the rhythm, the vibrant breath of the execution" (Damase, 1991, pp. 6–7).

Sonia Delaunay did not limit her art to painting. She was the first to apply abstraction in decorative art and fashion, abolishing the boundaries between the Fine Arts and the minor arts, and with colour she created clothes, a second skin for objects and women's bodies. She covered an incredible range of objects with her simultaneously contrasting colours, from playing cards to glasses, from lampshades to curtains and cushions, from theatrical costumes to ordinary clothing and textiles. She also worked as an interior designer, creating film-set and costumes for the movie too, as in "Vertige", and in "Le Petit Parigot", directed by René Le Somptier, where one can appreciate her extraordinary capacity to make use of connections and rhythmic repetitions of geometric colour-forms in order to create relations between different objects, so that they become part of a whole and are no longer perceived as isolated elements: the impression is one of being surrounded and wrapped by a vivid, pulsating, homogeneous containing space.

Women's bodies were other spaces she worked on, as, for instance, in the theatrical costumes she designed for the 1918 London edition of the ballet "Cléopâtre", on commission by Sergei Diaghilev, where in Cleopatra's costume the body becomes part of the design, in the disk of the belly and of the breast.

Occasionally she would make clothes for herself and her friends. When the new Russian revolutionary government confiscated her estates in St. Petersburg, Sonia and Robert could no longer live on her private income. After a first commission by the Marquis d'Urquijo, she decided to enter the fashion business to support her family. In collaboration with a silk manufacturer, from the twenties to the mid-thirties she opened shops and ateliers, where her fashion creations—dresses and accessories—were sold to a wealthy, á la page international clientele, from the actress Gloria Swanson to the wife of the architect, Walter Gropius.

The shapes and silhouettes of her dresses are not so particular. What is however astonishing, new and revolutionary, is the introduction of geometric, abstract patterns in place of traditional floral prints, and her use of simultaneous contrasting colours. Another innovation was her mixing of very different materials, or the use of unheard-of ones, such as the raffia dresses with folk patterns she created for the Marquis d'Urquijo's four daughters at the beginning of her fashion career. No silk, no velvet, no precious embroideries: this came as quite a shock to the Spanish aristocrats! When in the twenties she turned to fashion design, this stage of her career represented not only an industrial application of her painting research, but it was also the continuation of a previous sporadic activity of hers that developed from a psychologically significant starting event.

In 1911 Sonia and Robert were expecting their first and only son. Pregnancy is a biologically, bodily and psychically transformative experience. Becoming a mother confronts every woman—consciously and unconsciously—with childhood memories, with early emotional states and fantasies connected with her own experiences as a child, and as an infant in close contact with her mother.

Mothers use to prepare a layette for their babies. Years ago they would sew or knit it themselves, while imagining and feeling their baby's body grow inside theirs, and at the same time psychically creating a mental/emotional containing space for the baby to come. Sonia Delaunay threw all her creativity and sensitivity to colour into a blanket she made for the baby with scraps of fabric and fur. She sewed together small, irregular pieces of different geometric forms, of contrasting colours and textures, to warmly wrap her baby's tiny body. The couple's friends regarded the blanket as a work of Cubist art, but Sonia maintained that inspiration had come to her from the traditional patchwork quilts of Ukrainian peasants.

Two years later she designed the first "simultaneous dress" for herself, applying the same technique. She made it to wear to the Ball Bullier, a dance hall in Montparnasse where she and her husband used to go dancing and listen to jazz music with friends. One could imagine the blanket, with its unusual combination of colours and fabrics, now wrapping her own body, warming little-girl-Sonia as well, but without cancelling out her grown-up woman's body: the different pieces of the patchwork were arranged in such a way that the dress revealed the female body's anatomy, its living architecture and movement. "On her Dress she has a Body" is the title of a poem that Blaise Cendrars dedicated to Sonia Delaunay.

Far removed from any patho-biographical bent, I do not believe that biographical data about an artist's life can explain his or her work. Nevertheless, such information can help us make some conjectures about some of an artist's emotional premises or experiences that may have influenced the work. They can thus enrich the way we read or interpret some thematic or expressive choices. By way of example, here is some information on Sonia Delaunay's life that I feel is quite telling.

When Sonia first met Robert in Paris in 1907, she had already shown keen interest in colour, painting fauve-inspired canvases, which were exhibited in 1908. Many years later, in her autobiography, she wrote that her love for colour was connected to childhood memories under the bright Ukrainian sun.

Sonia was born Sarah Stern in a small village near Odessa in 1885. Her parents were very poor and had difficulty feeding all their children. At age five she was adopted by her mother's wealthy brother, whose marriage was childless, and moved to St. Petersburg, Russia, never to return to her secluded village in Ukraine or see her natural family again.

In one fell swoop, she had lost the love of her parents, the voices and frolicking of her brothers and sisters, the yellow sunflowers, the blue sky and gay colours of the peasants' Sunday clothes. She could not show sorrow or regret for what she had lost. Her new parents had asked her to remain silent and forget. They changed her name too: Sarah first became Sophie, then Sonia; Terk was her new surname. New faces, new settings, everything around her had changed: parties and concerts and elegant people, travel all over Europe, an excellent education with French and German teachers. Sonia Terk—seemingly without suffering any emotional wound or trauma—grew into a brilliant, cultured young woman, with a growing interest in art. Despite the worries and perplexities of her adoptive parents, she insisted on going to France to study painting. Alone, at age 20, she moved to Paris in 1905, never to return to St. Petersburg. She had won her freedom and the opportunity to try and recreate, through art, the lost vibrant colours of her early emotional experiences under the Ukrainian sun.

Louise Bourgeois

When speaking about the French-American artist, Louise Bourgeois, we enter a completely different ambience. She was born in Paris in 1911 and exhibited her first works in New York in the forties, but she achieved success with the general public only at the age of seventy-one. When she died in 2010, she was famous worldwide and celebrated as one of the world's greatest contemporary artists.

Her artistic research spanned almost the whole of the last century, during which she explored a wide range of expressive styles beyond labels or trends.

When in 1939 she moved to New York with her husband—an American art historian—she understood that in her painting there was "timidity in the way the idea is presented". She turned mostly to sculpture and installations—I would say that sculptures and installations look more like strong, affirmative self-expressions, each one occupies external space.

She used and often mixed many materials together: hot and cold, hard and soft, fragile and tough; marble, wood, bronze, latex, fabric, glass, plastic, clay, and so on. Following the thread of my arguments so far, I will confine myself to only one particular aspect of her very long creative career, disregarding many other interesting paths of investigation. Just to remember at least a few representative works from her extensive artistic production, it is worth mentioning the "Femmes Maison" series, reflecting one of the main themes of her early works from the forties, to which she often returned later: women imprisoned, trapped in their homes, in their bodies, in their sexual and maternal roles. There are then many works about sexuality and body: these were the main themes of her artistic enquiry during the sixties and the seventies. The body was presented through part-objects, anatomical parts, sexual organs, or bio-morphic and anthropomorphic forms. One of the most representative is a sculptured form, with the title "Self-portrait"; it is is a biomorphic phallic shape, with breasts dangling from it, at once male and female: it is a combined object, a condensation of the primal scene, an omnipotent phallic mother. It evokes a primitive, strongly bisexualised, totem-like figure. The works of these years are often disturbing and provocative, at times ironically humorous. All these aspects are brilliantly summed up in the famous photo-portrait by Robert Mapplethorpe, "Fillette" (1968), in which Louise Bourgeois, wearing a long-haired fur, holds the sculpture of a penis under her arm like a baguette: the little girl has got her penis!

An impressive set of works are the "Cells". It is a series of installations she worked on from the late nineties. She said she intended to represent different types of pain: physical, emotional, psychological, mental, and intellectual pain. The cages of these Cells are *unheimlich* architectural spaces, installations that look like symbolic containers of mind objects, embodied in everyday objects and in sculptures arranged within. They are visionary, theatrical creations by which Bourgeois stages the ghosts of her past, the memories still living and haunting her inner world.

Her entire artistic production is an introspective journey into her past, into the strongly conflictual relationship with her father and mother. She used to say that her work was the story of her yesterday, compul-sively referenced today. Her artistic creativity was at the service of a "reconstruction of myself", "to solve my problems". Louise Bourgeois was well aware that for her art was a lifelong effort at self-reparation: each and every formal choice had a metaphorical meaning—as well as subjective emotional significance—that she was eager to explain.

In 1982 Louise Bourgeois published "Child abuse", in which she dis-played a series of her childhood and family photos, with a few images of her phallic works and a written text in which she reveals what had been the unspoken trauma of her childhood. Behind the façade of a happy, wealthy family, there was a story of betrayal, infidelity, and hypocrisy. There was a woman hired as a governess for the children, who slept with Louise's father. There was the mystery of her mother tolerating the situation and refusing to answer her daughter's questions. Little Louise could not possibly understand what was going on there, in such an atmosphere full of aggressive, erotic tensions. The despair and isolation she lived in made her feel "caught in a web of fear, the spider's web".

Her work, "Cell with Spider", is a cage completely covered and entrapped by the body and legs of an enormous bronze spider. Bourgeois explained that the figure of the spider in her works intended to represent her experience of and her feelings about her mother. Perhaps her most famous work is "Maman Spider", the installation exhibited at the Tate Modern in 1999. It portrays a gigantic, towering spider, protecting and imprisoning. Mothers, like spiders, weave threads, the affective threads of family relationships, in which one can be trapped.

A forceful, provocative confrontation with male tyranny over women and her own ambivalent feelings towards her father had already been widely expressed in her artistic work, culminating in "The Destruction of the Father" (1974), a cannibalistic childhood phantasy of devouring a tyrannical father.

After her public confession in "Child abuse" in 1982, there seems to have been a more decisive turn on her part to re-elaborate her complex, ambivalent feeling towards the mother figure. Indeed, many art critics point to the fact that in the nineties Bourgeois introduced new techniques and materials in her works, and this observation is interesting for the point I want to make. Frances Morris writes: "sewing is a technique that remained repressed in her practice for many years. Now, sewing has presented itself as a major focus of her work". (Morris, 2003, p. 22).

In those years, her expressive research entered a new stage in terms of plasticity and form. At the same time, symbolically, sewing made the artist assume the role of her mother, who used to run a tapestry and carpet restoration workshop where, as a young girl, Louise had occasionally helped out. The new direction of her artistic creativity seems to parallel the internal psychic processes of re-elaborating the female identification with her mother, and re-weaving the thread connecting the two women.

First Louise Bourgeois started hanging some of her own clothes in her installations—she often used to hang her works when exhibiting objects and sculptures. In an exhibion catalogue (2009) she writes: "Horizontality is a desire to give up, to sleep. Verticality is an attempt to escape. Hanging and floating are states of ambivalence". What comes to my mind is the image of the umbilical cord as a tie that needs to be severed, and the tragic ambivalence between the need/desire to be connected with the other, and the need/desire to separate and differentiate oneself.

Later on she began cutting pieces from her garments or other fabrics and sewing them together to create new artworks. Fabric is an unusual material for making sculptures and three-dimensional objects. Only dolls and toys come to mind. The themes of her last period are the same as usual, rooted in her personal emotional experiences, but universal as well: rage, aggression, fear of abandonment and longing for connectedness, love and hate, sexuality and motherhood, anatomy and emotions—all what have always been staged, plastically and brilliantly, in her works. But perhaps now Bourgeois has learnt to "play" with these objects of her mind, embodying them in soft cloth figures that she creates with needle and thread.

These last works are mostly small stuffed figures, some tender, others rather disturbing, represented in different situations and states of mind. The colour of the fabric is often evocative of skin. Other times, the external surface of the fabric sculpture is richly embroidered, as in the series of "Heads", which look damaged and threatening, tragic and solitary.

Greatly significant is the work "Heart": the different elements are arranged in a way that could evoke a stylised human figure—head, open arms, body. It is composed by threads unwinding from spools and ending with needles—which suggest connections with her family business and her mother. The needles are pierced in a red, plastic heart, which here is located in the lower part of the human-shaped form. The pierced heart is symbolic equivalent to wounded love feelings—of course—but here it occupies the place of the belly, so it is about visceral emotions and sexuality too. Moreover, needles and threads can speak of a wish and an attempt of reparation, of reconnecting.

In any case, I would suggest that cutting and then sewing in order to reconstruct a whole can be regarded as metaphorical expressions of mental processes not only of destroying and repairing, but of separating and rejoining as well, both neverending processes, whose artistic representation I have tried to investigate through the creative universe of two great women artists.

References

Benjamin, J. (1995). *Soggetti d'amore. Genere, Identificazione, Sviluppo Erotico.* Bari: Laterza, 1996.

Bourgeois, L. (1982). Child Abuse. *Artforum*, December.

Bourgeois, L. (1998). *Destruction of the Father. Reconstruction of the Father. Writings and Interviews 1923–1997*. M. L. Bernadac & H. U. Obrist (Eds.), London: Violette Editions.

AA.VV. *Louise Bourgeois per Capodimonte*. Catalogo della Mostra, Napoli: Electa, 2009.

Chasseguet-Smirgel, J. (1964). *La sessualità femminile. Nuove ricerche psicoanalitiche*. Bari: Laterza, 1971.

Chasseguet-Smirgel, J. (1984). *Creativity and Perversion*. New York: W. W. Norton.

Damase, J. (1991). *Sonia Delaunay. Fashion and Fabrics*. New York: Thames and Hudson, 1997.

Erlich, S. (2003). Experience. What is it? *International Journal of Psychoanalysis, 84*: 1125–1147.

Ferraro, F. (2001). Vicissitudes of bisexuality. Crucial points and clinical implications. *International Journal of Psychoanalysis, 82*: 485–499.

Ferraro, F. (2003). Psychic bisexuality and creativity. *International Journal of Psychoanalysis, 84*: 1451–1467.

Giuffrida, A. (2009). *Figure del Femminile*. Roma: Borla.

Lakoff, G., & Johnson, M. (1980). *Metafora e vita Quotidiana*. Milano: Bompiani, 2004.

McDougall, J. (1993). Sexual identity, trauma and creativity. *International Forum of Psychoanalysis, 2*: 69–79.

Morris, F. (2003). *Louise Bourgeois. Stitches in Time*. London: AugustProjects.

Parat, H. (1999). *L'erotico Materno. Psicoanalisi dell'allattamento*. Roma: Borla, 2000.

Rigotti, F. (2010). *Partorire con il corpo e con la Mente. Creatività, Filosofia, Maternità*. Torino: Bollati Boringhieri.

Stanford Friedman, S. (1987). Creativity and the childbirth metaphor. Gender differences in literary discourse. *Feminist Studies*, XIII, I.

Winnicott, D. W. (1966). The split-off male and female elements to be found in men and women. *Psychoanalytic Explorations*. Cambridge: Harvard University Press, 1989.

Woolf, V. (1928). *A Room of One's Own*. London: Penguin Books, 2004.

CHAPTER SEVENTEEN

Commentary on *Brodeuses*

Maria Teresa Palladino

The possibility for a woman to think of herself as a mother represents the end of a growth path and implies she has achieved a separation from her own mother with whom she can now identify without fear of being incorporated but remain sure of her individuality (Argentieri, 1982, 1985). This path seems to encounter obstacles whose various forms we see in our clinical work. One of these is pregnancies in underage girls which, as we know, are generally only apparent expressions of mature creativity. The aim of this paper is to highlight the difficulties that young girls sometimes encounter in dealing with their creativity, and the close relationship that seems to exist between this and the problems that have characterised relationships with their mothers. In this paper I will refer to the film "A Common Thread" (*Brodeuses*) to illustrate how complex the journey can be to being able to become mothers. Rarely has a film managed to explore this dimension with both delicacy and versatile depth.

The film tells the story of the adolescent, Claire, who is expecting a child whom she does not want, the result of an affair with a married man. The girl, who has hidden from everyone that she is pregnant and has a very difficult relationship with her mother, decides to work as an embroiderer, which is her passion, continuing the pregnancy while

213

at the same time intending to abandon the child after giving birth in anonymity. Claire meets Mrs Melikian, a mature woman who has recently lost a son, and who agrees to be her embroidery teacher. Both women are suffering and struggling to come to terms with the reality of the emotional pain they are experiencing. Spending time together, they help each other and in a reciprocal relationship that is also ambivalent at times. Mrs Melikian manages to resume contact with life and forge ahead despite the loss of her son, while Claire learns to love herself and find the strength to keep her baby.

In the first place, I think the film admirably expresses the psychic task of dealing with the idea of what could be inside one when one is pregnant. Can the baby really be growing? Or, as Claire says, is it a cancer to be thwarted with chemicals, a persecutory object to be evacuated? Is it something vital to take joy in as an expression of one's ability to generate, or is it something dangerous? I think every pregnant woman may ask herself these distressing questions at some point, forcing each of us to re-examine the deepest experiences of our internal objects. Is there an intact world inside us that can give rise to life? Or is there a disaster of death that confronts us with reprisals experienced by our love objects whom we have violently attacked in our imagination? I believe the film illustrates these universal questions very well because Claire's pregnancy is the fruit of an oedipal-like transgression, the child having been conceived in a relationship with a married man. Perhaps this is what increases Claire's desire to avoid acknowledging her pregnancy and leads her to feel the baby as other than herself, a hostile object that as such cannot be overcome libidinally.

I do not believe this is such an unusual experience. Those of us who work in various ways with pregnant women cannot help but see how even the most visible signs of bodily changes can at times be denied. Sometimes the pregnancy is refused and until the very end the woman tries to make it "untrue". At other times instead, in very young adolescents (and others as well), it is the difficulty of having to be clearly aware of one's capacity to generate, as if it were something reserved for "grown ups". It is an uncertainty that can unconsciously lead one to verify the ability to give rise to life, confirming that one is an adult and that one's internal objects are intact and undamaged. When the pregnancy really does occur, it is as if it were hard to realise that ... the test was actually successful: I am really pregnant! Unfortunately these situations are the causes of many abortions in the very young, but in others as well. Claire denies her pregnancy with others by saying she is ill, as well as to herself by avoiding the mirror and trying to ignore the changes in her body. She only acknowledges the situation with the assistance of her gynaecologist, who helps her for the first time face the fact that there really is a being inside her.

It is a woman, however, who is the intermediary between her baby and herself. This brings us to the second point I would like to underscore, and one I feel is central: Claire's relationship with her mother, and actually with all the female figures in her life. We can talk about them in various ways: as autonomous and complete figures, but also as representations of phases in the life of a girl and of her corresponding relations with female figures.

Claire's mother seems practically incapable of coping with her daughter's deep needs: she realises cabbages have been stolen from her field, but not that the girl is pregnant. Furthermore, in what I consider one of the most moving scenes of the film, even when Claire is ready to come to terms with her condition and attempts to make her pregnancy visible, her mother still does not see it, so that she has no chance for either welcome or warmth, or for refuge. Claire's mother seems more concerned about what is taken away from her than being able to take interest in the changes in her daughter, wearily trying to come to terms with her own femininity and her own needs in general. Hence the dream in which her mother affectionately strokes Claire's hair in an atmosphere of tenderness and caring ends with the violent image of her mother tearing it out in clumps.

Yet if it is true that Claire's mother is clearly an unfit mother, it is also true that all women at some point in the psychic life of a daughter are viewed as mothers potentially capable of pulling out the hair of the young girl who is growing and becoming a woman, daydreaming about stealing the femininity and power from the more adult one. From Snow White onwards, sooner or later there will be a wicked witch in the life of all young girls. Of course, as in Claire's case, the witch is even more wicked if there was not a caring and affectionate mother to begin with. In that case the need for indemnification becomes even more important for the daughters and feeds the hatred and competitiveness that finds full expression in adolescent dialectics. Nevertheless, situations are also complicated when there are not problems like those shown in the film. As we know, excessive closeness between mother and daughter can be just as dangerous if it involves a relational enmeshment that prevents a real separation. In these cases, it is not possible to have one's own desires as one has become the object of projected identifications tied to the needs of others. In both situations, it is hard to imagine presenting oneself as an autonomous person, either because one cannot make one's own way without looking back at the past due to a demand for compensation for what one did not have, or because one cannot think of oneself as having truly personal desires.

In the film we clearly see how Claire does not really know who she is at the beginning or what she really wants. Only gradually will she manage to leave enough room for her passion for embroidery and let it become a real chance at life for herself, allowing her to leave the frustrating work at the supermarket.

Now we come to the other key female character who appears in the film and is clearly in opposition to the real mother: Mrs Melikian. She immediately realises that Claire is pregnant and despite being overwhelmed by the grief for the loss of her own son can still afford to offer a mental space where Claire feels welcome and cared about. In this sense she appears to be a figure capable of seeing that another individual besides herself exists and to welcome, at least in part, that person's needs without forgetting her own and without forgetting her own pain.

Through their shared creativity in embroidery, which they are both involved in, Mrs Melikian is able to regain some contact with life (she puts lipstick on again) and Claire, now that a woman-mother is able to "see her", can gradually approach the reality of her pregnancy and consciously accept the bodily changes that will follow even though the possibility of actually keeping the baby is not yet a reality for her. It is their profound, practically unspoken, relationship with each other consisting of careful movements that draw one towards life again and the other to the prospect of giving rise to it. At a certain point, it also implies the need to deal with the pain with no easy way out, as might be the case by quickly replacing the dead son with the young girl. This is the context in which to view the attempted suicide of Mrs Melikian, whose relationship with Claire in a certain sense recalls life, but also the pain of losing her son. It is a very important episode that lets one know the depth of the feelings that are presented in the film, which deals with the complexity and facets of sentiments and in which relationships are represented that provide room for love, but also for pain.

As Paola Golinelli (2007) points out in her commentary to this film, the way out will be represented by the understanding between the two women, who regress into an entirely female world, in a dyadic relationship that excludes men. Moreover, it will allow them to medicate the wounds that both of them have suffered in their life stories and in which both become aware of their reciprocal need, making room for the femininity of each without one proving to be at the expense of the other.

The description of how Mrs Melikian slowly shows renewed interest in caring for herself is particularly moving. Claire's kindness towards her and her keen and curious expression as she calmly investigates the aspects of femininity she finds traces of in Mrs Melikian's house, where Claire herself now lives, are of immense help in this sense. It is in this relational context that one can believe that there is actually space for the birth of a baby.

When we think of Mrs Melikian, however, let us ask ourselves if we should think of her merely as a maternal figure who is really an alternative to Claire's natural mother. Or, on the other hand, should we also see her as the image of a post-oedipal mother who must in some way be accepted by each one of us to be able to claim one's own femininity and one's own possibility of becoming a mother? And in this same context, then, also revive the femininity of one's own mother or, otherwise be overcome by the bereavement of the loss of her own daughter who has now become a woman. In a certain sense, through Claire's relationship with the two mother figures, biological and substitute, it is also as if her story told the story of the passage of an adolescent phase to a more evolved phase of youth in which a pregnancy is possible because a separation occurred and with it a chance to identify with a maternal figure that permits one to become, in turn, mother.

Finally, I think it is important to make a few comments about the male figures in the film, and about the emotions they arouse in us even though they remain in the background of an all-female event. The first man in the background, poorly defined and evasive, is Claire's father, confirming that when things are not going very well between mother and daughter something is missing, a father who could not manage to be a figure of importance as a separating element between mother and daughter. Hence, perhaps, the daughter's desire to put herself between the couple, taking away in exchange what she thinks she never had, something that is very dear to the mother. Nor does it seem that the father had a more significant role in relation to Claire herself, in that fundamental function of recognising the vital role of his daughter's femininity that should underlie a teenage girl's debut in the world.

These aspects are completely absent in the film and as we are well aware they are also absent in the stories of many of our patients who were not helped to deal with that triadic dimension that allows them to think of themselves as separate people capable of looking at the world from several perspectives inasmuch as they are involved in more than one significant relationship. The baby's father seems to have just as little importance, not sketched as a person but only sketched in his status as a married man who wants to stay out of trouble. In the film, however, as what happens with the female characters, changes take place that have to do with the arrival of other characters on the scene.

Two of them are the other important male figures. The first is Lacroix, the tailor, who, without appearing and in the words of Mrs Melikian, is like a father who can appreciate the embroidery work and thus symbolically Claire. It is interesting that he does not appear in person, but that his presence is guided by the female figure, first of all as evidence of the need for the mother to recognise the importance that the father has for the daughter. The second is Guillaume, the friend of the son who died. Working through his own personal bereavement, he seems capable of reawakening Claire's desire for a male figure at her side, as well as presenting himself to Claire as a figure potentially in contact with the baby who will be born. Two very different figures, therefore, each with a very specific function, proving that the work of growing did happen to Claire and on several levels.

Claire does indeed seem to be much more mature. She is even able to meet her responsibilities towards her "foster" mother, the woman whom Claire helped to get closer to life and who is now able to begin to mourn the loss of her dead son. Part of the path seems to have been accomplished and ties have been created on a foundation that can now evolve. A place in the mind of a mother was found and this opened the possibility of thinking of an interior space able to accommodate her child. Therefore, it is only within the relationship with a substitute mother, and the perspective through which another woman sees and recognises the pregnancy has it been possible to find a space to accommodate a child who can now be born.

References

Argentieri, S. (1982). Sui processi mentali precoci dell'identità femminile. *Rivista Italiana di Psicoanalisi, 28*: 371–376.

Argentieri, S. (1985). Sulla cosiddetta disidentificazione dalla madre. *Rivista Italiana di Psicoanalisi, 31*: 397–403.

Golinelli, P. (2007). Brodeuses (Sequins): The sparkle in the mother's eyes. *International Journal of Psycho-Analysis, 88*: 243–252.

CHAPTER EIGHTEEN

The voice of the mother in *To the Lighthouse*

Nadia Fusini

"Ihave an idea that I will invent a new name for my books to supplant 'novel'. A new … by Virginia Woolf. But what? Elegy?". (*The Diary of Virginia Woolf*, ed. by A. Olivier Bell & A. McNeillie, 1980, vol. III, p. 34).

It is 27 June 1925, and the writer is ready for her new book. She already knows its proper name, but she does not know its genre, its kin, its kind. She has no idea under which genre, or gender, or name to register it in the Literary Registry. But she anticipates its tone: it is going to be an elegy—to the Lighthouse. She has no doubts as to whom the elegy will be dedicated. That "to" is a preposition which does not indicate here movement towards a destination; it is not just the vector of movement from one place to another, concluding in a possible or impossible arrival at the Lighthouse. It is a dative case: the recipient of an offering, a gift.

Thus, Virginia Woolf writes for the Lighthouse: facing towards that light, and thanks to that light. What she writes for that light is also a gift. The Lighthouse is at the centre of the novel, as a place with which contact—if not the gaze turned towards it—is denied. Standing tall, it is the fire that directs the eye, a vertical structure that rises up like an exclamation point, a signpost in the flat and horizontal landscape of the sea mass, and of memory.

Yes, memory: for the Lighthouse is the lighthouse of her childhood, of the long summers spent as a little girl with her family at St. Ives in Cornwall; and *To the Lighthouse* will contain, in fact, all those memories. If I insist here on memory, on the elegiac tone, it is because *To the Lighthouse* has to do with nostalgia and memory.

Perhaps it is always so with the work of art; it is thanks to memory that life resuscitates in the work of art, adding to real experience new layers of meaning. After all, is not this the way meaning is always arrived at—years afterwards? Always après coup? Is not meaning come upon, like we get to the Lighthouse, because we are led there not so much by will and desire, as by the memory of and longing for what we have missed?

There is the existential and philosophical question of this great, truly great, work of art—so great precisely because of the radical nature of thought on life and art which it sustains and contains, brings and bears. It is in effect by writing that Virginia Woolf, mature by now— she is over forty—reaches the Lighthouse, completing a journey which in its making produces this chef-d'oeuvre—among the greatest of the twentieth century.

* * *

In the beginning Virginia Woolf says: the father is to be at the centre of the Lighthouse. "The centre is father's character, sitting in a boat, reciting We perished, each alone ..." (Woolf, 1980, pp. 18–19). The novel (Virginia Woolf will forgive me if I use the term she rejects, I know I am using it imprecisely, approximately) is to be "fairly short; to have father's character done complete in it; & mothers; & St. Ives; & childhood; & all the usual things I try to put in—life, death, & c." (Woolf, 1980, p. 19), as she writes on 14 May 1925.

However, during the writing, the mother slowly takes on much greater importance than the writer had originally intended. For it is Mrs Ramsay who, in the end, becomes the absolute protagonist of the novel. The reaction of Vanessa, Virginia's sister, confirms this. On 11 May 1927, immediately after reading the book, Vanessa writes:

> It seemed to me that in the first part of the book you have given
> a portrait of mother which is more like her to me than anything I

could ever have conceived of as possible. It is almost painful to have her so raised from the dead. You have made one feel the extraordinary beauty of her character ... it was like meeting her again ... it seems to me the most astonishing feat of creation to have been able to see her in such a way. So your vision of her stands as a whole by itself and not only as reminding one of facts ... I am excited and thrilled and taken into another world as only one is by a great work of art. (Woolf, 1977, p. 572)

Virginia Woolf herself is amazed: she did not think she knew her mother so well. Mother had died when Virginia was thirteen years old. There is something "astonishing" about the discovery, for her too (which leaves us readers disconcerted as well), that she had recreated, by writing, the memory of someone she did not "remember", did not "know" so well, after all. On 22 May, Woolf replies: "But what do you think I did know about mother? It can't have been much—I suppose one broods over some germ".

This thought of Virginia's confirms that there is something tremendously powerful, and strange, in writing. It proves that writing can be a true, actual conversation with ghosts, an alchemy that blurs the clear boundaries between life and death. A ceremony in which the quick and the dead, the dead and the living beckon to each other, exchanging visions. What is even more extraordinary is that in the play of memory strange metamorphoses occur, and as a consequence the facts of reality are distorted.

Once the idea of the novel comes to her, however, Virginia Woolf does not start straightaway: "I must write a few little stories first, & let the Lighthouse simmer ..." On 14 June 1925 she is still thinking about it, "perhaps too clearly"; on 27 June she confesses that she is still "making up 'To the Lighthouse'—the sea is to be heard all through it". But then on one particular day, walking through the streets of London, so dear to her, she conceives *To the Lighthouse* "in a great, apparently involuntary, rush", as she recounts in *Moments of Being* (A Sketch of the Past, in *Moments of Being*, J. Schulkind, (Ed.), 2002, p. 92). Thus her mother, who had obsessed her with her absence, is born again.

Mrs Ramsay is Julia Stephen: beautiful like her, a woman like her, and a mother like her; while Virginia Woolf, if anyone, is Lily Briscoe, the deuteragonist in the dramatic action—plain (that's how Virginia sees herself!), not exactly a woman, never a mother. In a condensation which shifts any preestablished sort of biographical realism, Lily Briscoe is a painter, like Woolf's sister Vanessa. Virginia appears in the novel in other disguises and under other names: she is Cam, who does not want to fall asleep and is afraid, she is Nancy playing in the big pools of water at the seashore; she is Rose, who chooses the jewels for her mother to wear in the evening, she is Mr Ramsay even, who resembles her own father—whom Woolf herself resembles—like him defenceless, in that he has a pathetic sense of his own inadequacy, with a vocation for failure … Like him intellectual, living in the mind …

The point is that everything becomes complicated in the process of writing, where, as in dreams, the most bizarre combinations are possible, while a secret thread weaves a fictional, imaginary web infinitely more revealing than the original, realistic autobiographical germ.

* * *

The theme of the novel, as I have said, is not the more or less possible arrival at the Lighthouse. The theme is the Lighthouse itself, the light emanating from it, and illuminating the heart and mind of a woman, Mrs Ramsay, who knows how to allow herself to be touched by the lighthouse. The lighthouse is erect, but it is also a liquid, soft light that touches the island and the people and things on it and makes them fertile—the lighthouse is the Mother. But it is also the Father: naked, erect, it dominates. The ambiguity, the multiple valency of the images is fundamental to reading. Reading, or at least my reading, does not aim to establish an interpretation resulting in a definitive meaning of the story, but rather to respect its poetic richness. Reading is not translating what is written in the text into other words: it is listening to the resonances that it generates, the interlacings that are inscribed into the poetic fabric of the text. It is through this attention to language that we readers will be able to grasp certain meanings, certain movements or rhythms—one of these movements or rhythms being precisely a tension moving us readers towards the experience of con-fusion—the fusion-with of opposites. Only if man and woman will be capable of melting, fusing and con-fusing into one another—"coalescence" might be the word; only if the woman is capable of allowing herself to be penetrated by the man and become a mother; only if the man will be capable of being enthralled by the female medusa, of becoming concave to receive the female power—only in that contact a fecundity will be achieved, that might (we are in the world of possibility, of latent power) give meaning and order to the world. This is a poetic, not a psychoanalytic, truth that Virginia Woolf offers to us: a truth of the psyche that she discovers in her writing.

As I said before, there is another woman in the novel as well: the woman artist, the virgin Lily, intact and untouchable. For her, the body desired is the maternal body: it is the mother that Lily, an orphan (like Virginia), loves in Mrs Ramsay—the Mother as woman penetrated by man and the light of the Lighthouse; by man and the inviolate light, which she receives and opens to. Passively, in a sense, although she herself is active in nurturing life in the one, and light in the other.

These two women hold the stage, with various stand-ins who repeat the two archetypes with minimal variations. Minta Doyle, for example, is the same type as Mrs Ramsay, but of inferior quality. Prue is exactly like her mother and dies in childbirth. Cam, who is more like Lily, is placed on the side of her father and brother, a new Electra. In these different characters, the woman as mother and the female virgin take each other by the hand and conduct the female dance, introducing archaic configurations into modern, personal mythologies.

For this is a novel of memory and childhood: of that age and time when imagination and reality are most confused and commingled, when the Mother is at the centre of all things. "Certainly there she was, in the very centre of that great Cathedral space which was childhood; there she was from the very first. My first memory is of her lap; the scratch of some beads on her dress comes back to me as I pressed my cheek against it" (A Sketch of the Past, in *Moments of Being*, J. Schulkind, (Ed.), 2002, p. 93), writes Virginia Woolf in *Moments of Being*. These are all details which return in the novel referred in turn to James or Cam. But if the germ of the "novel" is autobiographical, in its development, it becomes more and more symbolic, "poetic"—that is, creative. "What is creative, creates itself" says John Keats–exactly.

Virginia Woolf, like Lily Briscoe, does not aim at representative realism: she does not wish to paint a portrait based on resemblance. With *Jacob's Room* and *Mrs Dalloway*, Woolf has already demolished the very notion of "objective representation". Indeed, the writer repeatedly professes in her diary that she is seeking a different form, a different phrasing even, and a different name for what she is writing, which does not fall within the existing genres. She is seeking above all a "different reality". If she has a talent she recognises as her own, it is "to have so acute a sense of something", which coincides with "a consciousness of what I call 'reality': a thing I see before me, something abstract; but residing in the downs or sky; beside which nothing matters; in which I shall rest & continue to exist. Reality I call it. And I fancy sometimes this is the most necessary thing to me: that which I seek", as she writes on 10 September 1928.

Even before this, on 27 February 1926: "I have a great & astonishing sense of something there, which is 'it'.—It is not exactly beauty that I mean. It is that the thing is in itself enough: satisfactory; achieved". A ruthless severity of the mind, united with an extremely particular sensibility, compel her to the encounter with that "thing" that is beyond reach, elusive—a reality so different from the one reached in the "frightful" method of the realist writers.

For her, life ("life is my question", "it's life that counts", she continues to repeat) is beyond the "real". It has a different unity of time and place. It belongs to the possible and is incorporated into the antecedent— in the same way that the mother is there from the beginning. We always come late into being what we are, we always come late into existence: we learn how to live, how to speak—we enter in a conversation which has always begun before, don't we? When Virginia Woolf addresses "life" she is not seeking the common sphere of existence; on the contrary, in order to reach what she calls "life", she must separate herself from everyday life. "One must get out of life", she maintains, in order to enter into "reality". "When I write", she continues, "I am merely a sensibility" (22 August 1922).

* * *

But we need to understand precisely what that word—"sensibility"— means for Virginia Woolf; a word often inappropriately used with reference to her writing, as though it were the emblem of a decidedly feminine, intuitive, sensitive quality; an imagination that is excessive because lacking in logic. This is not the case here. With Virginia Woolf we find ourselves face to face with a completely new "sensibility", an absolutely unique vision which the writer is able to achieve, thanks to her extremely fine perceptive faculties, and by virtue of the arduous challenge she takes on. The "sensibility" she speaks of is rather pure receptive intuition, which she achieves through the discipline of silence and the exercise of her art.

Virginia Woolf is capable of an extremely profound silence of the self (the same which Mrs Ramsay produces in the novel, when she is sitting by the window and the Lighthouse casts its light upon her). It is through that extinction of her personality (a quest she shares with a poet such as T. S. Eliot) that she is able to listen to "a universal voice", as Kant would say. Putting this unheard sound to work, resolving it in language, is the experience of the writer, Virginia Woolf, the difficult task she assigns herself. In this sense, Virginia Woolf literally sets out on a "journey towards language", to say it with Heidegger. In travelling this road, language is no more than the way to move beyond. Beyond, but where?

* * *

For Virginia Woolf, there is the strong, acute, precise sensation of some-thing beyond the power of language, beyond the realistic dimension of the word, its time—which is the time dimension of conversation, upon which the realistic novel is sustained. She has a perturbing sense that there is something, that is the "thing", but she does not know "how to grasp it". Nevertheless, "for the love of it": for love of this neutral, nameless thing, she writes. That nameless it is not the same thing which realists speak of. "I haven't that 'reality' gift", she states. She adds: "I insubstantise, wilfully to some extent, distrusting reality—its cheapness. But to get further. Have I the power to convey the true reality?", she asks herself on 19 June 1923. Virginia Woolf puts eve-rything at stake on this question: every moment of desperation and of euphoria depend on the failure (necessary, repeated), or success (ephemeral, inconstant) of such an attempt.

The writer embarks on the quest relying on her own senses. She relies on her intuition. Thus she discovers the truth of that primary commu-nication with the world which is sensation. The "I" of Virginia Woolf is not a "personality" (to use a word that is also dear to her friend, T. S. Eliot), nor the subject of thinking and doing, ending in the person, personage, or character. It is an absolutely impersonal "I think" which has its source in the imagination. It is the imagining "I"—the field established by the indivisible tie between the sensible and the intelli-gible. In other words, the imagination for Virginia Woolf is the way, or the means, which unites sensibility and intellect—the deep root which in that knot protects, and assures, and assists in the birth of a properly human intelligence. Spontaneous, receptive, every human being in his or her existence comes in touch with a dimension of profundity, which in itself would remain inaccessible, if it were not for the imagination. The imagination stirs this deep end, it lifts it up into the word, gives it image.

* * *

There are three movements in the novel: the window—where mother and son make a party, threatened by the presence of the father, who comes to separate the incestuous couple; time passes—when the flood of time descends upon the empty house: "the most difficult abstract piece of writing" that she has ever attempted, writes Virginia Woolf on 30 April 1926. And the Lighthouse—when the two actions left unfinished (or perhaps forbidden by the presence of the mother) are completed: Lily's painting and the actual excursion to the Lighthouse. The closeness, the proximity to the maternal body seems to have frozen the action in the first part. The mother says "yes", but also holds back. The movement of everybody else in the book keeps coming back to her, turning back to the matrix, while she sinks ever deeper into the "heart of darkness"—an expression in which there resonates, in a lesser but not less intense resurrection, an echo of the same epiphany (and the same horror), that Conrad, a writer Woolf loved, believes he had to seek in distant navigations. More urgent, more imminent, closer, still it is the "darkness" that absorbs Mrs Ramsay, for it is the darkness that we find at the bottom of the soul.

If Virginia Woolf offers us the possibility of saving ourselves, she does so by placing all good in a woman, Mrs Ramsay—the woman who, because she is a mother, sees and feels the impending, disintegrating forces of chaos which surround us, and concentrates and collects herself and finds in herself the cosmogonic power to "set lands in order". She literally brings about the rebirth of the cosmos. She makes it possible to dwell under the heavens, on earth, precisely because she accepts to be the guardian of an earthly place, which she protects: hers is the grace that makes things human. Indeed, she is Dike: the power of connection. She brings light. Ultimately, she is the Lighthouse that assures the orient of cosmic light.

There are two scenes, or rather two epiphanies of maternal power in the book. One is at the end of the first part, in Chapter Nineteen. In reading that passage again, I would like you to be especially aware of the visual—cinematic one might say—quality of Woolf's language. Right from the beginning, you may remember how we are plunged into the novel *in medias res* (a type of dramatic opening à la Yeats), where we catch a fragment of the dialogue between mother and son, which immerses us into an amorous relation which the father interrupts.

Thus the maternal "yes" opens the novel. "Yes", says the mother to the son: and thus she bestows and promises the possible, she opens and solicits desire. Conversely, the father says "no": the journey to the lighthouse is going to be impossible, it depends on the weather. While the mother's word takes life in a circle of love, in an embrace that does not tear the veil of illusion from reality; the father rends and tears the illusions. He establishes a relation of simple truth between language and reality, so that the intellect must conform to the thing, and desire must limit itself to reason.

It is the first act of the novel that declares the lighthouse as the precluded centre of action; the prohibition falls upon the son with the result of making him impotent with regard to his own desire, while at the same time foregrounding as the theme of book the suffered tension of the subject in relation to the world.

Almost immediately, the "oedipal" nature of the novel comes to the surface: two adverbs (the maternal "yes" and the paternal "no") clash with equal force, and with them, two laws and two postures with regard to life come to the fore: the father's "no" and the mother's "yes"—which of the two will win?

The father, it would seem: in fact, there is no excursion to the Lighthouse. The weather does not allow it. Thus the father wins on the basis of his idea of reality. And yet, another triumph, sanctioned by the last words in this section—"For she had triumphed again"—concludes this first movement. But what sort of triumph is hers?

At the end of the chapter it is precisely "she" who triumphs, the mother, and her triumph consists in silencing him. It is he and she on stage and she triumphs. He turns to her with a silent entreaty: "He wanted something—wanted the thing she always found it so difficult to give him; wanted her to tell him that she loved him." But she could not do it: "she never could say what she felt ..." Then Mrs Ramsay turns and looks at Mr Ramsay, and triumphs: "for though she had not said a word, he knew, of course he knew, that she loved him ..." (Woolf, 1994, p. 89).

This is how Mrs Ramsay triumphs—she wins through the imposition of silence, like the laying on of hands of the miracle worker. Beauty and truth, silence and ripeness of meaning coalesce in her as they do in the work of art; the resulting effect is a splendour that dazzles. Revealing the vanity of words, the futility of verbal expression, beauty mercilessly places us face to face with the emptiness and impotence of language.

Without saying a word, Mrs Ramsay points to the idiocy of knowledge: she shows how Mr Ramsay, the philosopher, is unable to explain the power of the beauty and truth, before which he bows, capitulates. He thus realises that between beauty and knowledge there is a line of demarcation. Or rather, if beauty is truth, it is precisely because beauty brings about the manifestation of that division. Impenetrable, inexplicable, beauty is mute. In this it is law. Like law it lives off the effect of distance.

* * *

Law and desire coalesce—at times in a gloomy light, evoking the thread spun and then cut off by the Fates. Right at the beginning, you may remember, Mrs Ramsay has her knitting needles in her hands, which sparkle and mingle with the sharp and cutting ray of the Lighthouse. Assimilated into the same symbolical configuration, the Lighthouse and the woman vibrate in unison. In her fullness as symbol, in her abstraction as icon, Mrs Ramsay is life and death, over which the Lighthouse watches in its protective function. Mrs Ramsay guards the anonymous potency of life and death, which she appropriates for herself in the silence of her beauty. From the remains, the fragments, she creates unity—the all-important task which the poet Eliot entrusted to his poem, *The Waste Land*. In the desolate house of the summer holidays, the power of chaos lurks at the doors, presses at the windows. The insidious night is shut out at Mrs Ramsay's orders: "Light the candles", she says; and thus what before was dispersed, scattered, apart, comes into unity, and we see "a party around a table, for the night was now shut off by panes of glass, which, far from giving any accurate view of the outside world, rippled it so strangely that here, inside the room, seemed to be order and dry land, there, outside, a reflection in which things wavered and vanished, waterily."

The true face of Mrs Ramsay is thus manifested when we see emerge in her face and essence the anonymous face and essence of the mother: who stands at the centre of the room, as of the island, as of life, and transforms chaos into cosmos.

The second epiphany, to which I wish to call your attention, occurs in Chapter Seventeen, which opens with this question: But what have I done with my life? The main point of view in this scene is Lily's, whose gaze focuses on Mrs Ramsay, seated at the head of the table, like a goddess on her throne.

A little earlier, when she had descended the stairs, Virginia Woolf suggested the regal image that still surrounds her. She sits like a goddess on her throne, but her realm, she feels, is in disorder. As in Eliot's *Waste Land*, there is an echo of the story of the Fisher King "I sat upon the shore/Fishing, with the arid plain behind me" (Eliot, *The Waste Land*, in *Collected Poems*, 1963, p. 79, ll. 423–424), who is powerless to bring order to his lands, we know, because of a virile wound which puts at risk the fecundity of the whole world. With Eliot we fear for our salvation. (We know what saves Eliot, the Church: but we do not believe that the same redemption will come to our aid.)

In *To the Lightouse*, what saves us is the Mother. The person who "sees" is Lily—the other woman: she sees Mrs Ramsay both in her simple and more complex manifestations; like when wrapping herself in folds that make her invisible, she ventures into places we cannot penetrate and call "darkness". Even in the places where no-one is able to follow Mrs Ramsay, in that darkness, which is also a silence, Lily follows her. She sustains the different light, which others call "darkness". The fascination of those "shadows" Lily goes after and through and with Mrs Ramsay, is the fascination of another light that she does not see, but obscurely feels it must exist. Mrs Ramsay embodies it.

Indeed, when Mrs Ramsay is not there anymore, chaos breaks in. The house becomes inhuman. At the heart of the book, "Time Passes", is a true "wedge of darkness", a gem set between the living presence of Mrs Ramsay and her memory. Here time plunges into destruction: she was the Measure, she was the Balance, the Proportion and now, without her, all is weightless, measureless and chaos plunges infinitely. It is the advent of an impersonal force, of an automaton, which we might also call fertility, if it was not for the fact that it is presented rather as an excess of it, an insensibility of nature which dissolutely perverts its munificent bloom into a "brute confusion and wanton lust".

Without Mrs Ramsay this force would, might triumph. If this does not happen, it is because even in death she does not disappear, she hovers and her image, gliding over the walls of the empty house, evoked by the walls themselves, draws on or guides, like the light of the Lighthouse, Mrs McNab and Mrs Bast to lend their efforts to the salvaging of the house, which like a ship seems to be drowning into the billows of time. Thus, even though Mrs Ramsay is no more, the destructive power of time is curbed by lesser—but always female—gods; demons and witches, ministers all the same of a power at work against the crushing force of death. A merciful and charitable power evidently still inhabits the house even if only as memory; there hovers about the house—albeit in oblivion—a beneficent creative force (which in this novel bears the name of Mrs Ramsay, while in Forster's *Passage to India*, for example, it is Mrs Moore).

This is a dimension of reality with modalities similar to the aesthetic sphere. In a more original opening of will, of intentionality, similar to the work of art, the world which Mrs Ramsay creates is connected to the perception of a presence, resting in an intermediate realm between imagination and feeling; suspended to the instant when sensation is going to become words, feelings, to the instant when it is still matter in the state of emerging, in a condition of perpetual origin—what Virginia Woolf calls "the creative state of mind." To this dimension is offered incarnation in the Lighthouse.

This is what Lily would want to paint: that is why she has no need of the real image. It is not "resemblance" that Lily wants, but the essence of Mrs Ramsay. Or better, she would want to portray that central transparency gathered in a light, which infinitely surpasses the reproduction of an image: the light which is the essence of Mrs Ramsay is not to be found in what the image conveys—not because Mrs Ramsay hides herself or conceals something; on the contrary, she herself being light, she irradiates light. If light is her essence, she in turn believes that light is the essence of life. Ephemeral creatures—lovers of light, that is, we men and women love the sun, the day, and if we thrust ourselves into the heart of darkness, it is to bring to it the heat and clarity of light. In the same way, in a moment of sudden intensity, in unison with the long ray of the Lighthouse Mrs Ramsay reaches that wedge of darkness, where, sheltered from the light, ignorant of meaning, something comes about that is before meaning, before the word. This latency, this "before"— must be allowed to be. We need know that this darkness is, exists, we have to accept it—we must not remove it. From time to time one must go and touch it with the mind and the heart—with the soul. This darkness must be remembered, re-cor-ded—kept in the heart, as the Latin root of the word shows.

This is what Mrs Ramsay does and Lily sees it, and learns from it. True artist that she is, she learns how to perceive subtle gradations of reality, minimal variations in the scale of light, states of visibility that border on invisibility, obscure passages veined with light; and to penetrate the "firewall of the invisible" (that is what Van Gogh called it) with organs and senses which in the trial do not burn.

* * *

With peremptory clarity and perfect simplicity Virginia Woolf writes in her diary on 28 November 1928—she has now finished the Lighthouse: "Father's birthday. He would have been 96, 96 yes today ... but mercifully was not. His life would have entirely ended mine. What would have happened? No writing, no books;—inconceivable. I used to think of him and mother daily, but writing the Lighthouse, laid them in my mind." By writing therefore, Virginia has placated the "invisible presences", or ghosts: she has dethroned, deposed, buried them. "And now he comes back sometimes", she continues, "but differently. (I believe this to be true—that I was obsessed with them both, unhealthily; & writing of them was a necessary act.)"

The presence having given way to absence, and laid down arms before it, the writing moves in that vacuum; from the ashes of the sacrifice the work of art is born. The writer could not be clearer. In the same way it is clear what engages Lily with regard to her painting, that will be "done" when Mrs Ramsay is gone; when she has learned to bear the grief of absence, the pain of loss. In effect, it is from the pain suffered from that absence that will arise the "pathetic" impulse which will permit her to accomplish her doing, her painting.

Placed before the thing she wanted to paint, that is Mrs Ramsay, she felt she could not do it: the thing itself deprived her of power, deposed her—to return to the image that Virginia Woolf uses for "her" phantasms. Which is like saying that creation has to do with the capacity (Keats called it "negative capability") of bearing the emptiness, distance, separation.

* * *

"I meant nothing by *The Lighthouse*"—Virginia Woolf admits to her dear friend Roger Fry in May 1927. She means: the linguistic dimension of the Lighthouse is not communicative, narrative, discursive; it is symbolic. It works according to a measure which emphasises the rhythmic nature of language, its power of harmonious connection. Things are held together in language, not thanks to a logos that ties the words to meaning, creating a relation of sense between them which is the same of common, prosaic speech; rather they are gathered in the "non-communicative" quiet and silence, where they line up one next to the other in response to sound. This is how Mrs Ramsay holds things together. "She was glad … to rest in silence, uncommunicative." That way she is happy: when she rests "in the extreme obscurity of human relationships". In silence. "Aren't we more expressive thus?" she asks, thus making room for an extraordinary language, taking words away from our habitual mode of representation.

Or better yet: this is how Virginia Woolf approaches the only happiness that is rightfully hers, which is the right of every true creator—the happiness, the felicity of expression.

References

Eliot, T. S. (1922). The Waste Land. In: *Collected Poems*. London: Faber and Faber, 1963.

Woolf, V. (1927). *To the Lighthouse*. Oxford: Oxford University Press, 1992.

Woolf, V. (1976). *Moments of Being*. J. Schulkind (Ed.). London: Pimlico, 2002.

Woolf, V. (1977). *The Letters of Virginia Woolf*. N. Nicolson & J. Trautmann (Eds.). 6 vols, vol. III, London: Hogarth.

Woolf, V. (1980). *The Diary of Virginia Woolf*. A. Olivier Bell & A. McNeillie (Eds.). 5 vols, vol. III, London: Hogarth.

PART IV

LIVING CREATIVELY IN SOCIETY

CHAPTER NINETEEN

Happily ever after: depictions of coming of age in fairy tales

Cecile R. Bassen

F airy tales are stories with enormous staying power. They are told over and over, handed down from one generation to another, throughout the world. They derive from collective efforts, and circulate in multiple versions reconfigured by each telling, but retain a basic plot structure despite rich cultural variations. They were traditionally told by women to young children. There are written references to "old wives tales" as far back as Plato (Tatar, 1999). Their widespread and enduring popularity suggests that they speak deeply to something in all of us. In his landmark book on the meaning and importance of fairy tales, Bruno Bettelheim (1977) suggested that fairy tales endure because they speak to children's psychological conflicts and important developmental issues.

Many fairy tales are so widely told that they become basic knowledge shared by everyone within a culture. Their universality suggests that fairy tales not only reflect cultural beliefs but also perpetuate them. Maria Tatar, a scholar of folklore and literature at Harvard, has suggested that fairy tales are "arguably the most powerfully formative tales of childhood" (Tatar, 1999, p. xi). She has also pointed out that they operate like magnets, with each adaptation picking up relevant aspects of the culture in which the tale is being told (2012). I would take her metaphor one step further, and note that fairy tales also exert a powerful magnetic pull on our unconscious perceptions and beliefs—influencing children as they construct and revise conscious and unconscious beliefs, and continuing to resonate unconsciously in adults who remember and tell these tales.

Classic fairy tales offer us striking and memorable images of women. Many depict vulnerable young girls and powerful older women: evil stepmothers, witches, and fairy godmothers. I will explore two well-known fairy tales in this paper. My aim is to explore what they tell us about unconscious perceptions of women, as well as the impact of these tales on how girls and women experience themselves.

"Cinderella" and "Snow White" are iconic fairy tales with striking similarities: in both, a beautiful young girl with a dead mother is badly mistreated by a selfish and evil older woman. The heroine has done nothing to merit this mistreatment, but her innate grace and beauty arouse spiteful envy. She endures her plight virtuously, seemingly without hostility or even complaint. Her salvation and happiness rest on winning the love of a prince, who has the power to rescue her. Cinderella's coming of age creates an opportunity for her to escape from a situation in which she is powerless by winning the love of the prince. Snow White is in a similar situation, with the added element that her coming of age places her in great danger since her beauty provokes the murderous hostility of the ageing Queen.

Let us start with "Cinderella": the story of a young girl mistreated by her envious stepmother and stepsisters. This iconic tale originated more than 1,000 years ago, and it has hundreds of variants around the world with the heroines going by many different names (Tatar, 1999). The variant we know best was written down by Charles Perrault in France in 1697; this is the version used in the 1950 Disney film (Tatar, 2002). Perrault's Cinderella is as humble, virtuous, and kind as she is beautiful. When Cinderella's stepsisters are invited to the prince's ball, she fixes their hair without resentment, helping them to look as beautiful as possible. In contrast, her stepsisters are depicted as selfish, grasping, and vain. Cinderella's selflessness is rewarded by magical aid from her fairy godmother. Perrault's heroine is the epitome of patience, to the point of passivity. Although she is in tears after her stepsisters go to the ball leaving her home in rags, it is her fairy godmother who gives voice to Cinderella's wish that she too could go to the ball, and who makes it possible by supplying her with a gown, a coach, and coachmen.

Perrault's version ends with an explicit moral—grace (defined as goodness and selflessness) is priceless and will win a man's heart; but "if you wish to shine and gad about" you will get no help from godparents and "your life will never have great events" (Tatar, 2002, p. 43). In other words, women will be rewarded for selfless beauty (like Cinderella, whose beauty was hidden under cinders and ashes), but not for narcissistic striving. If you submit patiently to your lot in life, someone with power will single you out and come to your aid. Your true qualities will be recognised, and you will have earned the right to shine—to exhibit your beauty. Eventually you will gain everything you have dreamed of, by marrying a rich and powerful man.

The Grimm brothers recorded a different version of "Cinderella" in Germany in 1812, roughly a century after Perrault. There is no fairy godmother in their story, and their Cinderella takes more action on her own behalf—repeatedly asking to go to the ball. When her stepmother refuses, she appeals to her dead mother who, while dying, had promised to aid her if she was good.

The two tales also differ on the issue of revenge. Perrault's Cinderella is remarkably free of any desire for revenge. After winning the prince's love, she invites her stepsisters to live in the palace, helps them find noble husbands, and they all marry on the same day. However, the Grimms' tale ends with violent retribution. First Cinderella's stepsisters mutilate their feet at their mother's urging in a futile attempt to win the prince; then they are blinded by birds at her wedding. Earlier in the Grimms' story, Cinderella's dead mother sent all the birds in the sky to aid her; now it is birds that take revenge. Note that this cruel punishment is not attributed to Cinderella; we are left to assume that it is her dead mother's doing, or divine retribution. Although the Grimm brothers do not include an explicit moral like Perrault, their message is even starker: goodness is rewarded, but selfish striving is severely punished. (In other versions of "Cinderella", the stepmother is also punished; in one Chinese variant called "Lin Lan", after the evil stepmother and her ugly stepdaughter kill the heroine, she returns to life and they both die (Tatar, 1999).)

Strikingly, except for his decision to marry the woman who becomes her stepmother, Cinderella's father plays little or no role in either version. He does nothing to prevent his daughter's mistreatment. What are we to make of this? The most likely explanation seems to be that this is a tale about rivalry for the father's affection, disguised by elimination of any reference to the father and by focusing instead on rivalry for the prince. The story of "Cinderella" makes sense as the fantasy resolution of a young girl's oedipal longings—if she endures feeling and being powerless in relationship to her mother and older sisters, and waits until she comes of age, she will eventually outshine them and win the man of her dreams. The heroine's selflessness and passivity can be understood as a defensive disavowal of her forbidden wishes, with all her rivalrous feelings projected onto others.

There is strong evidence for the oedipal origins of "Cinderella". Academics who study fairy tales classify the numerous versions of this story into two distinct categories (Tatar, 1999). Although most of us are only familiar with versions that centre on Cinderella's mistreatment by spiteful women, there are many examples of the other category— exemplified by tales like "Donkeyskin" (also recorded by Perrault). The heroine of these tales runs away from home and hides her beauty by wearing a hideous animal skin, after her widowed father insists on taking her as his wife. Often the heroine is a princess, whose dying mother extracted a pledge from her husband, the king, that he would only remarry a woman more charming and attractive than she, or a woman whose finger fits her wedding band. Typically the princess in hiding works as a scullery maid under the harsh supervision of an older woman, and receives magical help from a second older woman. Like Cinderella, she ends up winning the heart of the prince when he sees her dressed in an extraordinary gown. She is identified by a ring, which fits her slender finger, instead of a glass slipper (Tatar, 2002).

Although oedipal issues are overt in "Donkeyskin", the young girl's wishes are explicitly disavowed, with all the responsibility for them attributed to her father and to the promise her mother extracted from him. The heroine flees from her father's interest, relinquishing everything she is entitled to as the king's daughter, and would be entitled to as his wife. Here too, the heroine is rewarded for her selfless behaviour—with marriage to a prince, and reconciliation with her father.

Before exploring the implications of the enduring appeal of "Cinderella", I would like to turn to "Snow White", another iconic tale with hundreds of variants. Two of these variants are widely known today: the Grimm brothers' version, first published in 1812, and the version depicted in the 1937 Disney film. I will refer to aspects of both which highlight how Snow White is portrayed.

Although Cinderella's beauty is emphasised as both the source of her mistreatment and the key to the prince's heart, an even greater emphasis is placed on the significance of beauty in "Snow White". The Grimms' version begins with Snow White's mother musing on her wish for a child as beautiful as the scene she observes out her window: white as snow, red as blood, and black as the wood of the window frame. Snow White's stepmother is obsessed with being "the fairest one of all" (p. 83), and will stop at nothing to prevent Snow White from surpassing her (Tatar, 1999). She is depicted as prizing beauty above all else, while virtually the only thing we know about Snow White's mother and about the prince is the value they also place on beauty. The prince is love struck when he sees Snow White in her glass coffin. He tells the dwarfs "I can't live without seeing (her)", evidently needing nothing more than her inert beauty to "honor and cherish her" (Tatar, 1999, p. 89).

In essence, this is the story of an older woman determined to destroy a young rival. She drives her from the only home she knows, and makes multiple attempts on her life. Snow White is sheltered and rescued by the dwarfs, and later revived by the prince; in contrast to "Cinderella", there is no good maternal figure to aid her. In fact, Snow White is vulnerable to the Queen in disguise because she wishes to see the old peddler woman as good; she seems oblivious to the risk she is taking by trusting her. Although the evil Queen is identified as Snow White's stepmother, it is noteworthy that in the initial version recorded by the Grimm brothers, she was Snow White's own mother (Tatar, 2002).

"Snow White" appears to be another tale with disguised oedipal origins, in which a woman panics over being surpassed by the growing beauty of her daughter as her own beauty wanes. While Snow White's father is absent without explanation, the huntsman who is unable to bring himself to follow the Queen's order to kill Snow White may be a father surrogate, caught between his wife and his daughter. The absent father may also be represented symbolically by the mirror the Queen consults as the absolute arbiter of attractiveness (Gilbert & Gubar, 1979).

Oedipal aspects are in fact explicit in some earlier versions of "Snow White", in which the older woman's envy and hatred originates in her fear of the young girl as a rival for her husband's affection (Bettelheim, 1977; Tatar, 1999). One of the earliest known versions, "The Young Slave" recorded in Italy in 1634, ends with the heroine's uncle turning his wife out of the house when he eventually becomes aware of her cruel mistreatment of his niece (Tatar, 1999). However like the father in "Cinderella", explicit references to oedipal rivalry have been eliminated from the versions of "Snow White" we know best, and explicitly oedipal variants of both tales have fallen out of favour (Tatar, 1999).

As in "Cinderella", Snow White's rivalry with her stepmother is disavowed and entirely projected onto the evil Queen, while Snow White is depicted as innocent, naive, and good-hearted. In the Grimms' version she is only seven, however many elements make it clear that "Snow White" is the story of a young girl coming of age: Snow White is described as "growing up and becoming more and more beautiful" (Tatar, 1999, p. 83), so that her beauty surpasses the queen's and wins the heart of the prince; she assumes the role of an adult woman by keeping house for the dwarfs; and she marries by the end of the story. It is also clear that Snow White is interested in her own appearance, since she is tempted enough by the corset laces and the comb the disguised Queen offers her to ignore the dwarfs' repeated warning to be wary of her stepmother and not to let anyone in the house. As Bettelheim noted, "this suggests how close the stepmother's temptations are to Snow White's inner desires" (Bettelheim, 1977, p. 211). However, even when it comes to these innocuous wishes, Snow White is depicted as reacting to temptation instead of being the agent of her own desires. Unlike Cinderella, who delights in her beautiful gowns, Snow White plays no role in the dwarfs' decision to display her body in a glass coffin.

Snow White is in a completely passive and reactive position throughout this story. She is attacked by the Queen, who subsequently tempts her with feminine wares, and she is asleep in a coffin when the prince falls in love with her. There is a striking disavowal of Snow White's romantic longings, let alone her rivalrous wishes. In the Grimms' version, as soon as Snow White awakens the prince tells her, "I love you more than anything else on earth. Come with me to my father's castle. You shall be my bride." The prince is described as being "overjoyed", but all that is said of Snow White is that she "had tender feelings for him and she departed with him" (Tatar, 1999, p. 89). Since Snow White revives when the prince's servants jostle her coffin, Snow White and the prince appear to be accidental beneficiaries, rather than agents, of their good fortune.

However, a century later, the heroine of the 1937 Disney film is portrayed as being far less passive and Snow White's romantic yearnings are made explicit. When the film begins, it is evident that Snow White has already endured mistreatment since she is cleaning the castle dressed in patched clothing. She makes a wish that a prince will come and find her. Her wish is granted and it is love at first sight, but Snow White is frightened and runs away. Later Snow White signals her interest in stepping into the role of an adult woman by acting like a bossy mother with the dwarfs. She also sings of her yearning in "Some Day My Prince Will Come". Bettelheim (1977) and others (Macquisten & Pickford, 1942) have suggested that Snow White's biting into the poisoned red apple symbolises her yearning for forbidden knowledge and sexual maturity. This is made explicit in the film when the disguised Queen offers Snow White a magic wishing apple: "One bite and all your dreams will come true—there must be someone your little heart desires." Although Snow White's acknowledgment of her desires places her in danger, it also brings her what she longs for. In addition, the Queen selects a poison named "sleeping death" and we are told that the victim can only be revived by love's first kiss, so that Snow White's romantic longings are depicted as both the source of her danger and the cure.

We empathise with Snow White and experience her as the Queen's innocent victim, since she is free of any rivalrous wishes or hostility. After everything she has endured, Snow White's wishes seem all the more justified (as do Cinderella's). All the rivalry is attributed to the Queen, and it is strongly condemned and punished in most versions of this story, often with a gruesome death. In the Grimms' tale the evil stepmother is made to dance in red-hot iron shoes at Snow White's wedding until she dies. Although this punishment is not attributed to Snow White, it seems to be more than a coincidence that it occurs at the moment of her triumph—her wedding, just as Cinderella's stepsisters were also punished at her wedding.

In summary, both "Cinderella" and "Snow White" depict a power-less young girl coming of age, overcoming adversity and winning the love of a prince. Both tales emphasise the heroine's kind temperament and innocent heart. The heroine appears to triumph by virtue of her inner and outer beauty, and the aid she receives is depicted as something she has earned or deserves as a goodhearted, innocent, and uncomplaining victim. Her patient endurance is rewarded, in contrast to the selfish strivings of her rivals. Both tales warn against the dangers of temptation—Cinderella must exercise self-restraint and leave the ball before midnight, while Snow White places herself in great danger when she succumbs to her desire for feminine wares and the poisoned apple. As a further warning, in many versions selfish behavior is severely punished.

Both tales present disguised versions of the oedipal situation. Bettelheim (1977) suggested that fairy tales speak to children's anxieties about their oedipal strivings, and help children cope with their fears. He noted that many tales mirror girls' oedipal fantasies by splitting the mother into two figures: the pre-oedipal good mother and the evil oedipal stepmother. "For the oedipal girl, belief and trust in the goodness of the pre-oedipal mother, and deep loyalty to her, tend to reduce the guilt about what the girl wishes would happen to the (step) mother who stands in her way" (Bettelheim, 1977, p. 114). This coupled with the fact that the heroine wins the prince, not the father, reduces the girl's fear of losing her mother's love. As Bettelheim noted, guilt about sexual and aggressive feelings and oedipal longings frequently leaves children feeling dirty and worthless, so that every child can identify with Cinderella, who is relegated to sit among the ashes (p. 243). For the young girl who feels she deserves to be degraded because of her secret wishes and angry feelings, the notion of being treated so badly helps to justify her feelings and absolve her guilt.

Bettelheim suggested that fairy tales like "Cinderella" and "Snow White" speak to the young girl's conscious and unconscious guilt, and the fact that they end with the protagonist's triumph reassures the girl that the same thing will happen for her. He felt that these tales provide a hopeful message that the girl will get what she desires when the time is right; that she will receive help and support from adults who will recognise how special she is, and will endorse her desires when she comes of age.

Yet it seems to me that these fairy tales offer a very mixed message. Although Cinderella's period of servitude and Snow White's sleep can be understood as marking the time the young girl needs to wait until she comes of age, they also convey that passive endurance and self-lessness will be rewarded, but not active striving. The vilification of active striving as selfish and the severe punishment Cinderella's step-sisters and Snow White's stepmother receive may be a projection of the young girl's disavowed guilt, but they reinforce the belief that competi-tive wishes and rivalrous strivings deserve to be punished. In addition, although winning the love of a powerful man can be understood as the fulfillment of the young girl's oedipal longings, the heroine's depend-ing on the prince for her rescue conveys the message that the only way for a woman to achieve power is through a man.

As many feminists have pointed out, these fairy tales reinforce problematic gender stereotypes with their emphasis on beauty, the virtues of passive endurance and selflessness, and the love of a powerful man as the solution to powerlessness (Gilbert & Gubar, 1979). They embody a stereotyped view of women that has been passed down and internalised for generations. Andrea Dworkin captured this in 1974:

> We have not formed that ancient world (of fairy tales)—it has formed us. We ingested it as children whole, had its values and consciousness imprinted on our minds as cultural absolutes long before we were in fact men and women. We have taken the fairy tales of childhood with us into maturity, chewed but still lying in the stomach, as real identity. Between Snow-white and her heroic prince, our two great fictions, we never did have much of a chance. At some point the Great Divide took place: they (the boys) dreamed of mounting the Great Steed and buying Snow-white from the dwarfs; we (the girls) aspired to become that object of every necrophiliac's lust—the innocent, *victimised* Sleeping Beauty, beauteous lump of ultimate, sleeping good. Despite ourselves, sometimes unknowing, sometimes knowing, unwilling, unable to do otherwise, we act out the roles we were taught. (Dworkin, 1974, pp. 32–33)

Feminists have tended to reject fairy tales like "Cinderella" and "Snow White" as products of a patriarchal culture, and to attribute their stereotypes to men's self-interest in dominating women, in order to protect their power. They have also proposed reality-based explanations for these tales, including the long history of women's economic dependence on men and the high incidence of death in childbirth, which left many children dependent on stepmothers in the past (Gilbert & Gubar, 1979).

However, these explanations do little to explain the enduring appeal of fairy tales, particularly in the present day. Parents are still telling little girls the stories of "Cinderella" and "Snow White", and variants of these tales continue to be made into movies. Two major Hollywood films about Snow White were released in 2012: *Mirror, Mirror*, and *Snow White and the Huntsman*. I will comment on these films later in this paper; for now I only want to note that both of them change a key aspect of the story—neither film depicts a passive Snow White being rescued by the prince.

Although this seems like a major departure, a close reading of the tales recorded by Perrault and the Grimm brothers shows that they are primarily concerned with the relationship between the female protagonists. Despite their oedipal origins, there is relatively little focus on romance and virtually no attention paid to the heroine's relationship with the prince. The Disney studio introduced Snow White's romantic longing, and ended their films with the heroine going off into the sunset with her prince. Although we think of fairy tales as ending with "and they lived happily ever after", the Perrault and Grimm versions of these tales actually end by focusing on what happens to the heroine's female rivals. Prior to his moral homily, the last paragraph of Perrault's tale focuses on Cinderella's reconciliation with her stepsisters (Tatar, 2002), while the Grimm brothers end both "Cinderella" and "Snow White" with the punishment their persecutors receive. What sense can we make of these endings?

Contemporary psychoanalytic thinking offers us a way of understanding the enduring appeal of these stories, and their emphasis on the mistreatment of a young girl by her mother or mother-substitute. Psychoanalytic developmental theory has enlarged our understanding of the dilemma that the young girl faces in attempting to separate from her mother and achieve autonomy, without relinquishing her tie to the mother she depends on. As many have noted, the fact that the girl's mother is both her primary source of nurturing and her same-sex parent complicate the girl's strivings to individuate and her subsequent oedipal rivalry (Dinnerstein, 1976; Hoffman, 1999; Kulish & Holtzman, 2008; Tyson, 1982, 1989).

As the Tysons (1990) put it, "Caught in the dilemma of struggling for autonomy while still in a state of dependence, the little girl often feels hostile and angry toward her mother" (P. Tyson & R. L. Tyson, 1990, p. 260). Envy is a universal characteristic of children, and young girls desire and envy all that their mother has which they do not. The young girl's envious wishes and her desire for autonomy create anxiety about threatening her relationship with her mother, and lead to fears of retaliation. Her hostile and destructive fantasies of taking mother's power for herself are projected onto her mother, heightening her fears of retaliation. Subsequent competitive feelings and oedipal rivalry further heighten these fears, which are reactivated in adolescence and at various points in the lifecycle. Yet girls simultaneously seek to retain their ties to their mothers, and each girl has an ongoing need to identify with her mother in order to consolidate her own identity as a woman (Tyson, 1982, 1989).

Contemporary analysts have suggested that girls' fears of endangering their relationship with their mothers frequently result in a need to disguise or repress their aggressive feelings and rivalrous wishes. Inhibition of a subjective sense of themselves as aggressive agents often becomes a pervasive defense (Hoffman, 1999; Kulish & Holtzman, 2008). As Dianne Elise put it: "Not only can a girl's anger get in the way of her relationship with her mother, her relationship with her mother … can get in the way of her anger" (Elise, 1997, p. 512).

We can see the expression of these conflicts, dilemmas, and habitual defences in "Cinderella" and "Snow White". Anxiety about separating from and competing with her primary source of nurturance may explain the heroine's passivity, despite the fact that her mother is supposedly dead. All of her envy, rivalry, and hostility are projected onto an evil woman, who is neither daughter nor mother. Her wish to take her mother's power for herself is projected onto her rivals, who are portrayed as robbing her of her rightful place. The gruesome punishments endured by Cinderella's stepsisters and Snow White's stepmother are a simultaneous gratification of the girl's hostile wishes and a reassuring rejection of aggression—a statement that hostile behaviour will be punished. The girl's wish to continue to depend on her mother is gratified by her fairy godmother, or expressed in relationship to her dead mother. Rather than actively opposing her mother, Cinderella is depicted as wanting only what her fairy godmother or dead mother provides for her. Her reconciliation with her stepsisters in Perrault's tale can be understood as representing the young girl's wish for an oedipal resolution which allows her to win a man's love without having to sacrifice her relationship with her mother or sisters.

In her 1964 paper on "Feminine guilt and the Oedipus complex", Janine Chasseguet-Smirgel proposed a psychological origin of the enduring appeal of witches and fairies:

> I believe that a child, whether male or female, even with the best and kindest of mothers, will maintain a terrifying maternal image in his unconscious, the result of projected hostility deriving from his own impotence … This powerful image, symbolic of all that is bad, does not exclude an omnipotent, protective imago, varying according to the mother's real characteristics. However the child's primary powerlessness … and the inevitable frustrations of training are such that the imago of the good, omnipotent mother

never covers over that of the terrifying, omnipotent, bad mother.
(Chasseguet-Smirgel, 1964, p. 107)

Chasseguet-Smirgel (1964) and others (Benjamin, 1986; Bernstein, 1993; Kulish & Holtzman, 2008; Reich, 1940) have also noted that the powerlessness the young girl feels in relationship to her mother may be perpetuated in her turning first to her father and later to other men as objects of dependent attachment, to help her separate from mother. This may help to explain why the heroine's powerlessness is resolved through the power of a man in many fairy tales.

In other words, I am suggesting that the emphasis on passivity and dependence, and the portrayal of active striving as selfish in both "Cinderella" and "Snow White" is a reflection of developmental issues that all young girls and their mothers struggle with: intense ambivalence about the young girl's autonomous strivings and oedipal rivalry, and fears about whether their relationship can survive the girl's age-appropriate envious and aggressive feelings. The inevitability of mother's ageing as the young girl comes of age lends a basis in reality to the Queen's fears of being surpassed by Snow White, especially if the young girl's coming of age occurs as her mother is entering menopause. In addition, every mother needs to come to terms with negative feelings towards her children, including envious feelings about being surpassed.

At the beginning of this paper, I suggested that fairy tales both reflect our beliefs and perpetuate them. "Cinderella" and "Snow White" alert us to issues that our female patients of all ages are likely to struggle with. Our clinical literature and our practices are full of examples of women with conflicts about asserting themselves and fears of expressing anger. Many adult women consciously or unconsciously equate asserting themselves with being selfish and unlikable. While there is a tendency to see this as a product of externally imposed repressive cultural attitudes, the roots run deeper. These beliefs originate unconsciously in the dilemma girls experience in negotiating their relationships with their mothers.

Many women are anxious about retribution for active strivings, which they consciously or unconsciously fear that their mothers would reject as a challenge to their authority—whether their mothers are living or dead. Unconsciously, many women believe that the only way they can retain their mother's approval and love is to remain dependent, a carbon copy or a narcissistic extension who denies any wish to separate, compete, or surpass. These fears surface in a variety of relationships in their every day lives, and often become a prominent part of the maternal transference. They manifest defensively in deferential behaviour and the inhibition of assertion and aggression, and in a wish to experience the analyst as an idealised fairy godmother. They may also manifest in anxiety that the analyst will not be interested in hearing about their accomplishments and success, and will only respond positively to their problems, or that their independent thinking will not be tolerated, let alone valued. Women may fear that their female analysts will be threatened by their looks, their romantic success, and/or their fertility.

Many women idealise selflessness, often with the idea that it will eventually be rewarded, or a belief that it is the only route to being loved. Some women fear that assertion and success mean being alone, losing not only mother's love but also any chance of happiness with a partner. They have difficulty enjoying their own industriousness and success, fearing that it makes them unlikable, and will deprive them of being cared for or taken care of. These fears may be experienced in relationship to men, who are perceived as wanting to be in charge and wanting everything their way, just as mother did. Women who have internalised a fairy tale definition of "happily ever after" believe that their happiness will come from being loved by and dependent on a powerful man. If the stepmother in "Cinderella" and "Snow White" is the repository of all the traits that women disavow as unlovable, then the absence of the father in these tales may reflect the unconscious assumption that only selfless women can hope to attract and retain a man's love, while powerful women end up alone.

Fears that independent thought, active striving, and success will result in feeling isolated or alone are of course heightened in women whose mothers had significant difficulty tolerating their wishes for autonomy. Some of our patients had mothers who were threatened by their independence and success; many had mothers who had difficulty tolerating their anger. For women struggling with any of these issues, tracing the origin of their conflicts, fears, and symptoms back to their relationships with their mothers is essential. When one of my patients recently said, "I wish I could say what I want without feeling isolated as a result", she was speaking about her relationship with both her mother and her husband at that moment. It has been helpful for her to recognise that her fear that her husband will get angry if she expresses her point of view originates in her relationship with her mother.

Perrault recorded his fairy tales 300 years ago, the Grimm Brothers recorded theirs 200 years ago, and the Disney studio's *Snow White and the Seven Dwarfs* was made three-quarters of a century ago. In recent years, there has been a great deal of emphasis on raising strong girls, and more widespread acceptance of assertion in girls and women. The passive selflessness of Cinderella and Snow White is no longer a consciously held cultural ideal. If fairy tales evolve over time, how do modern day versions deal with these issues? I'd like to conclude by taking a look at four films about fairy tales released in 2012. There were three films about Snow White; notably, all of them depict her as a brave and resourceful heroine who learns to fight her own battles with the help of male mentors, and she ultimately confronts and defeats the Queen in two of the three.

Mirror, Mirror is a comic take on "Snow White", which makes the oedipal underpinnings of the fairy tale explicit, albeit in reversal. Although the Prince is clearly interested in Snow White, the greedy Queen wants his fortune and is determined to marry him. The prince is an inept laughingstock who is incapable of taking care of himself, let alone rescuing Snow White. Snow White rescues the hapless prince repeatedly, and ultimately frees both the prince and her father from the evil Queen's black magic. The message of the tale has been altered significantly: goodness will triumph if you are strong and resourceful, but not if you are weak and vulnerable. While Snow White is neither passive nor dependent, there is an interesting twist: she needs to be stronger than the prince and her father in order to save them all.

The heroine of *Snow White and the Huntsman* is even more active and resourceful. She leads an army to take back the kingdom from the evil Queen, eventually killing the Queen in one to one combat. The huntsman is portrayed as mentor, protector, and romantic interest; he turns against the Queen and chooses to help Snow White. While several men who are enamoured of her aid Snow White, she becomes powerful in her own right and is depicted as following her destiny as her people's saviour. Instead of marrying at the end of the film, she is crowned Queen of her own kingdom.

Although they differ in many ways, both films alter the story we are familiar with by giving us a Queen whose villainy devastates the entire kingdom and harms everyone in it. It is as if it is necessary for Snow White to save others as well as herself in order to justify her activity and resourcefulness. (This is also the case in *Ever After*, a 1998 comic update of "Cinderella" with a resourceful, altruistic heroine who takes action to save a wronged servant, and ends up rescuing the hapless prince as well as herself.)

In *Blancanieves*, a 2012 silent Spanish film also based on "Snow White", the evil stepmother is a nurse who isolates and imprisons the young girl's paralysed father, who was once a famous bullfighter, then kills him and attempts to murder the heroine when she realises that they have been spending time together behind her back. This Snow White is an innocent, good-hearted, and resourceful heroine, who (after being rescued and sheltered by dwarfs) achieves success and the love of the crowd when she unconsciously follows in her father's footsteps. Yet she pays an enormous price when her prowess and fame lead to envious murderous attacks. She falls into a coma after taking a bite of her stepmother's poisoned apple and ends up as a circus freak on display whom men line up to kiss, with a tear rolling down her cheek. In this film, Snow White's assertive triumph ends in tragedy, and the men who love her are powerless to save her.

Another major Hollywood film about fairy tales was released in 2012. *Brave* is a brand new tale, with a different take on a young girl coming of age. The story centres on the harm the heroine does to her mother when she asserts her autonomy. Merida is a resourceful and independent princess who is used to doing as she pleases; she is neither passive, nor patient, nor selfless. She is appalled and angry when her parents insist it is time for her to marry the suitor who wins a competition for her hand. She impulsively buys and uses a magic potion in an attempt to change her mother's mind; this ends up placing her mother in grave danger. While much of the film concerns Merida's attempts to save her mother, she has difficulty accepting responsibility for what she has done and tries to blame the witch who sold her the potion. The film makes it clear that this problem lies between Merida and her mother, and that nothing can be solved by placing the blame elsewhere.

Here is a young girl who opposes her mother and asserts herself unwisely but ultimately ends up closer to her mother, in a relationship of love and mutual respect. By the end of the film, we see both Merida and her mother as strong. The contrast with "Cinderella" and "Snow White" is striking. *Brave* gives us a portrait of a mother and daughter struggling mightily with the daughter's insistence on choosing her own path, without either of them demonised as the source of all the aggression or characterised as an innocent and selfless victim. We get a partial picture of coming of age, in which the young girl's strivings to assert herself and the powerful struggles between mother and daughter are acknowledged. But it is notable that the men in this film are depicted as weak (like the prince in *Mirror, Mirror*, and the dwarfs and the heroine's father in *Blancanieves*), and there is a complete disavowal of Merida's romantic wishes, and of any rivalry with her mother as a woman.

That rivalry is either projected or disavowed in all these films, just as it was in earlier versions of "Cinderella" and "Snow White". It appears that girls' wishes for autonomy have become more acceptable to us, so that the heroines of our contemporary fairy tales can be depicted as resourceful and independent. However their feminine wishes, including the wish to be beautiful, their competitive feelings towards their mothers, and their oedipal longings still remain too unacceptable to be acknowledged, so they need to be projected or disavowed. All the destructive greed and envy, rivalrous feelings, and preoccupation with beauty are still projected onto an evil older woman, where they become the object of our fascination and condemnation, since these are attributes which we also long to disavow.

Both "Cinderella" and "Snow White" end when the young girl comes of age and marries. What happens to all of the girl's projected and disavowed wishes feelings, and fears once she becomes a married woman herself? Anne Sexton depicts this transformation in her 1971 poem "Snow White and the Seven Dwarfs", in her simple and chilling description of Snow White at her wedding, while the wicked queen dances to her death in red-hot iron shoes: "Meanwhile Snow White held court, rolling her china-blue doll eyes open and shut and sometimes referring to her mirror as women do" (Tatar, 1999, p. 100). It seems to me that we return to these fairy tales over and over again, telling them in old and new versions, because they address the complex wishes and fears stirred up in mothers and daughters, as we vicariously anticipate the daughter's coming of age and experience our own longing for an illusory, unobtainable "happily ever after".

Acknowledgement

An earlier version of this paper was presented at a conference on "Images of Women" co-sponsored by the Seattle Psychoanalytic Society and Institute and the Committee on Women and Psychoanalysis of the

International Psychoanalytical Assocation in Seattle, WA on 6 October 2012.

References

Benjamin, J. (1986). The alienation of desire: women's masochism and ideal love. In: J. L. Alpert (Ed.), *Psychoanalysis and Women: Contemporary Reappraisals* (pp. 113–138). Hillsdale, NJ: The Analytic Press.

Bettelheim, B. (1977). *The Uses of Enchantment: The Meaning and Importance of Fairy Tales*. New York: Alfred A. Knopf.

Bernstein, D. (1993). *Female Identity Conflict in Cinical Practice*. Northvale, NJ: Jason Aronson.

Breen, D. (Ed.). (1993). *The Gender Conundrum: Contemporary Psychoanalytic Perspectives on Femininity and Masculinity*. London: Routledge.

Chasseguet-Smirgel, J. (1964). Feminine guilt and the Oedipus complex. In: C. Zanardi (Ed.), *Essential Papers on the Psychology of Women* (pp. 88–131). New York: New York University Press, 1990.

Dinnerstein, D. (1976). *The Mermaid and the Minotaur*. New York: Harper & Row.

Dworkin, A. (1974). *Woman-Hating: A Radical Look at Sexuality*. New York: Penguin Books.

Elise, D. (1997). Primary femininity, bisexuality, and the female ego ideal. *Psychoanalytic Quarterly, 66*: 489–517.

Elise, D. (2008). Sex and shame: the inhibition of female desires. *Journal of the American Psychoanalytic Association, 56*: 73–98.

Gilbert, S. M., & Gubar, S. (1979). *The Madwoman in the Attic*. New Haven, CT: Yale University Press.

Hoffman, L. (1999). Passion in girls and women: toward a bridge between critical relational theory of gender and modern conflict theory. *Journal of the American Psychoanalytic Association, 47*: 1145–68.

Kulish, N., & Holtzman, D. (2008). *A Story of Her Own—The Female Oedipus Complex Reexamined and Renamed*. Lanham, MD: Jason Aronson.

Macquisten, A. S., & Pickford, R. W. (1942). Psychological aspects of the fantasy of Snow White and the Seven Dwarfs. *Psychoanalytic Review, 29*: 233–252.

Reich, A. (1940). A contribution to the psychoanalysis of extreme submissiveness in women. *Psychoanalytic Quarterly, 9*: 470–480.

Sexton, A. (1971). "Snow White and the Seven Dwarfs". In: M. Tatar, (Ed.), *The Classic Fairy Tales* (pp. 96–100). New York: W. W. Norton & Company, 1999.

Snow White and the Seven Dwarfs (1937). Walt Disney Movies DVDb.

Tatar, M. (Ed.). (1999). *The Classic Fairy Tales*. New York: W. W. Norton & Company.

Tatar, M. (Ed.). (2002). *The Annotated Classic Fairy Tales*. New York: W. W. Norton & Company.

Tatar, M. (2012). Snow White: beauty is power, *New Yorker* blog, June 8. Available at www.newyorker.com/online/blogs/books/2012/06/snow-white-and-the-huntsman-and-fairy-tales.html, accessed 6 October 2013.

Tyson, P. (1982). A developmental line of gender identity, gender role, and choice of love object. *Journal of the American Psychoanalytic Association*, *30*: 61–86.

Tyson, P. (1989). Infantile sexuality, gender identity, and obstacles to oedipal progression. *Journal of the American Psychoanalytic Association*, *37*: 1051–1069.

Tyson, P., & Tyson, R. L. (1990). *Psychonalytic Theories of Development: An Integration*. New Haven, CT: Yale University Press.

CHAPTER TWENTY

Cultural altruism and masochism in women in the East

Jhuma Basak

In this chapter I examine the sociocultural and psychological construct of self-sacrifice, leading to possible masochism in the women of two Eastern societies, India and Japan. Before doing so I will mention the emotional experience of shame which may often lead to unconsciously inflicting moral pain on the self by the mechanism of hiding. This dual aspect of what is visible and what is hidden and invisible is active in shame as well as in masochism. Japan had been on a pioneering journey in its exploration of its "shame culture" especially in women (Benedict, 1946/1967; Kitayama, 1985). I also indicate the treatment of women's identity as mothers and caregivers in the two societies and how it affects them psychologically by generating and nurturing self-sacrificial qualities in them. I will illustrate the self-sacrificial qualities of a "good mother"/care-giver, or "altruistic" qualities, often leading to the development of moral masochistic feelings, in a clinical vignette of a patient who experienced depressive guilt, which may often hinder creative explorations in a woman and clinically impact on the emotional wellbeing of women in some Eastern societies.

255

Interface of culture and psychoanalysis

In 2005, Lansky wrote that it was only in the last thirty years that shame had gradually become a major theme of exploration in psychoanalytic literature. Okano (1994) suggested a cultural conspiracy to avoid discussing shame in psychoanalytic theory, although exceptions were Piers and Singer (1953) and cultural anthropological research on the "shame culture" in Japan had led to works such as Ruth Benedict's (1946/1967), *The Chrysanthemum and the Sword*. However, after Kohut's (1971) influential work, *The Analysis of the Self*, considerable attention was given to the study of shame in such cultures.

Shame is an affect that the individual wishes to remain hidden, as well as to hide the subject content that induces the shame. There is also the danger of its likely emergence and the affect rising into consciousness. We experience shame when we are exposed to ourselves or others as unlovable, inferior, or deficient. Shame leads to conflicts with moral standards, ideals, role expectations and the individual fears rejection and disgrace, whereas guilt is concerned with transgression and prohibition and indicates subsequent retaliatory punishment. Shame is always about a flaw or a lack in the self, guilt is about harming the other.

Freud (1919e) initially saw masochism in women as originating from sadism which had been turned around upon the self. In 1924, he described three types of masochism, feminine, erotogenic and moral masochism, with one of the main purposes of moral masochism to gain glory and love from others. In 1933, Freud further suggested that social proscriptions for suppression of aggression in women ignited a feminine tendency towards masochistic impulses.

Later women analysts such as Karen Horney, Nancy Chodorow and Juliet Mitchell challenged the construction of the Oedipus complex as a culturally political construction of patriarchy, propagated by classical Freudian theory. Before them, women's pre-oedipal attachment was yet to find its full significance in the psychoanalytic theoretical discourse and its inclusion the complexity of female sexuality came more into light. Suddenly a return to sexuality was recognised, and a reexamination of femininity and female sexuality/love was called for. It is interesting to note that in 1921 Girindrasekhar Bose, the founder of psychoanalysis in India, was exploring pre-oedipal attachments between mother and child in his book on the concept of repression. In Japan three psychoanalytic theoretical developments, Heisaku Kosawa's Ajase complex, Takeo Doi's concept of amae and Osamu Kitayama's (1985) concept of the "don't look" prohibition, focused on the mother as the locus of psychoanalytic construction rather than the father, unlike the Western model. Kosawa and Bose are said to have gifted Freud with their works on pre-oedipal attachment, although these did not become known to the rest of the world until much later.

By offering women a secondary position of sexuality (through the process of denial of their primary pre-oedipal attachment to the mother), patriarchy simultaneously offered women a culturally depressive position which was a consequence of a fundamental disavowal of a woman's primary self. This female depressive position was reinforced by family and culture, especially in the East. The negation of a fundamental core of their being, their self (including sexuality), could bring significant emotional harm. In this way, a socioculturally driven and sanctioned depressive position could be constructed for women, particularly in the East. The glorification of motherhood in Eastern societies, and the strong distinction between the sexual object and the love object added to the complexity of their position in society. Subsequently, any claim of their sexuality to be pleasure-driven and not *utility driven* (such as motherhood and reproduction), would bring a deep sense of excessive guilt. The burden of this guilt could leave her with an intense amount of ambivalence towards her own body/sexuality/self as well as motherhood. This ambivalence in turn may be projected into other women (for example, jealousy between mother-in-law and daughter-in-law, or between mother and daughter). This may indirectly encourage women towards a reinforced masochistic position as their only form of *glory or pleasure sanctioned* by family and society which is free of guilt—a form of glorious pleasure which was not possible to attain directly but is sought indirectly through masochism.

Helene Deutsch (1930) suggested that masochism was rooted in the psychobiological experiences of women's menses, defloration, childbirth, and child care. Added to that, sociocultural expectations and familial sacrificial norms re-emphasised a societally depressive position for women, making it more difficult for her to break free of the cycle of masochism, while in 1937 Horney expressed the view that masochism found much deeper satisfaction by losing the self in something greater—dissolving the individual in its self-sacrificial offerings to life and civilisation.

One of the chief reasons for the development of a masochistic personality may be the childhood traumatic loss of a loved object, and a life-long yearning for that lost love which may often turn into unconscious self-reproaches, introjecting the object as persecutory. However, in an Eastern cultural context, as in India, nurturing of masochism in women is often related to an altruistic level in its relation with self-sacrifice towards others in the family, and society at large. A virtuous quality such as "devotion" may become a pathological trait if extreme. When in therapy such individuals may often experience deep shame at their lifelong concealed private self being revealed—the shame of revealing their own desire for pleasure of any kind. Desires for self-satisfaction are encouraged by family, society, and culture to be unconsciously suppressed, and the outburst of these in therapy may often bring about deep shame in the person, subsequently rendering the self further unacceptable. Thus, they prefer to keep such desires hidden and yet internally suffer a conflict between their hidden private desires and glorified public self or duty. Therapeutic intervention has to be delicately timed and may be time consuming. In Mrs P.'s case below, the therapeutic rapport, external support from family and friends and other sublimatory processes within the patient helped her to travel a path of introspection about her life-time conflicts, and gradually develop a freer self.

Clinical vignette: patient's background

Mrs P., aged fifty-six years, was by profession a physics schoolteacher. Her father died of heart-attack when she was an infant and she hardly remembered him; her mother who was a teacher brought up the entire family of five children, Mrs P. being the youngest. Mrs P. had been married for over thirty years and was the mother of two grown up successful daughters.

Mrs P.'s life history told us about her growing up in a very disciplined and culturally oriented family where education was considered most important. After the death of her father, the family had a long period of financial difficulties but her mother tried not to let her children and their education be affected by it. Mrs P. had deep admiration for her mother who would teach in a school during the day, do the household chores, take care of her children, and at night sew clothes to sell to neighbours and school colleagues to earn extra money. Mrs P.'s values and principles were built on such lessons of her mother's sacrifice.

Over time, Mrs P. turned out to be even more admirable in her self-sacrifice for her own family after her marriage. She wanted to be a doctor but gave up her studies because her family could not afford it. After marriage she finished her Masters through correspondence course. Her days were spent looking after her child (the first daughter was born in the following year immediately after her marriage), doing household chores, and at night she would study for her correspondence course after her child and husband were asleep. Initially they lived in a one room apartment with hardly any space—but with her savings over years their status in society moved upwards till they finally bought a spacious flat in a smart locality. Eventually she found the school job where she had been teaching for seventeen years.

She was brought for therapy by her elder daughter (who was herself in analysis with a colleague of mine) with symptoms of constant crying and feeling unloved by her family, especially by her daughters. In the initial sessions she refused to talk at all since she believed there was nothing wrong with her and felt that if she was feeling unloved by her family, why should she talk to an "outsider" (i.e., the therapist) when she would rather talk to her family. But she found her daughters were impatient with her. They could not go on listening to her complaints repeatedly. As she gradually started to open up, she even mentioned that her elder daughter brought her for therapy so that she and her family could continue to disregard Mrs P.'s agony and lead their individual happy lives. Nobody cared for her pain.

Process and treatment

The therapeutic treatment started with three sessions a week, face-to-face gradually moving to the couch. She was in psychoanalytically oriented psychotherapy for two and a half years, and showed considerable improvement before she decided to discontinue (when she felt she could take good care of her own self, and felt happy with her life and self in equilibrium).

Excerpt from the thirty-sixth session (three months)

MRS P.:   I feel that all my sacrifices for my family have been futile.
ANALYST: What makes you feel like that?
MRS P.:   What do you mean by asking that? After all these months if you still have to ask me that question then what kind of

an analyst are you? Sometimes I think you are so stupid, so dumb! Don't you know, can't you see that my two daughters are completely selfish, that they only care about their career, their friends, their fun and parties ... For all these years I have cooked for them, learnt special dishes to cook for them, saved every penny possible so that they could have a comfortable life style and not suffer like me, sat every evening with them when they were in school to make them do their homework, make them study ... Their father did not do any of this! He only earned money, and came back home and watched TV! It was me who sacrificed my own joys to bring joy into their life. And now they have no time to listen to my pain—they send me to a professional therapist who is paid to listen to me! Of course all you care at the end of the day is the money that I pay you! You are such a beggar!

(I could feel a need in Mrs P. to provoke me, to belittle me—in a way projecting her own sense of feeling "small" for having to come for therapy in the first place and that, too, to someone much younger than her—to which I did not react, thereby indirectly letting her know that she could express anything that she felt like in the session, including negative feelings against me).

A: Perhaps you would like your daughters to make the same sacrifices for you as you once made for them.

MRS P.:   Isn't that expected from your own child? I did that for my mother, why will they not do for me? I remember in my childhood I used to come back home from school, while other children would go outside to play I would finish up the kitchen work, wash the dishes, so that when my mother came back home from school she would have less work to do. And my daughters? They just treat their home like a hotel! They leave their dishes in the sink as if their servant mother is there to wash their dirt!

A: I can understand how it upsets you to see your daughters like this when you had sacrificed so much for your mother and then again for your daughters ...

MRS P.:   So why shouldn't my children do that for me? Don't I deserve that? Have I not been a good mother to them to deserve these little self-sacrifices from them? (She was almost in tears … silence, and then I asked quietly).

A: What kind of self-sacrifices from your daughters would make you feel satisfied?

MRS P.:   At least that would make me feel that they care for me! What about not going out with their boyfriends and taking me out for dinner or a movie or accompany me for shopping?

(Here it seemed like an unconscious desire of Mrs P. to take that special position in her daughter's life that their boyfriends had in their lives, in a way to be more important in their lives than their boyfriends … Technically speaking, here she was not encouraged into fantasy regarding these desires in her as this was a psychoanalytically oriented psychotherapy rather than psychoanalysis four to five times a week on the couch).

A: But isn't it natural that at their age they would rather do all that with their friends or boyfriends than with their mother?

MRS P.:   But why? I never did that when I was their age. I was always so committed to my mother, concerned about her wishes. I have given them all the freedom, and now look at them how they abuse it!

A: Does it disturb you that your daughters seem to have more freedom than you did?

MRS P.:   (Raising her voice she said …) Not at all! They can do whatever they wish! Who am I to them? They can have all the fun in the world while I slave for them! That's what I did all my life, and see what it has got me now!

(I was left with questions—as it was obvious that motherhood alone had not been able to bring satisfaction, what else did she want, what might her hidden desires be which if life offered her would bring her satisfaction and happiness).

Countertransference

In the initial stage I often felt quite irritated with Mrs P.'s constant emphasis on being right and always perfect, as if she was a strict headmistress in session, with her the teacher and me the student. I felt like a child within the therapeutic set-up. I needed to reflect to free my ego from what felt like her over-powering superego. I was surprised to observe my fear of being disapproved by Mrs P. and could feel how her daughters might have felt with her persecutory gaze. She was extremely elegant, composed, cultured—a pinnacle of perfection. Once I could free myself of this persecutory fear, I often felt sad for Mrs P., identifying with her tremendous self sacrifice and devotion towards her family and children, and the denial of all her desires in order to be this highly glorified woman and mother. I was reminded of my own mother (who had also lost her father in her early childhood, her struggles growing up and later her self-sacrifices for the family). I also identified with Mrs P.'s indirect ways of controlling her daughters' freedom and independence by invoking guilt in them with her symptom of constant crying. One immediate result of therapy was to free her of her depressive symptom of constant crying and feeling unloved.

Excerpt from the 124th session (just under a year)

A: You seem to be very quiet today ...

MRS P.:   Yes ... I feel sad ... I wonder why I had to deny myself for so long ... It's true that all I did was for my family, and I have no regrets for that. But now when I am nearing sixty I feel there is hardly any time left for me to do all that I once wanted to do. My daughters have their own life now ... my family seems to be doing quite okay even if I don't cook everyday or keep the house spic and span like before ... (Sounding a little cheerful she continued) ... The other day I was quite amused to see that my elder daughter was dusting the rooms because she was expecting some of her colleagues to visit the house ... Maybe I should have left them on their own a long time back, then they probably would have taken more responsibility of the house ... I wonder where did I go wrong ...

A: You did what you believed to be right—that's all that we can do ...

MRS P.:   But at times I feel angry—angry with myself, angry with all of them. All of them are so bloody selfish, my husband, my daughters. All these years they never really cared what happened to me, to my wishes and desires.

(This is the moment that I recognised that Mrs P. conveyed the probability that she was internally ready to shift from her masochistic position and move towards claiming a proactive full life that would enrich her individually).

A: Perhaps you too did not find an opportunity to express that clearly.

MRS P.:   That does not mean that they will not understand! What is a family for then? What is the point of loving your family?

A: Did you care for your own wishes and desires before this?

(A long pause followed ... Mrs P. continued)

MRS P.:   You know what, now I feel jealous of my daughter's independence! Somewhere I know that I want them to include me in all their fun because I don't want to lose out any more on life. But I don't know where to find that now.

A: Is that what made you cry for so long?

MRS P.:   (Quiet ... Long pause—I let the pause grow)...

(I quietly ask ...)

A: What about your friends, your husband?

MRS P.:   (Gently answers) Yes, I have been thinking along those lines ... I guess its alright for me to want to be happy too! (She smiled) ... It feels a little strange with my husband because its been a long time since we did things together ... (short pause, continued laughing gently) You know, it feels strange but just now when I told you that I want to be happy, somewhere I felt scared inside—what if it goes away if I express it too much or even want it too much.

A: Why should it go away?

MRS P.:   What if others become jealous of my happiness and their evil eye sets on my happiness?

A: Like how you perhaps felt jealous with your daughter's happiness?

(Long pause ... then quietly she said)

MRS P.:   Perhaps ...

A: But their happiness was still there, and still is, it had nothing to do with what you felt.

MRS P.:   Yes, true ... Maybe then I too can be happy ...

Excerpt from the 216th session (one and half years)

MRS P.: I have a piece of good news to share with you! I have finally joined an acting course in an amateur theatre company! I have always wanted to do this—I would really like to be on stage! The first and the last time I did that was when I was in my high school! I remember how much I loved it—the whole preparation, excitement, and then finally being on stage! Wow! Being on stage feels so great! I remember how my teachers had also praised me for my acting in school! I feel so happy that I am being able to do some of the things that I have always longed for!

A: That surely calls for a celebration!

MRS P.: Yes, I know! But I feel kind of embarrassed to share my happiness with my family! What will they think of me?! At this age I am doing all this! Somewhere I feel guilty that all of a sudden I am thinking about all my happiness over my family—will they not find it selfish?

A: I am sure there is no harm in being a little selfish! (We both laughed with Mrs P. gradually moving towards developing a more benign superego.)

Countertransference

It was very satisfying to see the gradual change in Mrs P.'s life, how she actively started choosing a happier life for herself, and her return to the stage and acting (I myself had once had a very active performing life on the stage). This was also a very significant point of reflection for me as it brought immediate attention to my mother's life-long attachment with the arts and culture as possibly her sole path of sublimation, and subsequently liberation and joy, against familial and social showering of glorified gender roles such as motherhood. As therapeutic rapport developed, Mrs P. could feel free enough to voice her anger and frustration with her family and the unfairness of life in general towards her life's struggles, gradually moving emotionally towards her therapist. This helped her to feel lighter in her sessions over time. That was a turning point in her depressive state towards more of a life drive. In the long run, the intention had been to go into depth psychology so that the inherent masochistic quality in her personality could be eased. As she started feeling free of her own masochistic demands on herself, her demands on others also started to relax. The initial harsh superego was becoming a more flexible benign one and this helped her over time to actively participate in seeking happiness for herself. Following this, in her own pursuit of happiness she also became more tolerant towards others in her family (especially her elder daughter). As a result her object relationships with her immediate family started improving.

Conclusion

In contemporary psychoanalytic investigations, with the shift in focus to pre-oedipal mother–child bonding, Nancy Chodorow (1989) argued that during the pre-oedipal phase, due to the mother's deeper maternal identification with her female child than with her male child the process of separation and individuation is made more difficult for girls, and may subsequently lead to incomplete self-other distinction in the girl child. This feeling of oneness between mothers and daughters may hinder the girl's capacity to internalise the dyad which may further create obstacles in her pathway when she needs to delve deep into her emotional core for creative explorations. Due to her difficulty to let go of her symbiotic tie with her mother, and further fail to internalise a symbolic representation of that pre-oedipal idyllic feeling derived from her earlier symbiotic loss, a woman may often find it difficult to traverse the creative pathway of an artist. However, the very lack of it may generate feelings of desire, and since desire is a symbolic expression of the will to transcend limits, it may be that once the capacity for solitude has been achieved by a woman, it would be more stable and robust in nature. This will not be a smooth process for a woman to initiate since a fundamental obstacle has been, and continues to be, the problematic sociocultural learning of the taboo in "desiring" at all. Added to this intrapsychic struggle of the woman to negotiate so as to liberate her personality to its full is also the multi-layered sociocultural and political repression of women that she has to face in order to find her voice of freedom. While, however, society had tried to fill this lack in the woman by glorifying motherhood, the politics of this is being challenged by the changing views of self-aware, informed women of contemporary times.

References

Benedict, R. (1946). *The Chrysanthemum and the Sword*. Cleveland: Meridian Books, 1967.

Chodorow, N. J. (1989). *Feminism and Psychoanalytic Theory*. New Haven, CT: Yale University Press.

Deutsch, H. (1930). The significance of masochism in the mental life of women. *International Journal of Psycho-Analysis, 11*: 48–60.

Freud, S. (1919e). A child is being beaten: A contribution to the study of sexual perversions. *S. E. 17*. London: Hogarth.

Freud, S. (1924c). The economic problem of masochism. *S. E. 19*. London: Hogarth.

Freud, S. (1933a [1932]). New introductory lectures on psychoanalysis. *S. E. 22*. London: Hogarth.

Horney, K. (1937). *The Neurotic Personality of Our Time*. New York: W. W. Norton.

Kitayama, O. (1985). Preoedipal 'Taboo' in Japanese folk tragedies. *International Review of Psycho-Analysis, 12*: 173–185.

Kohut, H. (1971). *The Analysis of the Self*. New York: International University Press.

Kosawa, H. (1934). *Two Kinds of Guilt Feelings—The Ajase Complex, Japanese Contributions to Psychoanalysis*, Vol. 2. Pub: Japan Psychoanalytic Society. (2007).

Lansky, R. M. (2005). Hidden shame. *Journal of the American Psychoanalytic Association, 53*: 865–890.

Mitchell, J. (1974). *Psychoanalysis and Feminism: A Radical Reassessment of Freudian Psychoanalysis*. New York: Basic Books, 2000.

Okano, K. (1994). Shame and social phobia: A transcultural viewpoint. *Bulletin of the Menninger Clinic, 58*: 323–338.

Piers, G., & Singer, M. (1953). *Shame and Guilt*. Springfield, IL: Charles C. Thomas.

CHAPTER TWENTY-ONE

Horses and other animals: some background obstacles to female creativity in Russia

Marina Arutyunyan

> I am a horse, and I am a bull,
> I am a woman, and I am a man
>
> —*Russian folklore*

Here I will explore how some aspects of Russian history and culture created or maintained a mix of contradictory attitudes and representations, which despite all conscious efforts at integration often result in representational splitting at societal and individual levels and for many women a masochistic character structure presents obstacles to their using their capacity for creativity freely. Using clinical vignettes from four women patients including dream material I hope to explore this. I will start with a brief sketch of the broader picture.

Some aspects of Russian history and culture in the twentieth century

The history of Russia is contained in overcoming its geography wrote the prominent Russian historian, Ivan Solonevitch (1991). The vast multiethnic empire embraced very different cultures, divided into European and Asian parts within an absolute monarchy and the supremacy of the Russian Orthodox church, a patriarchal state where Enlightenment ideals found their place, and the first free public schools, hospitals, and educational orphanages had been established as early as the eighteenth century. A country with one of the most progressive divorce and inheritance laws for wives and widows, and increasing chances for higher education for young women, with serfdom only abolished in the second half of the nineteenth century, it became no less confusing after the 1917 Great Russian Revolution and the gradual establishment of the despotic USSR communist regime. The decrees of the Revolutionary government in 1917, the 1918 constitution of Russian Federation and the 1924 constitution of the USSR gave everyone over eighteen years of age equal electoral rights, equal rights to work and leisure, to free education, freedom of religious choice, freedom of speech, and equality before the law. They guaranteed women equal rights with men in all spheres of civil life perhaps earlier than most of Europe. Quotas for female representation in all government and higher educational and other socially important structures were established to make equality possible. Paradoxical as this may seem, but logically indeed in a perverse "Orwellian" sense, one of the most democratic European constitutions was the 1936 Russian one, when Stalin's terror was already blossoming. It peaked in 1937: millions of people from the highest to the lowest rank were imprisoned, tortured, humiliated, starved to death or shot after a trial, which had been a mockery of justice.

In some sense—also with a perverse flavour—women might be seen as somehow privileged. Several centuries of humiliation of serfdom, the bending of individual will in strictly organised hierarchical monarchy, the wars of the nineteenth century, the two devastating world wars, the bloody civil war of 1917–1919, and to an extent the disastrous state terror of 1924–1953 concerned men in the first place physically and probably psychologically. One might speculate perhaps simplistically that the history of Russia had produced a specific type of "man": infatuated with power (identification with aggressor) but heavily traumatised with an almost permanent threat of mutilation and death, and narcissistically injured by socially implied humiliation. Both could probably be described in terms of a castration experience transmitted and consolidated from one generation to another. Of course, this state of affairs calls for intermittent explosions of idealised heroism, or/and narcissistic rage and blind revengeful hatred that for a short time might reverse the positions but changes nothing in terms of structure. Thus the complementary woman figure comes to the fore.

When in the 1980s to 1990s I interviewed married couples in a research project, I was deeply impressed by an image of a female respondent. She described her idea of marriage in the following way: "Imagine a man hanged by the neck, and a woman embracing his feet and pushing him up, thus keeping him alive. Sometimes, when he has enough breath he can pat her on the head, and sometimes he kicks her, and sometimes establishes himself firmly on her head". This bitter fantasy struck me with a mixture of grave disappointment, sorrow for a man with his self-esteem so vitally endangered, but a view of him nevertheless as despicable, and pride at the female self-sacrifice and wisely hidden mightiness. Guilt is of course implied; there is clearly something murderous here.

The difficult task of preserving man's dignity by compliance to patriarchal law while at the same time keeping the split-off or repressed secret of her own "phallic" powers for herself is vividly illustrated by Russian/Soviet author Maxim Gorky (1972) in his autobiographical novel, *Childhood*. He depicts there his grandparents who brought him up, emphasising the difference in character, physical size and strength between them: the grandmother was tall, mighty, strong, tireless, calm, knowledgeable, and capable of doing a lot of work in the household and the shop, while the grandfather was small, thin, easily excited, easily exhausted, shallow, and obsessional. Each Saturday he whipped the children for their misdeeds, which had been meticulously counted by him for the whole week. If he met with resistance he went out of control, and could become dangerous to the child. Then the grandmother interfered, restricting him—and she was beaten, and in order to let him do this she had to bend, otherwise he would not be able to reach her hair. Afterwards she consoled the assaulted child and soothed his wounds. Obviously she was extremely careful to treat her husband's narcissistic wounds properly. Looking at these scenes through the author's eyes one cannot help seeing the allusion to a specific version of Joan Riviere's (1929) concept of "womanliness as a masquerade", but the seduction here goes more along the lines of masochistic adjustment to man's narcissism than to oedipal conflict. I tend to think that this phenomena of masking with femininity one's own intellectual, technical, and physical abilities and autonomy, hiding it from oneself or letting it be exercised in a split way is very typical for Russian women of all social strata, while Riviere seemed to confine this more to intellectual women.

This type of gender interaction is probably not specific to a certain national type; one can meet something like this in European literature, especially describing a working class milieu, as Emil Zola did. The particularity of the Russian constellation might be more in the enormous inconsistency of social, economic, legal, and religious or/and moral pressures shaping gender identities on a societal level. The self-abandon of a woman to her "fate" often personified by a man might be an implicit cultural ideal. Then the more cruel and unfair this fate, the more weight it gives her virtues, or at least the more chance to be pitied and forgiven by her superego.

When many years ago I was hospitalised in a small rural town I witnessed an unmitigated circle of cruelty and masochism: each weekend several men were brought there wounded or dead from drunken fighting, drunken driving or suicide, and one or more women maimed or killed by their drunken husbands. These women lived with their abusive husbands for many years, often carrying the main responsibility for the family's wellbeing. One of these women shared a room with me; her hand had been chopped off by an axe when her husband aimed at her head but she covered it with her hand. From one day to the next I watched how her pain, her enraged decisiveness to leave him forever and give him up to justice diminished, giving way to helplessness ("who needs me with one hand?") and masochistic revenge ("he'd always have his crime before his eyes") and manipulative plots ("now when he is guilty he'd have to take care of me"). It was evident that her obvious "innocence" versus his obvious guilt played a big part in this dynamic, that her whole life with her husband was a system of provocations and assaults, and that she used to identify herself with "a working horse", who was extremely tired and deserved rest—I think from her superego demands.

The following lines by the nineteenth century Russian poet, Nicolai Nekrasov, who was well-known for his sympathy and guilt towards "simple people" and especially his adoration and compassion for peasant women are often quoted: "There are women in Russian villages … she'd stop the (male) horse who has gone wild, she'd come into the burning hut" (Nekrasov, 1982, p. 1/IV)—obviously to save someone in misfortune. One can see the image not only of self-sacrificial moral behaviour, but of triumphant force here, she is able to do something that culturally belongs to a man, and better than he can—because he is dead, absent, crippled, struck with cowardice or in another way incapable. So to the pet-house of Nietzsche (1990), who wrote that women are still cats or birds, or cows at best, the other animal should be added from the epigraph: a horse (feminine noun)—mighty, but seemingly easily tamed, hard working, compliant, containing, humble but with a hidden ability to go wild and make her own way and even to destroy her master.

Patient A

Patient A requested analysis after she had had a dream of killing her husband. She was terrified by the fact that the dream-murder had been "shown" to her in all its detail—she had been strangling him, he was passive and helpless, his eyes pleading, his tongue protruding—but the horror that had turned it into a nightmare and woken her up had been realising that not only had she been merciless in a dream, but that she had felt pleasure. She used to think of herself as a nice person, tolerant, and avoiding conflicts, hard-working with appropriate earnings, and a good mother of two children, trying to do her best for the family. She was aware of her dissatisfaction with her marriage and with her selfish, jealous husband but she used to think of him as a big child, who only needed wise covert guidance and enough praise to make him "behave", an attitude which, she admitted, had not really worked and was exhausting. Her sexual desire, once strong, had diminished and she felt increasingly averse to sex, though she did not think consciously of having an affair. She had never considered divorce before the dream, although there would be no financial or other losses as she was completely independent. This was a beautiful but tired horse gradually becoming mad and suddenly becoming aware of her deep hatred and rebellion.

Patient B

Patient B is complex and I will try to follow only one relevant line. This twenty-one-year-old woman came for therapy because of sudden and severe panic attacks mainly linked to the prospect of final examinations at a very prestigious university, although she had not previously had any problems, and with the need to write her thesis and the mere thought of a possible future job. Her father was a hugely influential government figure in a post-Soviet country, and he showered her with money on the condition that she had to give him full record of her expenses. She could buy herself an expensive car, exclusive underwear, haut couture dresses, rent a fashionable apartment, have private lessons in languages and music but she was not allowed to decide with whom to make friends or where to go for vacations, and she could not even dare to think about telling her father that she opted for therapy, so it had to be at a very reduced fee. From the beginning I was impressed with the simplicity of the splits in her thinking: she put it plainly that women could be only "hens or secretaries or blue stockings", and she meant it literally, not allowing any combination or any other idea except three types of derogatory images: a narrow-minded mother preoccupied with her child's eating and peeing, and letting the cock "do her"—a clear allusion to how she viewed the parental couple; a woman as a big man's sexualised servant, having no will or mind of her own, or a sexless dry creature involved in abstract matters because no one wanted her as a hen or a secretary. It was so confusing to hear her numerous recitals of this shallow circle of images until I gradually became aware of her desperate gender confusion and horror behind penis envy and the hatred of her mother that she expressed so unequivocally.

Her terror and disgusted denial of femininity might be seen in a dream, in which she saw a high hill almost reaching the sky, and at the bottom of it there were numerous women, some with babies, some without, and the babies were disgusting, but women cuddled them and kissed them, and looked like a pile of worms themselves; their evident enjoyment and satisfaction looked horrible. At the same time in association to the dream with great shame she related an episode that had probably been a last step before she decided about coming to therapy, betraying her enormous rage to men with their phallic attributes. At the university ball she had been dancing with a "very pretentious" young man and she felt that he looked at her as at an inferior, or may have said something that she had interpreted that way—and all of a sudden she took out a lighter and set his long expensive tie on fire. Her facial expression changed, her eyes blinked with triumph, and she added that the material flashed at once, and the man "was barely able *to save his face*". In the course of a long therapy this patient became more able to see an impossible dilemma created by her extreme idealisation of, and identification with, her father with his derogatory attitudes toward women, including his wife and daughter and his incestuous masculinity, her consequent envy and hate of men for their power, and of women for their receptive submission, and their creative and procreative capacities. She felt that she belonged nowhere, locked in castrative identifications with birds (innocence and stupidity), cats (seduction and treachery) or cows (purely biological motherhood) in accord with Nietzsche's saying, and probably also with worn-down working horses, including intellectual ones. Her panics and near delusional states were connected with the feeling that she had to make a fateful choice of identity—gender and otherwise—after the prolonged period of "latency" in all meanings, including latent perversion or even psychosis.

For me this case is illustrative of a cultural framework. The father gives his daughter full access to the highest possible educational chances and sends her alone to live in the megapolis with all accompanying possibilities and temptations, but at the same time demands that she follow a very traditional female socialisation path. While conscious of the contradiction he does not see it as such, making it clear that she is to be under control, and her education is considered mainly a sign of high status, for a better marriage choice, but is not really valued for its content. Or he would make use of her new knowledge as his "secretary", which would make separation impossible. While this example may not be typical, what is typical is the inconsistency and splitting of values.

Gender socialisation

In the research mentioned earlier (Zdravomyslova & Arutyunyan, 1997) this phenomena was characteristic for the Russian population in comparison with other European samples (Germany, Sweden, France, Hungary, Poland). For instance, the majority of Russian men thought that a woman had equal rights to have a job, but also believed that if jobs were scarce a wife should not apply for a job; the situation when a wife works while the husband does not was completely unacceptable for most men and for more than fifty per cent of women. About seventy-five per cent of men also declared that whether a wife worked or not, they expected the home to be cosy and orderly when they came home from work, and the children to be well-kept. No wonder that among the Russian female respondents the biggest percentage were those who expressed their dissatisfaction with married life and the work-family balance and they lacked self-confidence as mothers.

They also demonstrated the least optimism about their own future and the country's future, expressing a most fatalistic attitude about their own possible impact, although at the same time the largest proportion insisted that the quality of family life mostly depended on how cute the wife was. (One has to bear in mind that this data was obtained during a period of considerable turmoil soon after the breakup of the USSR, when the level of societal anxiety and regression was higher than in more stable times).

The peculiarity of gender socialisation in the post-revolutionary period since 1917 had to do with the fact that the country was compulsorily and extremely rapidly modernised, turning from a mostly agricultural rural state to industrialised and rather urbanised, from illiterate to universally literate, from absolute monarchy to "democracy"—all this, paradoxically, at the price of civil war and the gradual establishment of dictatorship. (In 2002 almost thirty per cent of all women of twenty-five to twenty-nine years old in Russia had university education; by the late 1970s women had a higher general educational level than men.) The rights and freedoms, which in many countries had to be earned like other democratic reforms from "below" had in the decades of political struggle in Russia been imposed from "above". The first Soviet decrees as early as 1917 not only declared electoral equality but also abolished church weddings, substituting civil registration of marriage (and even this was not obligatory for a recognised partnership), gave equal rights to all children even if born out of wedlock; divorce also became easy with both partners having equal economic rights; abortions were legalised as well as becoming solely a woman's decision. As a flavour of how it was, one of the first Revolutionary Government ministers, Alexandra Kollontai, and later a Soviet ambassador, was the propagandist of the "glass of water" theory: sex is a natural need of a person, who when thirsty drinks water, when they feel like having an intercourse they have it; it does not depend on a particular character of an object, man or woman. Friendship or comradeship is different; here spiritual values are involved.

It soon became obvious that the excessive liberties of the early twenties were in contradiction with the new power establishment, and the Stalinist period was characterised by reaction. The new absolutism demanded a high level of control of the private sphere, and sexual freedom again became anathema; abortions were prohibited under criminal law not only for the doctors but also for women who dared to have them illegally, the paternalistic state and family ideals were restored in a mixture of pseudo revolutionary and patriarchal ideology. The most prominent slogans cherishing a woman were: "a wife, a friend, a comrade (of the husband)", "motherhood is a first honourable duty of a woman" producing soldiers and workers for society.

Returning to Joan Riviere's concept of defensive femininity, the superego confusion of a Soviet woman seemed sometimes to lead to extremes of guilt and shame in both directions: she might feel ashamed for the lack of self-confidence, initiative, self-realisation, achievement (similar to Slavoj Žižek's "post-modern superego" (1999, pp. 3–6)), which calls for, as it were, "defensive masculinity", and simultaneously felt guilty for having this "masculine" quality and resorted to feminine masquerading.

Patient C

Patient C, a woman in her fifties who had been deserted by her wealthy husband for a young partner, was absorbed by guilt for "if she were a *true* woman she wouldn't have lost him"; she had a fantasy that if she were "light" (a bird) or sexually seductive (a cat) he would be more attached to her; she was deeply ashamed at the same time of her dependency and sorrow as betraying her lack of self-sufficiency. Her husband used to reproach her for her social underachievement and to compare her to more self-assertive professional or bohemian women. She berated herself both for her compliance and rebelliousness, for paying attention to her own work and educational achievements at the expense of family values (her parents would not have approved). She had a dream where she saw herself on top of the high mountain, watching how enormous statues of gods and goddesses fall down, burying people under them. At that moment she felt relief and excitement.

Patient D

Patient D made a sharp division in her perception of her husband as a "night husband" versus a "day husband". The latter was paranoid and despotic, and she "behaved wisely", well aware of her own fear and rage, feeling very guilty about murderous wishes at times. The former restored her positive sense of femininity with his incessant desire for her body. She felt ashamed of her clinging and at the same time felt guilty for insufficient humility, which she confused with femininity; during the day she created an impression of a very independent woman with "masculine" smartness and firmness. She was inhibited in her ability to enjoy work and family life, seeing these more as duty and burden, or a narcissistic extension or a proof of her value than a source of joy. She had a dream where a boy and a girl came into her analyst's office, the girl was cute and well behaved and had a conversation with the analyst, the boy meanwhile was frantically dirtying everything with brown colour.

Integrative discussion

This spectacular dream image conveys the identity dilemma I am trying to describe. Femininity in the cases mentioned was strongly associated with passive submission and covert seduction while masculinity was associated with phallic-anal features; this was not only about (suppressed) aggression turning to violence but about having power of extension and filling the space. All those women had deep conflicts about creativity, intellectual flexibility, and self-presentation. Patient A was not able to take any leading role in her job although she had been promoted several times; patient B who excelled in her studies like a "good girl" but also in an effort to prove that she was not a brainless "hen" like her mother, was completely unable to work productively and to earn money. Patient C was prone to the states of deep psychic confusion and physical dizziness reminiscent of Danielle Quinodoz's (1997) "emotional vertigo" whenever she tried to formulate and express her thoughts to others, and patient D had bouts of anxiety and self-depreciation related to any possibility of making a mistake in her professional field so that idealisation/devaluation of her objects was necessary for self survival. All these women felt strong anxieties hindering development and use of their high intellectual and creative potential. Despite the differences of their respective life stories and levels of disturbance they seem united by a kind of distorted "phallocentricity" which deprived mother/woman/inner space of any considerable value in itself but which could also take a shape of a phantasy of a phallic mother castrating father or using him (and a child) as her own penis to penetrate the world.

The primal scene took the form of something very humiliating and destructive for one or both of the partners: a confirmation of female incompleteness (patient A), powerlessness and dehumanisation of a woman and her creative space versus grandiosity of a man (patient B), swallowing of the father to fill the "empty space" (patient C), and castrating him to secretly appropriate his powers and covering this crime by becoming a victim, having to take life-long care of the impaired husband (patient D). Identifications with mother, highly charged with negative and sometimes even life-threatening projections, made the "feminine" process of accepting something belonging to the other from outside (penis, semen, ideas), transforming it inside, and giving to the world some mutual creation to be happy with and proud of, problematic. Inner space is not represented as a transformational one but as hollow or greedy or even filled with rotten remains. Now the identification with father is associated with robbery, horrifying envious competition (with him and with the mother) and the corresponding castration threat as it means having "grown" and shown the (anal) penis. Quinodoz's notion that "in some female patients the inhibition of curiosity may go hand in hand with penis envy and with the anxiety that one's family circle (parent substitutes) might find out that … displaying a curious and adventurous spirit is a way of parading a penis equivalent" (Quinodoz, 1997, p. 98) is applicable here, although in the context I am trying to explore I would substitute "many" for "some" and would add that this is especially conflictual if the father's penis is experienced as easily extricated (patients C and D) or on the contrary father is equated with the phallus (patient B).

Coming back to the wider context, I think that the massive societal mutilation of men and women in their individual power of agency and creative wills under the totalitarian rule producing very confusing messages about gender roles had become a facet of transgenerational traumatic experience that may have played a part in the confusion of normal psychic bisexuality with external and internal castration. Thus in many cases this would have abnormally complicated cross-gender identifications—the latter being indispensible for creative processes.

I have not touched here on the very profound topics of treatment of the body, bodily privacy, and sexuality in Russian/Soviet culture, which would be extremely important in understanding female guilt and masochism and male shame and self-destruction in this culture. Nor have I explored another important theme in terms of gender identity conflicts which would have been the specifics of oedipal relations in "matriarchal" families within a "patriarchal" context. Here I have tried only to show how the weight of Russian history and culture maintained a mixture of contradictory attitudes and representations, which militated against a fuller expression of female creativity, whether on personal or societal levels.

References

Gorky, M. (1972). *Childhood.* Complete works, vol. 15. ϕscow: Nauka.

Nietzsche, F. (1990). *Thus spoke Zarathustra.* Moscow: Interbook. (in Russian).

Quinodoz, D. (1997). *Emotional Vertigo: Between Anxiety and Pleasure* (The New Library of Psychoanalysis, 28). London: Routledge.

Rivere, J. (1929). Womanliness as masquerade. *International Journal of Psychoanalysis, 10*: 303–313.

Solonevitch, I. (1991). *People's Monarchy.* Moscow: Poenix. Reprint from 1973, Buenos Aires (in Russian).

Zdravomyslova, O., & Arutyunyan, M. (1999). *Russian Family on the European Background.* Moscow: Editorial URSS.

Žižek, S. (1999). You may! *London Review of Books,* vol. 21, N 6, 18 March. www.lrb.co.uk/v21/n06/slavoj-zizek/you-may. Last accessed 19 October 2013.

CHAPTER TWENTY-TWO

Is healing possible for women survivors of domestic violence?

Nicoletta Livi Bacci

In 1991, together with a group of women activists in the Florentine feminist movement, I founded The Artemisia anti-violence Centre, in order to support women and children victims of violence and abuse. The name of our association comes from a seventeenth century female painter: Artemisia Gentileschi who was raped by a colleague painter. Artemisia courageously filed a complaint and in the court case that followed, the first in history for rape, Artemisia was subjected to severe humiliations including public gynaecological examinations and having her thumbs crushed to force admission of a presumed "truth", which she never gave in to. Although the aggressor was found guilty Artemisia was never fully believed. This episode however profoundly marked her artwork, with the rape chiefly exorcised in her beautifully painted representation of "Judith beheading Holophernes". This painting allowed Artemisia her symbolic revenge, in a dramatic role reversal, as Judith is a self-portrait and it is she who beheads Holophernes with icy determination, certainly a reprisal for the rape she had undergone. I thought it important to tell Artemisia's story, whose theme is that of female creativity, because Artemisia represents a shining example of female resilience. This is what we would wish to occur within our crisis centres and women's shelters. We would like to transform pain into creative projects.

The first anti-violence centres and women's shelters in Italy were founded in the late 1980s, in Bologna, Milan and Rome, and represent an important change within the feminist movement. Mass demonstrations began to decrease but the movement entered a more operative phase with renewed energy. From discussion groups women started taking action and putting their experience and knowledge into practice. The new issues became "create" and "transform", the creation of social women's places in order to transform a given reality, where the objects of transformation are both women involved in the project and society. The new anti-violence centres found their expression in this new context. As time went by, especially during the late 1990s, battered women's shelters sprang up all over Italy. In 2008 the national association, D.i.Re, was born, a network of sixty counselling centres and shelters. Their methodology and political approach set them apart from similar public and private institutions and services which were opening at the same time all over the country. The approach adopted by battered women's shelters is based on establishing a strong relationship between women and the enhancement of the female gender. This is the starting point from which a healing process may be activated, a process which focusing on women's needs and interests may produce self-determination, autonomy, empowerment, and legitimises women's subjectivity. From this point of view working tools are organised taking into consideration women's choices and offering resources without imposing conditions. This approach is based on the need to give good services within a feminist perspective. It is is an approach not founded on power since violence is rooted in men's use of power and control within interpersonal male/female relations. Women's centrality, their choices and desires, are fundamental criteria for the birth of reciprocal trust, the acquisition of autonomy and the consequent exit from a violent situation. In this way, values of cognitive thinking, desires and planning abilities, all aspects profoundly undermined by the violence suffered are recovered, helping to bring back self-esteem.

Almost every Italian battered women's shelter consists of two separate places: a public one, accessible to everybody, which receives calls for help and provides counselling of various kinds: legal, psychological, self-help groups etc. Then, the secret shelters for high risk situations, which welcome single women or mothers with their children whose psycho-physical safety is in danger. Every two days in Italy a woman is killed by her partner or ex-partner. In fact "femicide" accounts for one of the principal causes of death of women between sixteen to forty-five years of age. Escaping and breaking up a violent relationship represents the most dangerous moments for women. Secret shelters—while official protective and safeguarding measures are being arranged in accordance to the law—are the one place capable of offering real protection to women and children at risk. For this reason safety is a priority, although empowerment and healing from abuse require more than finding safety. My work in the Artemisia Association consists in being the person responsible for the shelter and following the progress of women guests. Working with battered women within a shelter represents an interesting, important, and very special experience, although difficult given its heavy emotional impact. Women who approach our crisis centre for psychological support or legal counselling mention only their most problematic experiences, which sees them in the role of victims. In the shelter's daily life other difficulties and shadow areas begin to emerge, especially regarding their relationship with their children, so that it is possible to observe attitudes, beliefs, and perceptions of reality in greater detail, which reveal the different levels of damage caused by the exposure to violence.

Besides the visible, external signs of abuse, such as bruises and wounds, there are other less visible aspects such as confusion, bewilderment, sense of impotence, relational difficulties, lack of contact with reality, difficulties in their relationship with their children. Furthermore by living, sometimes for many years, with a perpetrator women develop and interiorise coping strategies that help them survive, such as manipulation and lies, that they will continue using with the shelter professionals. As Giuliana Ponzio explains in her book, *Un Mondo Sovvertito* (*A Subverted World*): when a woman enters a centre and especially when she asks for hospitality in our secret shelters, she starts on a difficult and contradictory path. Entrance to the shelter is dramatic and requires strong support on the part of the staff. To begin with the woman is dazed, in an unknown place, confronted by a void. She is also frightened by having broken away from a relationship that for many years she has tried to hold together. In any violent relationship, apart from physical abuse there are also insults and judgments and women increasingly see themselves through the eyes of their perpetrators, gradually sharing his values. To have run away from him means reversing the behavioural pattern she has adopted so far, consisting in passively submitting to his desires, the alternative being suffering violence. We have to cope with a woman whose violent partner is still well embedded in her mind and plays out his part, making her feel guilty. Inverting this process is extremely difficult as one interferes with cognitive structures. For years, the woman has used various strategies which allowed her to stay within the relationship, now the situation is reversed, she must elaborate new systems to come out of it, to find herself again, which requires a completely new set of strategies. Both counselling centres, which do not set a time limit on this process and especially shelters, where women may stay for up to six months, provide an interesting insight into the day-by-day evolution of a mental process which consists of a review of reality, for instance having been beaten for a trivial incident, being forced to have sexual relations, or being subjected to jealousy (not love, but control). A shelter is an opportunity for women to undertake positive reframing, in a long and difficult process, especially in the case of women who come from a culture where abusive behaviour finds social consensus.

The priority of a shelter is to stop violence because only in a safe place can women re-plan their own and their children's lives. This starting point guarantees security and protection, without which it would not be possible to increase their empowerment, which will ultimately allow women to resume control over their lives. It is of the utmost importance that leaving home be her own choice because the right to make choices directly contradicts the stereotyped sex-role notion that women require someone stronger than themselves, a parent or a husband, to take care of them, and the role of the professionals working in the shelter is often seen in this light. Yet it is not possible to subtract oneself from an abusive situation without self determination and taking responsibility for one's choices, where control and decision making must ultimately lie exclusively with the woman. The professionals working in the shelter must facilitate and support but without ever replacing the women in taking decisions. It is important that shelter professionals are not perceived as those who will resolve all women's problems and therefore control their lives. So the main goals of the officials working in the shelter must be:

- Encouraging women to take care of themselves
- Helping women to assess the effects of battering

- Favouring social support
- Helping women to increase economic resources and have social contacts
- Supporting mothers in their relationship with their children
- Challenging cognitions and reframing
- Increasing skills
- Helping women increase their abilities and potentials.

* * *

Taking care of themselves is taking care of basic physical and emotional needs. Self-nurturing can for the abused woman be an issue in itself, but remains important as it helps her to achieve a healthy standard of living. During this process it is essential for the battered woman to be supported in understanding her emotional needs, in identifying how to obtain them and accepting the fact that this is her right. Attention to nurturing the emotional self is as important as nurturing the physical self. It is also important to help women develop the necessary strategies to cope with the effects of trauma. These can include depression, anxiety, phobic behaviour, panic attacks, eating and sleeping disorders and many others which might require specific treatment and therapy. They might also include aggressive behaviour towards their children, and towards the shelter professionals.

* * *

It is useful to *help women to assess the effects of battering* and the way in which violence is represented in our society. Increasing their knowledge about violence towards women in society is useful because it provides a framework for seeing that their abusive situation is part of a widespread problem which is not only theirs. Battered women often consider themselves "mad" so that "normalising" their reactions to abuse can be empowering. It is equally important to provide information about legal options such as protective orders, the process of criminal prosecution and the civil action available, because the more they are prepared to deal with the legal system the more they can demand an effective response.

Anti-violence centres should *favour social support* and have an advocacy role to increase the responsiveness of institutional systems regarding the problem of violence against women and children. This means applying pressure to pass new legislation, ask for economic resources, promote inter-institutional networks that will accept the social responsibility of supporting women and their children who have been victims of violence. Women must also be encouraged to ask for help and learn how to cope with often complicated bureaucratic realities. Activating external resources is essential to counter the isolation in which an abused woman feels herself in. It is also vital that the woman meets and exchanges information with other female victims of violence. This too will lessen her sense of isolation and help her to perceive her own situation no longer as unique, but one of many similar cases.

* * *

A fundamental duty of a shelter professional is to help the battered woman *increase economic resources and social contacts*. For some women, leaving an abusive relationship is difficult due to lack of sufficient economic resources. Some women may have a family that supports them but many others, especially where migrant women are concerned, do not have anyone to provide economic and other tangible support during the time of transition until they can manage to earn enough money to keep themselves and their children. Battered women shelters provide this bridge and women are very happy to use it, yet the time spent in our shelters is often insufficient to recover enough economic autonomy for themselves and their own children; this can lead them to fear that their children might be taken into care because of their difficulties in providing for them. It is therefore fundamental for a woman who has left an abusive partner to obtain sufficient financial resources to provide for her new single-parent family.

* * *

The experience of many years tells us that helping the battered woman recover some of her own *skills and potential as a mother* not only is important but a further means of empowerment in her healing process. A mother's ability to meet the needs of her children is almost always damaged by protracted exposure to violence. Healing this important aspect not only enables the battered mother to reestablish a healthy loving emotional relationship and authority with her children, but also allows her and them to feel more supported and secure. Mothers who have been victims of domestic violence do not often realise to what extent their children have been involved in the situation, or what consequences it has had on them.

The shelters' professionals have an important role in *challenging cognitions and reframing* based on the fact that knowledge, emotion, and behaviour combine in a triple system within which these components are interdependent. Protracted exposure to abuse can provoke a sense of guilt, a feeling of impotence, or lack of control of the outcome of events, and the minimisation or denial of violence, of its severity and effects. All this makes up an internal barrier which prevents a battered woman from seeing violence in its various forms. Correctly indentifying this helps women to recognise that violence is functional to exert power and control over their lives. Labeling the partner's behaviour as abusive moves from a position of denial to one of recognition. If we do not help women to accept the reality of their abuse we collude with their possible minimisations and denials. Helping the battered woman to recognise the gravity of the violence she has undergone needs a lot of support from the shelter professionals as she may feel her life is a failure or that her life is over. Many female victims of abuse blame themselves for the violence they had suffered, or they feel responsible for their partner's abusive behaviour. It is important to help the battered woman to attribute the responsibility of violence correctly to the abusive partner, thus shifting or redirecting the woman's energy from attempting to justify the abuse or looking for ways of coping, to taking care of herself. This does not imply that she should not recognise her own responsibilities. Sometimes female victims of violence delegate responsibility for their safety to other people including the support workers. Some women think that no one, including themselves, can guarantee their safety and wellbeing. It is fundamental to help the battered woman examine her goals—which may or may not include safety as primary—and take responsibility for meeting them. It is also possible that she will not be able to achieve total control of her life, but she can have control of her actions when attempting to meet the goals that she has planned for herself and her children. Accepting responsibility for her own decisions being aware of the obstacles in meeting them is an important factor so as to have control over her own safety and other aspects of her life.

It is my conviction that it is not possible to escape a violent situation without reassessing the *stereotypes related to gender roles* that circulate in our society. Many socialised sex-roles stereotypic beliefs are dysfunctional for women in general, for battered women in particular. For a woman to have suffered abuse for either a brief or longer period may reinforce further dysfunctional convictions, preventing them from coping with the situation, this can also lead them to think that they are not able to be in charge of their own life, because: "I don't deserve anything better", "my task is to look after other people, not myself","it is my duty to make the relationship with my partner work", "his blows and jealousy are also a sign of love".

* * *

Challenging these stereotypes can help women examine their own beliefs, some of which can have been adopted unconsciously, and can help women to *increase their own skills and potentials*. Sometimes women think that they cannot live without their partners. This may happen when the woman lacks her own economic resources or lacks the self-confidence necessary to use the resources she already possesses. After leaving an abusive relationship, many women learn that they are able to develop or engage in behaviours that they believed were previously unavailable to them. It is very important to help women recognise their behavioural, emotional, or cognitive barriers to decision-making. A battered woman may believe that she faces objective barriers whereas it is her fear and beliefs which prevent change. It could also be that, regardless of her actions, her beliefs or her coping strategies, a battered woman might find herself without guarantees for her own and her children's safety. Even after a restraining order, the woman might live with the uncertainty of not knowing when or where she may encounter her perpetrator. Therefore it is important for the shelter professionals to bear this possibility in mind in order that the woman is always on her guard.

On a final note I would like to say that this process, which on paper might appear so clear and problem-free, can encounter a variety of obstacles. It is a complex process with moments of deadlocks and even misunderstandings. With some women, one has the impression of an evolving process which produces effective changes, with others changes occur slowly and sometimes long after they have left the shelter, and with other women no changes seem to appear. Which is why it is vital for the support workers to have a regular supervisor to whom they can report their frustrations.

CHAPTER TWENTY-THREE

No peaceable woman: creativity in feminist political psychoanalysis—commemorating Margarete Mitscherlich-Nielsen (17.7.1917–12.6.2012)

Ingrid Moeslein-Teising, Gertraud Schlesinger-Kipp, Christiane Schrader, and Almuth Sellschopp

"One of the wisest thinkers of the post-war time, a role model in every respect" was a headline in German news (Feddersen, 2012) when Dr Margarete Mitscherlich-Nielsen died in Frankfurt, aged ninety-four, on 12 June 2012. She was able to combine psychoanalysis, feminism, and a critique of society in a creative way and made them uniquely accessible to a wide public. The "Grande Dame" of German psychoanalysis contributed essentially, together with her husband Alexander in post-war Germany with the book *The Inability to Mourn* (1967/1975) to the critical discourse on National Socialism which had been avoided till then, a topic to which she repeatedly returned. She helped to reestablish psychoanalysis in Germany, contributed creatively to the further development of the psychoanalytic theory of femininity and finally put her story and her views on ageing in her 2010 book *Die Radikalität des Alters* (*The Radicalism of Age*). In representing psychoanalysis she passionately dedicated herself to the themes and the cultural debates of her time and stimulated our creativity as female analysts. Until her death she preserved an impressive intellectual alertness and creativity, yet worked on a new book—about love, although she anticipated every day the possibility of her death.

Career

"If you want to be a real psychoanalyst you have to have a great love of the truth, scientific truth as well as personal truth, and you have to place this appreciation of truth higher than any discomfort at meeting unpleasant facts, whether they belong to the world outside or to your own inner person". (Anna Freud cited in Mitscherlich-Nielsen, 1982, p. 268)

For Margarete Mitscherlich-Nielsen, "the psychoanalytic talking cure is always jigsawed of two speeches: one in the analytical treatment rooms and the other in public spaces, for public engagement was for her always a dedication to psychoanalysis" (Leuschner, 2008, p. 378). Linking the different started from the cradle, so to speak: her mother was German, a teacher, who was close to the bourgeois women's movement and promoted the educational and personal development of her daughter. Her father, a physician, was Danish, descended from a Danish national-minded family and was undoubtedly a career model for her. Born in 1917, Margaret Nielsen grew up on the border of Denmark and Germany, which had a checkered history of national affiliations. The "crack", she later recalled, also went through her family—till the opposition towards National Socialism overcame this (Mitscherlich-Nielsen, 1994). Her desire for freedom in life and thinking and her sculptured political attitude resulted in difficulties in school in Flensburg and led during her medical studies in Heidelberg to surveillance and interrogation by the Gestapo.

In 1946 she met Alexander Mitscherlich in Switzerland, where she worked as a physician. They became a couple, while he was still married and father of six children. In 1949 their son was born, whom she first reared alone and with the help of a woman friend—at that time a difficult situation. When Alexander Mitscherlich founded the in-patient Clinic for Psychosomatic Medicine in Heidelberg, she continued her professional career there in the early fifties. Her son was then brought up by her mother, a decision with which she quarreled a lot, a struggle that is inherent in her work. Margarete Nielsen and Alexander Mitscherlich married in 1955. For decades, they formed a "life and thinking-community" of astonishing creativity and productivity; the couple were spoken of as "the Mitscherlichs". Her contribution to his work remained invisible for long periods, as often with the wives of successful men, as it was based mainly on cooperative teamwork. Even in *his* book on the perspective of "society without the father" (Mitscherlich, A. 1963/1969) *she* was involved; in *The Inability to Mourn* book she was named co-author (Mitscherlich, A. & M., 1967/1975). At the same time, she was head of training at the Sigmund Freud Institute and worked for *Psyche*, the main German psychoanalytic periodical and especially here, she supported enormously the quality of her husband's published work. Parallel to this, she published her own work and found her own topics. At the same time she repeatedly came back to the couple's main theme, the critical debate with National Socialism and its transgenerational effects into the future, as well as the necessity to remember and mourn.

Psychoanalysis and politics

After two short training analyses with Vilma Popescu and Felix Schottländer in Germany, Margarete Mitscherlich-Nielsen went to London for psychoanalytic training and analysis with Michael Balint in the late fifties; Alexander Mitscherlich's training analyst was Paula Heimann. The couple established contacts with the psychoanalysts who had survived the Nazis and were in exile in London leading to professional exchanges as well as personal friendships.

> "Further, I think that a psychoanalyst should have ... interests ... beyond the limits of the medical field ... in facts that belong to sociology, religion, literature, [and] history, ... [otherwise] his outlook on ... his patient will remain too narrow." (Anna Freud cited in Mitscherlich, 1968, p. 553)

In the vibrant discussion in London among the various psychoanalytic schools, Margarete Mitscherlich-Nielsen experienced a "new dimension of perception of myself, another psychoanalytic culture than I had previously experienced" (Mitscherlich-Nielsen, 1994, p. 328). At that time she became acquainted with the ideas of Melanie Klein, who emphasised the early dependency of the human being on the mother, a basis for conflicts throughout the life cycle. This concept remained for Margarete Mitscherlich-Nielsen a permanent element of her psychoanalytic thinking, even though the couple sympathised most with the Middle group, which included Paula Heimann, Michael Balint, and D. W. Winnicott (A. Mitscherlich, 1980).

Together with her husband, Margarete Mitscherlich-Nielsen worked to reestablish psychoanalysis in Germany. On the occasion of Sigmund Freud's hundredth birthday in 1956, Alexander Mitscherlich organised in Frankfurt and Heidelberg a series of lectures to which many psycho-analysts from around the world came together, some for the first time after the exile. Personal relationships with colleagues in London and in America made this possible. For the first time since 1933, psychoanalysis was presented to a wider public. In Frankfurt an academic ceremony took place attended by the German president, Theodor Heuss. The Hessian Prime Minister, Georg August Zinn, saw the penetration of the politics by psychoanalysis as the most effective protection against dictatorship: "A state in which the findings and the methods of psychoanalysis can not only interfuse deeply into the hospitals and medical consulting rooms, but also into the laws, into the penalty system, into the classroom and in the social professions, is probably somehow immune to dictatorships" (Berger, 1996, p. 48). The Sigmund Freud Institute as a psychoanalytic research and training institute, where the Mitscherlichs both worked from 1960 on, was established then in response to these activities.

"No future without memory"—Margarete Mitscherlich wrote many of her books based on this conviction. Together she and her husband wrote *The Inability to Mourn* in the 1960s. This striking title was often misunderstood as the Germans being unable to mourn their losses during the war, their deaths, loss of home, etc. However, the Mitscherlichs initially dealt with the loss of the beloved "Führer" as well as fantasies of being almighty, and of ideals which could not be mourned. They described in detail the inner consequence which the social reality of the Germans during and after the War had on the collective condition, suggesting that for many the inability to mourn becomes comprehensible on understanding the German way of loving: "It is wonderful to be the chosen nation ... We absolutely agreed with the leadership that knew how to connect typically German ideals with our self-esteem" (A. & M. Mitscherlich, 1967, p. 28). The fall of the "Führer" signified a traumatic devaluation of the ego ideal. There was barely any alternative apart from retreating to a collective depression. But according to the Mitscherlichs, the Germans chose another way. The Nazi past was derealised, made unreal. As well as the death of Hitler as a real person, it was particularly the ending of his representation as a collective ego ideal which provided a reason for mourning. He was an object on whom one projected responsibilities and he was an inner object. Losing him was the equivalent of losing a narcissistic object and therefore an impoverishment of the ego and the self. This had to be prevented and by a kind of emergency reaction all affective bridges to the past were unconsciously destroyed.

Mourning can only occur when an individual is able to empathise with—love—another object. After losing a beloved one, narcissistic affection leads to deflation which brings an emotional numbness which the Mitscherlichs called "autistic". The inability to mourn was preceded by our way of loving which was less about empathy and more about confirming self-esteem. The Mitscherlichs' main thesis was that the sensitivity of this way of life is a collective attribute of our character. This way of loving also explains the missing empathy for the victims of National Socialism immediately after the war. Collective aspect of states of such fierceness as National Socialism unleashed had an intense effect on all who were affected by language, education, and emotional attachment to such events. It is not surprising that the Mitscherlichs' working hypothesis, illustrated in their book by case studies, was quickly forgotten because of the other usage of the title *Inability to Mourn*. This diagnosis is bitter and as it has an inner necessity and logic, it had to be suppressed along with suppressing National Socialism.

Passion and honours

Margarete Mitscherlich-Nielsen was a training analyst and head of training for a number of years at the Sigmund Freud Institute and the German Psychoanalytic Association (DPV). During this time, she dealt repeatedly with the task and the difficulties in identifying useful eligibility criteria for psychoanalytic training (Mitscherlich-Nielsen, 1970) and wrote a number of clinical contributions (Mitscherlich-Nielsen, 1962, 1965; Mitscherlich, M., 1968, 1976). She was a member of the International Psychoanalytical Association and the DGPT (German Society for Psychoanalysis, Psychotherapy, Psychosomatics and Psychodynamic Psychology) where she critically observed the consequences of the institutionalisation of psychoanalysis. She joined the PEN centre of Germany and commented on films and authors, writing for example about Kafka. At times, she served on the advisory board of the Hamburg Institute for Social Research. She wrote several books: on the dynamics of internal and external conflicts (Mitscherlich, M., 1972), about ideals, role models, and their transformation, on women and repeatedly on the aftermath of the Nazi past in the present, on contemporary issues and social changes and the permanent need to remember and mourn in order to grasp outer and inner reality (Mitscherlich-Nielsen, 1973, 1979, 1992, 1993, 2000). She presented her topics in publications, media, and events and received a number of honours and awards, such as in 1982 the Wilhelm-Leuschner Medal, in 1990 the Honorary Medal of the City of Frankfurt am Main, in 2001 the Great Cross of Merit of the Federal Republic of Germany—for her "merits to the general welfare" and in 2005 the Tony Sender Award for female political involvement and commitment to gender equality. This award was presented by the Women's Department of the City of Frankfurt am Main, and the eulogy was by Alice Schwarzer, the prominent German feminist.

From 1982, after the early death of her husband, Margarete Mitscherlich-Nielsen acted until 1997 as co-editor of the magazine he founded, *Psyche*. Until recently she followed the development of the *Psyche* "as an honorary member of the editorial board with curiosity and benevolence" (Bohleber, 2012, p. 674).

As well as her academic and journalistic activities she worked as a clinician in her practice. Her special way of listening was probably influenced by her intense experience of working with psychosomatic patients. She had a particular way of dealing with transference and countertransference: she was able to enrich and condense situations in the here-and-now of the analytic dialogue which created deep evidence, something that is now referred to as a "healing presence" (Miller & Cutshall, 2001). Because of her sensitive and awake capability of resonance she was able to revive people and situations as if they were present, creating a mutual fantasy. One could feel her strong desire to make the past come alive in the present by eliciting details of the specific situation that experienced their symbolic compaction in the interpretation and sent back as a real presence into the past. Her analytic work implied the message to the analysand to accept that life goes on and analysis can never be completed. For herself this implied a reservoir for further thinking, as she said in her last interview. She liked to revive issues from the past, which were not worked through or resolved, seeing them in the light of new ideas and thereby created ways of taking part in an enterprise of being surprised by herself and of breaking free with the help of new thoughts and insights—even in old age.

Theory of femininity and feminism

Parallel to the intense collaboration with her husband, Margarete Mitscherlich had already in the early sixties devoted herself to women's issues. In West Germany the psychoanalytic discourse on the development of women, which had been destroyed by the Nazis, received from the late sixties significant impetus from abroad and through the women's movement, which had been reactivated by the students' movement.

Mitscherlich-Nielsen was aware of the history of the women's movement and its importance in Germany before the world wars. She was inspired by the discourses accompanying the student riots in the late sixties and seventies and was the first psychoanalyst in Germany who took up the currents of feminism. She recognised the possibility of recovering lost female creative potentials of thought and action in a lifelong process of emancipation, and realised, that not only the women themselves, but society would profit from this. She did not criticise Freud's work as such, but began fundamentally challenging his theory of femininity. In the papers she published on this topic since 1971, she criticised his patriarchal attitude and drew attention to the sadomasochistic dynamic between the sexes and the conflicts on dominance and submission in a woman's inner world (1971, 1978). But she thought of the psychoanalytic method that Freud had developed as fundamental and emancipatory because it made it possible to investigate the effects of societal double standards, individual taboos and inhibitions, and transform them. She therefore saw psychoanalysis and feminism as supplementing each other (1989) and Freud as a precursor of the women's movement: "His work taught us to make conscious the unconscious, and to realise our prejudices and misjudgements in relation to the role models of men and women at all!" (Sellschopp, 2013, p. 42).

Her theoretical revisions led to a dynamic idea about women and their development, whose main features are still valid. She revised the concept of the phallic monism and the myth of the vaginal orgasm on the basis of recent psychoanalytic, biological, and sexological findings (1975). Even more she criticised the intimidating effect that these and other psychoanalytic theories had on women, as well as the Freudian triad of masochism, passivity, and narcissism. She raised the question of whether the (male) gender identity of women psychoanalysts encouraged their adherence to the Freudian femininity theory, but could harm patients (1982).

Mitscherlich-Nielsen's first meeting with Alice Schwarzer in a television appearance began a lifelong friendship and cooperation. In 1977, she announced in the newly founded feminist magazine, *EMMA*, "I am a feminist." The German feminist discourse was significantly influenced by many of her lectures, articles, books, and her publishing activities as co-editor of the *Psyche*. She continued this work in her 1985 book on *Die Friedfertige Frau* (The Peaceable Woman; in English, *The Peaceable Sex*, 1987)—a title the irony of which was often misunderstood. She addressed the fact that "subliminally" remaining passive aggression and sadistic impulses of many women were transformed into a self-punishing "complaint and victimhood attitude", turned against the body, or acted out as devaluation and revenge towards others unconsciously. "We women should take care to not have illusions about ourselves or to commit ourselves to a wishful thinking. Our issue is also but not only the liberation of social enforcements; the hassles with psychic forces, in most of the woman's unbroken interiorisation of her social devaluation" (Sellschopp, 2013, p. 39).

Mitscherlich-Nielsen is said to have primarily depicted women as victims of National Socialist leadership and therefore freed them from any responsibility and blame. Anyone who knows her complete works cannot maintain this reproach. Perhaps the later feminists did not understand her irony. She almost prompted women to free themselves from the subordination deriving from fear of deprivation of love and to take on responsibilities themselves. While women's research has developed further and this thesis is no longer tenable, it is historically important and interesting. It seems unjustified to accuse Mitscherlich-Nielsen of anti-Semitism (Radovic, 2005) and completely misjudges her attitude and history.

Mitscherlich-Nielsen kept up the thesis of her book until 2011 while mellowing in others of her opinions: the rigorous diagnosis of the 1960s about the "inability" to mourn is seen more as an individual ability to mourn or not. Given the critical review after 1968 of the crimes during the period of National Socialism, it is no longer possible to refer to it as "collective". Seeing how her creative political thinking and action were a recurrent theme of life and how she was always able to see new aspects, to analyse, and to think, made meeting Mitscherlich-Nielsen in the last years of her life very intense.

Age

Mitscherlich-Nielsen continued the analytic discourse in her consulting room at the Sigmund Freud Institute till old age. The issues of clinical indication and newer treatment, technical challenges and developments of psychoanalysis were not her issue. She implemented the necessary changes and updating, for example of the theory of femininity. To preserve a lively and liberated thinking was as central to her psychoanalytic work as for her a way to withstand the hostility of age. Her family, her abiding curiosity about the world and her joy of thinking helped her to face physical deficits and insults. Her creative energies were focused on the socio-historical and scientific context, on the psychoanalytic questions and ideas arising there, as well as to the contributions that psychoanalysis could make to these issues. As with her husband, Alexander, she was a gifted ambassador and mediator of psychoanalysis in the public which in the end she estimated was penetrated by psychoanalytic ideas "at least superficially", as deep as enlightenment can reach in the complex political and cultural field of forces (Sellschopp, Moeslein-Teising, Schrader & Stoupel, 2012). She also commented on and interpreted the events of the time, as well as accompanying new social movements with interest and critical attention. With her death an era ends, "in which psychoanalysis in Germany had an influential voice" in which psychoanalysis was able to trigger societal debates and communicate "the psychosocial state of contemporary society" to a wide audience (Wirth, 2012, p. 25). However, she would have agreed that "the emancipatory potential of psychoanalysis would certainly be helpful for understanding future social and political processes" (Wirth, 2012, p. 25).

In an interview with Almuth Sellschopp (2013) four days before her death, she reflected on ageing and discussed the influence of the feminist movement to the quality of ageing. She did not generalise the influence of feminism to the process of ageing, but underlined the importance of an individual development. She emphasised the mature self-reflection of old women and found the differences between the sexes diminishing with growing age. When she was asked about the influence of the body—how the body shapes the psyche and vice versa, she said: "The integrity of the body guarantees your independence, if you don't like anything you can go away. In old age you lose these possibilities to flee and this is why ageing is the most difficult period in life to my mind. For me the possibilities to flee are to flee into thinking" (Sellschopp, 2013, p. 44). "When I can't sleep in the night … I'm going to sit in my armchair and say to myself: what is it you want to think about, what would you like? What did you not fully understand … Then I can choose and will always find something—these are moments of happiness, to think something new (p. 44)". There are a lot more discoveries, as she called them, possible in advanced age, if only there would be enough time. Liberated thinking, which also relinquishes body deficits as mortifications of the individual existence, was what she longed for in old age. The possibility of introversion of her thinking gave her independent mental power till the end. "I know I'll die soon, I could die every moment, that's all right … But the joy of thinking should not be gone before" (Sellschopp, 2013, p. 44).

Mitscherlich-Nielsen was fascinated by the fact that not much is known about dreams in old age and that sexuality and eros played such a big role in her dreams for such a long time. This belongs to the human being until the body starts to have pains, until the power diminishes concerning desires in reality. In wish fulfilling dreams in earlier times she was able to deny awkward reality, for example she could dream that she was still able to walk. Later she dreamed she was on tour with a walker, and laughing she said: "This is annoying, when you once realize you can't deny it" (Sellschopp, 2013, p. 45).

In her last years, we were able to work with her at various events and witness her wit, humour and an alert mind, spirited, quick-witted, and spontaneous. As part of the International Psychoanalytic Congress in Berlin in 2007, she participated with a presentation on the Committee on Women and Psychoanalysis (COWAP) panel, "Women and psychoanalysis in Germany". It was of concern to her to cooperate with us in COWAP activities, a committee for which she among other creative women had prepared the ground by her work (Mitscherlich-Nielsen, 2008). Even in her last year she appeared on television in well-known talk shows and was invited to scientific public events (Sellschopp, Moeslein-Teising, Schrader & Stoupel, 2012).

Farewell

Margarete Mitscherlich-Nielsen passed away surrounded by her family. Numerous relatives, companions, colleagues, friends came to her funeral service in Frankfurt. Sounds of the Pastorale inspired the participants' personal reveries as well as the final song by Edith Piaf, "Je ne regrette rien" (I regret nothing).

> "We all need ideals, models, goals by which we orient ourselves, we can strive for their achievement. Without them we are exposed to a feeling of emptiness, and the lively interest in the things of the world and our fellow human beings is lost". (Mitscherlich, 1978, p. 14, translated for this edition)

For us, then young women and psychoanalysts (in training) who did not want to live as our mothers did, Margarete Mitscherlich-Nielsen was an important ideal and model to work out our own ways. With her vitality and creativity, wit, humour, and with her personal radicalism in old age she remains in our memories.

References

Berger, F. (1996). Zur Biographie einer Institution. Alexander Mitscherlich gründet das Sigmund-Freud-Institut. In: T. Plänkers, T., Laier, M., Otto, H. H., Rothe, H. J. & Siefert, H. (Eds.), *Psychoanalyse in Frankfurt am Main* (pp. 349–372). Tübingen: edition diskord.

Bohleber, W. (2012). Zum Tod von Margarete Mitscherlich. *Psyche, 66*: 673–675.

Feddersen, J. One of the wisest thinkers of the post-war time, a role model in every respect. *Spiegel online*, Last accessed 13 June 2012.

Leuschner, W. (2008). Laudatio für Margarete Mitscherlich-Nielsen. *Z. f. psa Theo u. Prax., 23*: 373–379.

Miller, E. J., & Cutshall, S. C. (2001). *The Art of Being a Healing Presence. A Guide for those in Caring Relationships.* Place: Willogreen Publishing.

Mitscherlich, A. (1963). *Auf dem Weg zur vaterlosen Gesellschaft. Ideen zur Sozialpsychologie. Society Without the Father* (1969). New York: Harcourt, Brace & World.

Mitscherlich, A. (1980). *Ein Leben für die Psychoanalyse.* Frankfurt/Main: Suhrkamp.

Mitscherlich, A., & Mitscherlich, M. (1967). *Die Unfähigkeit zu Trauern.* München: Piper.

Mitscherlich, A., & Mitscherlich, M. (1975). *The Inability to Mourn. Principles of Collective Behaviour.* New York: Grove Press.

Mitscherlich, M. (1968). Contribution to symposium on acting out. *International Journal of Psycho-analysis, 49*: 188–192.

Mitscherlich, M. (1972). *Müssen wir Hassen? Über den Konflikt Zwischen Innerer und äußerer Realität*. München: Piper.

Mitscherlich, M. (1976). Wiederholungszwang oder Neubeginn. *Psychoanalyse in Europa: Bulletin, 9*: S. 26–33.

Mitscherlich, M. (1978). *Das Ende der Vorbilder*. (The Transformation of Ideals). München: Piper.

Mitscherlich, M. (1985). *Die Friedfertige Frau*. Frankfurt: Fischer ((1987), *The Peaceable Sex. On Aggression in Women and Men*. New York: Fromm International Publishing.)

Mitscherlich, M. (2010). *Die Radikalität des Alters*. (The Radicalism of Age.) Frankfurt am Main: Fischer.

Mitscherlich-Nielsen, M. (1962). Probleme der psychoanalytischen Technik in Bezug auf die passiv-feminine Gefühlseinstellung des Mannes. (Korreferat zum Beitrag von P. C. Kuiper). *Psyche, 15*: 345–354.

Mitscherlich-Nielsen, M. (1965). Über Schlagephantasien und ihr Erscheinen in der Übertragung. *Psyche, 19*: 24–39.

Mitscherlich-Nielsen, M. (1970). Was macht einen guten Analytiker aus? Literaturübersicht und kritische Erwägungen. *Psyche, 24*: 577–599.

Mitscherlich-Nielsen, M. (1971). Entwicklungsbedingte und gesellschaftsspezifische Verhaltensweisen der Frau. *Psyche, 25*: 911–931.

Mitscherlich-Nielsen, M. (1973). Probleme der Idealisierung. *Psyche, 27*: 1106–1127.

Mitscherlich-Nielsen, M. (1975). Psychoanalyse und weibliche Sexualität. *Psyche, 29*: 769–788.

Mitscherlich-Nielsen, M. (1978). Zur Psychoanalyse der Weiblichkeit. *Psyche, 32*: 669–694.

Mitscherlich-Nielsen, M. (1979). Die Notwendigkeit zu trauern. *Psyche, 33*: 81–99.

Mitscherlich-Nielsen, M. (1982). Gibt es einen Unterschied in der Identität von männlichen und weiblichen Psychoanalytikern? *Psyche, 36*: 267–276.

Mitscherlich-Nielsen, M. (1992). Die (Un) fähigkeit zu trauern in Ost- und Westdeutschland. Was Trauerarbeit heißen könnte. *Psyche, 46*: 406–418.

Mitscherlich-Nielsen, M. (1993). Was können wir aus der Vergangenheit lernen? *Psyche, 47*: 743–753.

Mitscherlich-Nielsen, M. (1994). Anmerkungen zu meinem Leben und meiner Zeit. In: L. Hermanns (Hg.), *Psychoanalyse in Selbstdarstellungen II* (pp. 313–342). Tübingen: edition diskord.

Mitscherlich-Nielsen, M. (2000). Schweigen, wegdenken oder trauern um die Opfer unserer politischen Vergangenheit. *Psyche, 54*: 234–241.

Mitscherlich-Nielsen, M. (2008). Erinnern, vergessen, verdrängen. Überlegungen zur Unfähigkeit zu trauern. *Forum d. Psychoanal, 24*: 64–67.

Radovic, L. (2005). Die friedfertige Antisemitin? Zwischenwelt, 1/2.

Sellschopp, A. (2013). Die Gedanken sind frei, kein Mensch kann sie wissen—Älter werden in Zeiten des Feminismus. *PIA, Zeitschrift für Psychotherapie im Alter, 1/1.*

Sellschopp, A., Moeslein-Teising, I., Schrader, C. & Stoupel, D. (2012). Friedfertige Frau—Quo vadis? Frauengenerationen in der Psychoanalyse. Margarete Mitscherlich zu ehren. In: M. Teising & C. Walker. (Eds.), *Generativität und Generationenkonflikte* (pp. 12–39). Tagungsband DPV 2011.

Wirth, H. J. (2012). Zum Tod der Psychoanalytikerin Dr med. Margarete Mitscherlich. *DGPT-MitgliederRundschrieben 03/2012.*

CHAPTER TWENTY-FOUR

Should we as psychoanalysts apologise to women?

I. Maria Pia Conte

Concerning this matter I find myself in a difficult position because of very strong and conflicting feelings. As a human being I am deeply indebted to psychoanalysis and am very grateful to my first analyst and my training analyst, because they helped me to get sufficiently in touch with myself and others to feel free to be, and to enjoy living my life as I am.

As a woman, on the other hand, I feel often attacked and belittled by the way women are represented in some psychoanalytic theories and by the way some analytic concepts have deformed the image of women's inner life in collective imagination. Among these concepts are: castration anxiety, penis envy, female passivity, and masochism.

What is more I miss the acknowledgement and the appreciation of women's own specific contribution to the mental development of mankind and I feel this is due to a powerful denial of the importance of the relationship of dependency as compared to the sexual relationship.

As a psychoanalyst I feel deeply concerned and drawn to try and find the reasons for this and possible ways of evolving from this situation.

I have the feeling, like many others, that psychoanalysts began investigating human development as if we were a one sexed species. Something akin to the famous myth of Adam's Rib.

Freud described infantile sexual development from his own perspective as a male growing up in a society that was sexually repressed and where men and women lived a condition of profound disparity. In describing sexual development the centre of his attention was the male genital and the anxieties he connected with it, mainly castration anxiety within the dynamics of the Oedipus complex. He denied the awareness of female genitals in our development, because he could not envisage the specific anxieties connected with them and attributed to women his own male anxieties in some way reversed and also distorted. In his writings, he assigns a phallic phase with the annexed castration anxiety, also to women as if these were the most important organisers in our sexual and psychic development.

From the beginning many women analysts, Melanie Klein among them, as well as male analysts have pointed out that males and females have each their own anxieties linked with their specific sexual organs, and have described our development as a two sexed species. But even now many analysts still describe female mental life using concepts derived from males' experiences with which in truth we cannot identify. I believe that in so doing they unconsciously contribute to perpetuate the power imbalance between the sexes existing in our society.

Perhaps in not challenging more directly these issues we behave like the victims of prolonged, insidious trauma and try not to stick our heads out in order not to make ourselves into targets, and we assume a kind of defensive attitude of "let them go on playing, so we can get on with our job".

In the prehistory of humankind it is recognised that the passage to Neolithic civilisation was fostered by the development of big, containing earthenware pots that allowed big quantities of food to be stored and preserved. These vessels have a great analogy with the woman's body. Their function was to contain, preserve, protect, receive, and give. They are centred on their cavity and the precious objects they contain. They seem the result of a projection in some concrete object of the life-giving qualities of the female body. In the same way it seems to me that we have developed our mental capacities in the image of what we have experienced in our mother's body through her life-giving qualities. We all start our life in our mother's womb. The sexual couple, in creative intercourse, through the connection between penis and vagina, provide a peer genetic contribution: the sperm and ovocyte meet in the uterus and give origin to a new being.

But we are mammals. From here on, during pregnancy and breast-feeding, our relationship with our mother differs enormously from the one we have with our father. In this period our life and our development depends on our mother. Sheltered by her body that gradually adjusts to our growth and needs, we begin a specific relationship of active dependency. Our bodies develop to meet each other, the placenta entwines and through the umbilical cord we get nourishing substances and get rid of our waste products. Through the construction of this link we experience the power of connection from which our survival depends. "My mother says I must have held on very tightly", I was told by a young woman born after five miscarriages. Through the placenta blood flows in both directions, bringing nourishment and disposing of waste substances.

This experience does not remain exclusively physical but is represented as the unconscious phantasy of a relationship with someone endowed with special qualities. This inner relationship shapes our emotions, our thoughts, and our mind. This is the first meaningful link of our life.

This experience is at the root of our mental life and is represented in omnipotent unconscious phantasies of having created around us a live object who can perpetually fulfil all our needs. These phantasies are tinted by the emotions that accompany a more or less successful satisfaction of our needs and are the precursors of our symbolic capacities.

When we are ready and come out, our relationship with our mother evolves and we actively seek a connection between our mouth and the nipple she offers us. We suck milk and we get rid of our waste, but our mother goes on providing for us and cleaning us for a long period. During pregnancy and breast-feeding we totally depend on her for our survival. This prolonged intimate asymmetrical relationship of dependency on our mother shapes our inner life.

The placental connection allows for a transmission in both directions of substances at such a minute level that it seems a foundation for the omnipotent phantasy that sustains the communicative process of projective identification. We acquire what we want from the person on whom we depend and we dispose in her of what we do not want.

Containing and being contained

While in the uterus we are contained in our mother's body, while breast-feeding we contain the nipple in our mouth. We can have feelings of total satisfaction and pleasure, both in being contained and in containing.

We need, we search for, we meet, we receive, we keep in, we grow, and we gradually relinquish our omnipotent phantasies and we recognise our mother as existing as a whole being who provides for us and with a life of her own.

In this period a mother needs, in her turn, to be sheltered, nurtured, and cleansed by someone: partner, family, society should provide physical and psychic containment in order to allow her to be available for her baby.

I have been pregnant while in analysis and many of my patients have been pregnant during our work. I am convinced that to have a dependent relationship in which we are psychically held, nurtured and cleansed has a great balancing effect and enhances our capacity to provide for those who depend on us while at the same time helps us avoid becoming stuck in the identification with the ever providing object. As psychoanalysts we should contribute strongly to foster awareness of a mother's needs during these periods. Often reality is quite the opposite and women are, on the contrary, at the receiving end of powerful projections by society.

Some analysts believe that the acknowledgement of father's phallus is at the origin of the development of human symbolic capacities. This seems to me an attack that tries to dehumanise the dependency relationship as if it were only physical, denuding it of the emotional richness that provides a powerful thrust to symbolise.

On the other hand the psychoanalytic technique has moved forward from focusing on the idea of a mutative interpretation to the acknowledgement of the mutative function of the working through in the psychoanalytic dependency relationship; from a magic wand we have moved on to the acknowledgment of the need of a minute exchange during a period of gestation. This deep, intimate, prolonged relationship of dependency between mother and child is so very relevant for each of us in our own development, but at the same time, seems to me under attack by those who feel left out.

Freud chose as a model of the complexities of human relations the ancient Greek myth of Oedipus. In more recent times we refer to the relation between the child and the creative parental couple, the couple in sexual intercourse from which the children are left out and with which they have to come to terms.

I think that it is just as difficult for fathers and siblings, male and female alike, to come to terms with the feeling of exclusion from the mother–baby couple while they are in such an intense relation of dependency. The tragedy of Oedipus has its origins in Laius' rivalry with his son and in his decision to kill Oedipus. Laius cannot accept sharing Jocasta's attention and care with their baby, and violently annihilates their relationship in competition with their son. Here begins the vicious circle of violence, deprivation, hate, and undue erotisation that provokes so much corruption, destruction, and death. The myth does not even say what Jocasta felt towards Laius after he had their son disposed of. Nor does Freud.

In the past few years I have been working as a volunteer in a centre for abused women. I have come to realise that very often the partners' physical violence begins during the first pregnancy. It seems to me that this apparently phallic behaviour hides a very primitive phantasy of an umbilical cord that cannot be disconnected as if this meant a threat to survival. The competition with the new baby is at the level of the possession of the woman's body as the exclusive provider of shelter, nurture, and cleansing.

Dependency

As foetuses and babies we experience a relationship with someone who can accept total dependency and allow us to develop gradually in safety our own capacities: to breathe, to evacuate, to explore, while she remains an individual in herself. Of this relationship that causes so much awe and admiration in every child there remains no trace in the description of human sexual development by those analysts who talk of castration complex, phallic phase, Oedipus complex. Unbelievable!

As children we all share this experience: as females, if we have had a satisfactory enough exchange with our mother we can hope to have the enormous pleasure of identifying not only with the person contained but also with the person that contains.

Ever since we are little girls we wish to become as important as our mother and all our life we work in our mind to be able to feel even with her and at peace. What trace of this do we find in psychoanalytic theory? To have babies would be just a substitute for the penis? This denial of the richness and of the complexity of women's inner life is unacceptable.

Awareness of the need of the penis

As I understand my experience and the work of many colleagues, we are soon aware of our inner organs and of their function in connection with our experience inside our mother, and of the need of some intervention from outside in order that a baby could get inside. So this first meaningful link that we experience as foetuses inside our mother's bodies is for us, females, doubly meaningful as we work through our identification, not only with being dependent inside but also with the one providing from outside.

I remember that, as a little girl, though I admired both my parents very much, I found my mother's and my grandmother's bodies really awesome. They seemed so bountiful, and I wondered whether I would ever become as interesting. Also, while I watched my elder sisters grow I was sure they would take all the nice men and there would be none left for me. But my worst fear was to become like some of my father's sisters. Three of them did not have any children, it did not matter for me that one was married, that was not enough. It seems to me that our predominant preoccupation as women is with the condition of our inner organs and with their potential to be full of babies for which we need the contribution of a man's penis. As often stressed, this is a very different scenario from wanting a penis of one's own or babies as substitute for a penis.

Power imbalance

In our struggle to grow we have to face the sexual relationship between our parents. There are other aspects of the parents' relationship that I find are relevant in the process of identification with each of them and especially with that of our own sex. The imbalance in power in the couple, confirmed or even amplified by society is felt by all children. This is again a topic that has been raised by many women analysts but has not been as yet acknowledged generally.

Growing, we have to face the fact that even if there was great reciprocal respect between our parents the power imbalance can still be felt: society and history are very unfair towards us women. This stimulates strong conflicts in our relationship with our fathers between affection and respect on one side and resentment for the unfair advantage on the other and with our mothers for the difficulty in understanding how they could put up with it. When I was a girl I wondered often whether it would not have been easier if I had been a boy. I might even have had a chance in the competition with my sisters and I would not have had only Heidi and Cinderella to chose from as models of identification.

Today we are more or less mistresses of ourselves and if we are lucky also our mothers and grandmothers were so, in some measure. But we must remember that in Italy in our laws, until the 70s, the father had the power in the family and until the 50s also the right to use corporal punishment even with his wife. So it is very probable that all our great-grandmothers were subordinated to some coercive control through a combination of physical, economic, social, and psychological means. Property, money, power to decide, education belonged to men. In short women depended on men for their survival, their initiative and independence of thought and action were permanently restricted.

Women in the past have had to learn helplessness, their attention was monopolised by men's laws and wishes, by the need to accommodate to the judgment of others: they could not express anger for fear of retribution, to the point of feeling worthless without a man, of losing the sense of their own self.

Unfortunately the description of a victim of prolonged subordination to coercive control, be it a prisoner of war, a hostage, a survivor of a concentration camp, a battered woman or an abused child overlaps painfully with some aspects of the female personality as conceived in some analytic theorising.

Passive, dependent, masochistic, self-defeating

This view of the female character undermines self-respect but is also dangerous because it supports abusers who maintain that women "like it". The clinical picture of women subjected to generations of coercive control is mistaken for the portrait of the underlying female character.

As I noted, from the beginning within the psychoanalytic movement there have been different views on female development and female personalities, as in a dissociative defence where two different beliefs coexist without it being acknowledged that they are mutually incompatible. It is a common defence used by perpetrators and their accessories to blame the victims; unfortunately it is just as common that as a result of the violence suffered the victim feels guilty. She feels such a deep disturbance inside due to the violation of her boundaries and of her own freedom as an individual that she resorts to searching for its cause inside and what is even more devastating she attacks her own inside trying to get rid of it. As we know, it takes a very long time and needs a lot of work to recover from a devastating experience like prolonged coercive control. As women in general we are slowly and painfully, generation after generation, recovering our sense of self and our sense of worth.

The psychoanalytic world has been open to women from the beginning, but not as open to our ideas and our capacities. Melanie Klein (1952/1975) dared express her own ideas but tried not to challenge Freud's views too directly. Not only it may be dangerous to stick one's head out too much, but we also need to feel that we are in a good relation with those on whom we depend, or have depended, like senior analysts, supervisors, and highly regarded colleagues.

To express critical views of our elders may evoke an enormous sense of guilt, even if we know we are right. Dobby, the house-elf in Harry Potter's books, had to arm himself when he described the bad deeds of his evil masters.

Women for women

I often meet with a distancing reaction when I talk of women getting together to think about themselves, I think there is a fear of women getting together, a fear in men and also in many women, maybe a fear of something dangerous like in the tragedy of the Bacchae. I also often find a fear to be categorised as the aggressive feminist, maybe lesbian.

For me being a feminist is a positive attribute. From 1973 I took part in the feminist movement in Genoa. I felt confused as a young woman, emerging from the 1968 students' movement where I had felt more gender-discriminated then in my own family. I owe the sisters in my group and in the movement the discovery that being a woman is a value in itself, and the pleasure and pride of having together contributed to a decisive change in our own lives and in the lives of the next generations. We earned the freedom of contraception, divorce, abortion as the woman's decision and most of all, the right to have a mind of our own. This did not help me enough to get out of my confusion and like other friends I decided I needed personal help and began my first analysis.

I believe, just the fact that we felt the need to meet amongst women was and still is felt as aggressive by men and other women; perhaps women getting together may be seen as seeking an opportunity to retaliate for the violence we have been, and still are subjected to, and as a possibility that we may stop sustaining male narcissism and let it go to pieces. The Bacchae do not recognise the son of one of them and tear him to pieces.

Thanking and apologising

While talking about women's functions I feel that I identify with them not only as a woman but also as a psychoanalyst.

In our work we accept the responsibility for a certain number of dependent relationships in which we try and provide psychic nurture and cleansing in a sheltered enough situation, in the sustained hope that those who accept to depend on us will eventually take us in and acquire the capacity to identify both with the dependent self and with the containing person, thus becoming an individual capable of establishing peer and complementary relationships.

For this reason I believe that as psychoanalysts we should first of all acknowledge the debt we have to women's functions and mind, and second strongly apologise for having up to now colluded with aggression, denial, and male narcissistic exhibitionism at the expense of women.

Respect for women's bodies means respect for our human minds, their capacities and their limits that may be also the boundaries within which we might feel and keep safe.

Reference

Klein, M. (1952). Notes on some schizoid mechanisms. In: *The Writings of Melanie Klein Volume 3* (pp. 1–24). London: Hogarth, (1975).

II. Laura Tognoli Pasquali

This paper stems from a dream I have in common with Maria Pia Conte. A dream that urges me to join my voice to hers. I do not know if the result will be good but sometimes two voices are better than one, especially if they break a silence that has gone on for centuries.

My dream is ancient, it is the same one that Euripides had, more than two thousand years ago, beautifully expressed through the chorus of women who accompanied Medea to her destiny of cruelty:

> Back to their source the holy rivers turn their tide. Order and the universe are being reversed ... Rumour shall change my life bringing it into good repute. Women's sex will be honoured and foul tongue's clamour sealed. (Euripides, 1985, pp. 410–415)

Plenty of water has flowed down the holy rivers since this doleful song was chanted and it is undoubtedly true that femininity, at least in our part of the world, is now taken into much more consideration than it was during the ancient times of Euripides or even during the much more recent times of my youth.

Yet, I do not think women's sex is honoured today.

I, and many women who live in a cultural background similar to mine, have the full support of men when feeling deeply offended by the situation of those remote countries where females are treated as ghosts without body and soul, forced into living behind a shroud that only a man can remove. It is a great source of strength to be able to share with male partners the pain over women's discrimination.

Yet, patriarchal attitudes persist in different ways in almost all cultures. Even in psychoanalytic culture.

Since the beginning, through its founder, psychoanalysis has refused to recognise the value and the specificity of mental and biological female creativity. According to Freud, since childhood the female "acknowledges the fact of her castration and with it, too, the superiority of the man and her own inferiority" (Freud, 1931b, p. 229). On the other hand, "... the boy discovers the possibility of castration by the sight of the female genitals" (1931b, p. 229). If boys see women as castrated men, it is no wonder that "a certain amount of disparagement is left in boys' attitude towards women"! The Freudian metapsychology of female development and its relationship with the male sphere stems from these initial considerations. Being considered a man without a penis takes for granted the fact that a woman should be envious of men. Being already castrated, girls do not go through the Oedipus complex and consequently are prevented from reaching the creation of a superego "and thus initiate all the processes that are designed to make the individual find a place in the proper cultural community" (Freud, 1931b, p. 229). Being seen as frightening castrated objects it is obvious that girls are bound to be depreciated by boys and worse, are bound to depreciate their own femininity considered "as the result of castration: a misfortune peculiar to themselves."

Freud was a man of his times: it appears clearly in the writing on female sexuality just referred to; nevertheless if we look at the group he founded there is no doubt that women could enjoy if not an equal position to their male colleagues, at least a very similar one there. There women counted and were given a voice and were even asked to enter and explore the mysterious continent of femininity! They did but it was as though they were male explorers, not female ones: the first women psychoanalysts have been much more Freudian than Freud.

In exploring the dark continent of femininity and in trying to give women the possibility of having their own Oedipus complex and consequently a superego, Helene Deutsch proposed that women not only agree to being castrated but convert their misfortune into a desire. So: "I won't be castrated" is converted into "I want to be castrated" (Deutsch, 1930, p. 52) by father, the object of girl's libidinal instinctual trend. With her theory Deutsch gave women a proper Oedipus complex but condemned them to masochism: "The women's whole passive-feminine disposition, the entire genital desire familiar to us as the rape-fantasy is finally explained if we accept the guilt that originates in the castration complex" (Deutsch, 1930, p. 52). It is as though Deutsch, in order to feel properly accepted by her psychoanalytic society, had to allow father Freud to rape her mind with his thinking. While it is hard to understand how a woman could be so out of touch with her own interiority as to negate her internal perceptions and consequently her emotions, it is very difficult to contradict a leader especially if the leader is a genius and even more if he is saying something that fits perfectly with the culture of the social environment.

It is obvious that if everybody around her, even her father and mother, tells a woman that her real nature is that of a man without a penis, she is very likely to consider herself inferior and to adopt masochistic strategies of survival. What should a humiliated human being do when feeling shame at being told she lacks a penis, superego, strength, and moral qualities, if not adopt a masculine identity or find a place in the second line of the social community wearing a masochistic, psychological burqa?

The mind cannot take any risks as it guides its body cautiously through the woods of reality. It looks for pleasure wherever it finds it, where it can get a hold of it, in the most unthinkable places, competing with others, tying alliances, settling on thousands of compromises. The mind's adaptability is both its strength and weakness. The freedom to think of things as they are, to say I like or I do not like this person, I want this thing or I do not want it, these are my feelings, is a prerogative of whoever feels strong and confident. It is a rare fact, it is what in analysis we call insight and when we find it we feel a thrill of pleasure. "If I could have admitted to have been like a dog"—a patient once told me—"I could have been helped to be myself."

You need a lot of courage to be yourself and perhaps you need to put the ocean between you and the ones who are saying what you are and how you should behave. Two women had this courage: Karen Horney from a new continent dared to contradict the leader while Melanie Klein, from the country where queens had been stronger than kings, brought about a real revolution in psychoanalysis starting from the theory of instincts, a pillar of Freudian thinking.

Horney emphasised the social struggle of being a woman in a world which considers objective all that is masculine and where even woman's psychology is viewed from men's point of view. She underlined how genital difference has always been the starting point on which to build the hinges of feminine and masculine development, while other great biological differences, such as the different parts played by men and women in the function of reproduction, were ignored. As a woman she asked herself in amazement how could psychoanalysis have forgotten to speak about motherhood "and all this blissful consciousness of bearing a new life inside oneself? ... and the deep pleasurable feeling of satisfaction in suckling?" (Horney, 1926, p. 329). As a psychoanalyst she dared to suggest that men too may have intense envy for motherhood.

Klein was not particularly interested in women and their psychology, she was too busy trying to follow the destiny of instinct once it had reached the object of its desire. She was too attentive to look out for the alternating events of envy and gratitude, love and hate, fear and yearning, emotions that become very alive inside the mother–baby couple. Soon she stopped speaking of instincts and their objects and started talking of the multi-coloured spectrum of emotions within mothers and babies. A baby who not only has an instinct aimed at possessing the mother but loves and wants to be loved as well as hating and feeling hated.

Klein talked of the deep intimate dependence between a mother and a baby that every individual, man or woman, has experienced at the beginning of life. An intense relationship that Maria Pia Conte thinks "to be under attack by those who feel left out" while Winnicott suggests that without a true recognition of this part played by a mother at the start of life, both on an individual and social level, "there must remain a vague fear of dependence. This fear will sometimes take the form of a fear of WOMAN, or fear of a woman, and at other times less easily recognised forms, always including the fear of domination" (Winnicott, 1957, p. 125). I think that both, exclusion and fear, if not recognised may set fire to violence against women.

To go back to Klein's work, here men and women are described as much more equal with their luck and their wealth, all liable to envy and be envied. A long time has gone since these "controversial discussions" were taking place between the old and the new world. Other analysts have appeared on the stage of psychoanalysis and many of them have spoken in favour of women. Among them I want to mention Winnicott who spoke of the unrecognised contribution of a devoted mother to society:

> Is not this contribution unrecognised precisely because it is immense? If this contribution is accepted, it follows that every man or woman who is sane, every man or woman who has the feeling of being a person in the world, and for whom the world means something, every happy person, is in infinite debt to a woman. (Winnicott, 1957, p. 124)

Now practically every analyst has distanced him or herself from the description of a woman as a human being lacking something (penis, superego, strength) and it is rare to hear in discussion mention of penis envy or women's masochistic desires to be raped. If sometimes, in clinical material, we come across these problems, it is clear that there is a pathological situation that has to be carefully analysed.

Yet concepts such as penis envy, castration complex, phallic phase, women's masochism, in spite of not being supported by clinical work as features of ordinary development, keep being transmitted in the institutes of psychoanalysis and remain as theoretical truths. Even now it is not unusual to read in psychoanalytic literature of a woman whose desire to have a child is interpreted as a substitute wish to have a penis, or to come across such statement as: "she is a phallic woman", an assertion that is offensive and ridiculous. A woman does not need to rob a penis to be aggressive, domineering, seductive, and bossy! She can do all this very well with her own weapons!

It is true that the majority of analysts have revised and reconsidered Freud's theories in giving women back their value but it is a slow process both inside psychoanalytic institutions and in the social network. Interestingly psychoanalysis, conveyed through the media, is overcrowded by females' unconscious desire to be raped, penis envy, phallic orders, spiritual fathers versus earthly mothers, language and culture as fathers' legacy ... the social environment is impregnated with these concepts. This is a serious matter. It is as though psychoanalysis has given intellectual substance to the "matter-of-fact belief" that women are somehow a bad copy of men, endorsing the cultural myth of Adam and Eve that sees women as born of a man to assure him of her good and passive company and to bear the guilt for sexual transgressions.

Although these primal concepts are now updated, they have remained in the collective imaginary as the real psychoanalytic truth. How many times we come across the idea, given as "deep psychoanalytic thinking" that if a woman has been raped or abused, even by her father, unconsciously she really wanted it? We hear it in psychoanalytic corridors even if the abuse is carried out in analysis!

So religious culture through its myths, social culture, through its patriarchal roots and psychoanalytic culture, through its theories, have condemned women to be despised as second class citizens and blamed for men's sexual transgression, namely rape and incest. Not as long ago, in 1999 an Italian judge in sentencing an eighteen-year-old girl who had the courage to denounce a thirty-seven-year-old man for raping her, described her as a liar and acquitted her rapist because the girl was wearing jeans, an outfit that obviously cannot be taken off, not even partially, without the active collaboration of the person who is wearing it. Maybe the judge confused jeans with the chastity belt he thought the woman should be wearing.[1]

Throughout the world there are serious problems of sexual abuse, gender discrimination, religious fundamentalism, genital amputations. Women are often denigrated and considered a personal possession of their male partners, badly treated both at home and in work. When women are allowed to work, their wages are less than those of men. In Italy, one woman gets killed each day by her partner and many women do not disclose rape for fear of being condemned to social pillory. It is tempting to remain silent, but is it right to do so, letting a subtle discrimination go on in psychoanalytic writing when we are confronted with this enormous discrimination around the world?

It is much easier for a woman, as Reenkola (2002) writes to let men talk about penis envy and the phallic phase as this is not her foremost concern. It is true that a woman has other considerable worries during her growth, worries that being specifically feminine are seldom mentioned in analytic writings. For me it would be much easier to remain silent and avoid the risk of being looked upon as an angry feminist, a troublemaker who fights for her rights without seeing that perhaps there is nothing to fight for.

Yet, I do not think it is right. As a woman I feel I have the duty to denounce the violence perpetrated on women, sometimes with the open and total consent of society, sometimes with a subtle sanctioning of the establishment.

As a psychoanalyst I have a strong need to make sure psychoanalytic thinking officially recognises that as human beings we all lack something, both men and women, and that it is this very limitation that pressures us to search for the other in a creative intercourse. This seems so obvious as to lead me to wonder how it could have happened that a member of the couple, even by psychoanalysis, has been depicted as the only one who has to bear the difficult burden of not being perfect! Personally I need to hear my psychoanalytic society discrediting the early theories on women's psychology and recognising them as harmful. That is where the cultural background of my analytic home is and where I wish to go back to my dream. How beautiful would it be if we as psychoanalysts could recognise our mistakes and apologise to women for the social and personal damage the theory of luck has done!

Then rumours would change a woman's life bringing it into good repute, while the holy rivers from their source onwards would turn their tide leaving man and woman the ability to rediscover themselves and to draw water from their own as well as from each other's source. We as women and men would feel freer to rethink and rewrite women's psychology.

Yet when for the Genoa conference on women and creativity I tried to organise a group to discuss this matter, I found many difficulties: at first those I asked to speak or to chair seemed interested, but then did not come forward as though I had proposed something wrong, tricky, or awkward. I knew it was not an easy group because we were bound to denounce our analytic home where personally I feel well cared for, where I have my best friends and the people I most value. The home I love and yet where I do not feel totally recognised as a woman with my female identity, with my defects as well as the richness of being a woman.

According to religion a male God has created the world, whose story was then written by man as "His-story". At least we psychoanalysts should not allow man to go on writing "his story" as though it were her-story too. It has done too much damage! It is time men and women united to rewrite their story because inevitably a new women's psychology will change that of men's too.

"Anatomy is destiny!" I want to start with this sharp statement, the one that has always scared me. I can see Freud with his beard, this overshadowing genius casting a curse on the race of women. I am paralysed, my first impulse is to deny everything, to say there is no difference between men and women but I get tangled up and stutter like a little girl who has been caught with all her unfitness. Luckily a voice inside tells me to quiet and reflect: I am not listening to a curse thrown against women's race, but to a destiny common to men and women. I cannot but agree with Freud.

I am and feel a woman both in mind and in body even if, taking into account those complicated crossed identifications of the mind and those chromosomes of the body that mix and extend themselves and twist beyond the laws of probability, I believe I have a good part of a male in me as well. Furthermore as a woman, with my female mind that has a part of maleness in it, I am curious to embark on a journey in the obscure continent of femininity.

Its earth is fertile and dangerous. It is full of caves that cannot be easily explored but seem to be full of treasures and hopes for future lives. It belongs to a magical world, thick with dark, primitive secrets, where reason has no tools to know, where eyes cannot see. It is a land dominated by forces that burst out primitive, unpredictable, intensely sensual, concrete. Forces that work through unknown mechanisms that appear and disappear in precise rhythms that only an attentive waiting can give meaning to. Lunar forces that govern the crops, provoke tides, induce births, give the beat of menstruation. If reason does not possess the tools to know everything, if truth is hidden like the other side of the moon, intuition arises extracting subtle perceptions and secretly connecting them till they are transformed into internal certainties that come and go but are never fully trustworthy. The unsettling uncertain knowledge bound to precise internal perceptions, the curiosity of entering mysteries that nature has kept secret, an illicit power, fragile and precious. It is easy to blow it off and quickly run to the man's home where everything is safe, clear, visible and certain, where solid beliefs take the place of intuition.

Yet we need both, beliefs and intuition, security and doubts, to see things and to imagine them. Men and women have the great opportunity to enjoy each other's body as well as each other's mind and joyfully discover its secrets!

To be healthy, strong, and creative, a couple must be able to count on a true emotional bond that originates in the identification of a reciprocal dependence and a basic diversity. The joy that comes from giving brings out the need to receive less humiliation. The pleasure to accept is strictly tied to the security of having something precious to offer in return. When the virtues of giving and taking are reciprocally organised by the laws of interdependence, gratitude and love help greatly toward tolerating the inevitable impulses of envy, disdain and fear towards that which is foreign and different and does not belong to us. This is not only true between a man and a woman but it is true of all those couples where two different worlds meet and intertwine. When one of the two members gives up his or her self-esteem to find it in the other, a very unbalanced relationship is established between the two, one of idealisation and submission, dominated unconsciously by envy and resentment: two ingredients which come to the surface if there is a break up and then have all the power to spark off violence.

Psychoanalysis has taught us to reason in biological terms. Mysterious bonds link mind and body: the body becomes ill with the fantasies of the mind, the mind shapes itself on the body's pattern, but not only that of a single body or a single mind. The circle spreads out through larger groups in a complex giving and taking schema through invisible, unconscious and still very concrete mechanisms. We can see the consequences, even though we may miss out the details. Not only anatomy is destiny, the social environment where we are born and grown is destiny too! The thread of the personal unconscious weaves itself so subtly in the sociocultural cloth that there is a continuous risk of remaining caught up in the hopeless attempt to discriminate between the two. But they may be so intricately interwoven that it is not possible to separate them.

I think psychoanalysis has given little space to study the enormous power the group has to forge human development.

The group and the couple

Perhaps we should start thinking in terms of what happens in the constantly changing dynamic encounter between man and woman inside the couple, how each one of them is affected and shaped by the other in his or her growth, and how both of them are unconsciously moulded and forged by the psychic nature of the social tissue into which they sink their roots. How envy and gratitude, love and hate are very strong passions active inside the couple but also spread in the social background in which the couple lives, generates new couples and dies. This passions are very strong forces active in moulding not only the relationship between the partners but their character. The social community not only provides the couple with food for thoughts but with a basic mentality and adamant believes of how man and woman should be and they should behave.

It is important that we follow the projections inside the couple and the group and try to understand how these projections are taken in to become part of the group mentality and of the individual's personality. In this book Irma Brenman Pick highlights the possibility of strong and dangerous unconscious projections when she asks herself:

> If there is this unconscious knowledge of the female sexual organs, why does the sexual development of the girl continue so frequently to be seen as the girl born only in "lack" (of a penis)? Might it be that the baby's "lack" is projected into the mother, and there is then a collusive consensus to support the inauthentic proposition that the "lack" remains lodged in her? (Brenman Pick, Chapter One, this volume)

The collusive consensus to support an inauthentic—could we say untrue?—proposition is the strong defense mechanism the group—in this case the psychoanalytical group—uses to maintain the consolidated truth passed on by its worshipped leader.

It is important that we follow the projections inside the couple and try to understand how these projections are taken in to become part of the personality.

We need to rethink the oedipal complex, the mother–infant relation, the role of father in the oedipal triangulation, the effect of ever-changing social ideas on the mental representation of feminine and masculine, father and mother.

I feel that more important than sexuality is the psychic exchange between man and woman, their growing together and forging each other to become what they are.

Together with the oedipal triangulation we have to consider the three dimensions of our identity: the individual, the couple, and the group. Each dimension needs the other to grow and develop fully but each one of them can suffocate the other and obstruct its full expression. It is through their mobility that our mental health, our physical and psychological development as well as the possibility to modify ourselves throughout time depend on. Three dimensions of our identity within which life articulates itself and creativity develops. The prospective change that the passage between one dimension and the other entails represents a dangerous space, a possible breaking point inhabited by ghosts, oppressive anxieties that threaten those who have to live through them. They come from far away, from the originating oedipal triangle, from the possible internal configurations of primitive characters—mother, father, child—that have constituted the pivotal points around which personal identity has defined itself: the intimate ability to live, to feel and to think. To be alone, to be in a couple, to be in a group.

Along the axis of this three-dimensional space of social existence transmitted through generations, we could see twining those varied manifestations of creativity and madness of our life that strongly depend on the cohesive force as well as on the exchanging and moving ability of these three intricately interwoven dimensions of our life. Very vital dimensions because if every psychoanalyst brings to the society his or her own individual dimension, if the choice of a partner, though affecting one's individuality, is one's own individual choice, the group we are sharing is the one we ourselves have contributed, and go on contributing, to build.

The group I would like to live in, the group where I would feel at home, the group where I need to grow in order to be able to express my creativity, is a psychoanalytic society where women's as well as men's sex is honoured.

I have enjoyed imagining new horizons for femininity which necessarily embrace masculinity too. The possibility of exchanging experiences, thoughts and feelings in a secure and supporting small group has helped me to find the strength to disclose my dream and export feelings, experiences, and some emerging ideas into the larger and more frightening group.

To use the words of a COWAP colleague: "We do not have answers, only questions and a great desire to build".

Note

1. Information gathered in an article by A. Stanley in the *New York Times* Archives, 1999, titled "Ruling on tight jeans and rape sets off anger in Italy".

References

Brenman Pick, I. (2014). Creativity and authenticity. In: L. Tognoli Pasquali & F. Thomson-Salo (Eds.), *Women and Creativity: A Psychoanalytic Glimpse Through Art, Literature, and Social Structure* (pp. 3–13). London: Karnac.
Deutsch, H. (1930). The significance of masochism in the mental life of women. *International Journal of Psycho-Analysis, 11*: 48–60.
Euripides. (1985). *Medea*, H. N. Coleridge, Trans. The Internet classics archive.
Freud, S. (1931b). Female sexuality. *S. E., 21*. London: Hogarth.
Horney, K. (1926). The flight from womanhood: the masculinity complex in women. *International Journal of Psycho-Analysis, 7*: 324–339.
Klein, M. (1944). The emotional life and ego-development of the infant with special reference to the depressive position. In: *The Freud-Klein Controversies. (1941–1945)* (pp. 732–797). London and New York: Tavistock.
Reenkola, E. (2002). *The Veiled Female Core.* New York: Other Press.
Winnicott, D. W. (1957). The mother's contribution to society. In: *Home is Where We Start From* (pp. 123–127). Ltd Harmondsworth, Middlesex: Penguin Books.

AFTERWORD

Frances Thomson-Salo

We have been on a rich journey in this book from what is shared in the consulting room to creativity in different kinds of art works, literature, and film, as well as the everyday creativity in overcoming obstacles to intimacy and coupling, and of being able to allow the female body in particular to be receptive to grow and nurture an infant human being. We have also experienced the large, small, and unseen creativity in culture and society and the cities we live in, and the creativity that may come out of the perversion of violence in relationships. Many themes weave in and out of the chapters, such as the fairy tale of Snow White, needlework with its creativity, the feeling of being trapped shared in the artwork of Louise Bourgeois and Joan Rodriqez. Dreams that are dreamt by the patient to be understood in the creativity of analysis or therapy feature in many of these chapters.

I would like to finish quoting some of Laura Tognoli Pasquali's words in the previous chapter for the poetry contained in them about the continent of femininity that:

> cannot be easily explored but seem to be full of treasures and
> hopes for future lives. It belongs to a magical world, thick with

dark, primitive secrets, where reason has no tools to know, where eyes cannot see. It is a land dominated by forces that burst out primitive, unpredictable, intensely sensual, concrete. Forces that work through unknown mechanisms that appear and disappear in precise rhythms that only an attentive waiting can give meaning to. Lunar forces that govern the crops, provoke tides, induce births, give the beat of menstruation. If reason does not possess the tools to know everything, if truth is hidden like the other side of the moon, intuition arises extracting subtle perceptions and secretly connecting them till they are transformed into internal certainties that come and go but are never fully trustworthy. The unsettling uncertain knowledge bound to precise internal perceptions, the curiosity of entering mysteries that nature has kept secret, an illicit power, fragile and precious. (Tognoli Pasquali, chapter twenty-three, this volume)

We would like to thank all friends and colleagues who have been on this journey with us and to think that Mariam Alizade would have enjoyed the journey too.

INDEX

325

Mother and Child Department 123
mother–baby relationship
    creative 5, 18
    exclusion from 305
    fusional tendencies and 16
    Klein and the 313
mother's identity 6
mourning 291
Much Ado about Nothing 39
Müller, J. 51
Muscetta, S. 146

narcissistic omnipotence 40
National Socialism 291, 294
National Socialist leadership 292
National Socialists 181–182
Navarro, J. B. 153
Nazi persecution 175
Nazi regime 186
need of penis, awareness of 306
negation 106
Nekrasov, N. 270
Neri, N. 159.
*New Introductory Lectures on Psycho-
    analysis and Other Works* (Freud)
    61
Nietzsche, F. 271, 273
nothing (term), 39–42
nothingic order 42, 44, 53, 56, 58
nothingness 40–42
    anxiety and 41–42
    fertile 42
    in women 42
    sexes and 41–42

objective representation 225
observation family 30
O'Connor, F. 123
Odent, M. 121
oedipal complex 319
oedipal triangulation 319–320
Oedipus, myth 71–72, 305

Oedipus complex 38, 43–44, 70–71,
    247, 256, 302, 305, 311–312
Ogden, T. H. 22–23, 25, 27–28, 33
Okano, K. 256
oligospermia 125
originary anxiety 41
"Origin of the World, The" (Courbet)
    43, 57
over-inclusive conception, of gender
    38
oversound 22

Parat, H. 198
parental couple
    precocious childhood and 72, 99
    procreative intercourse of 71–72
    sexual intercourse of 72
parental sexual relationship,
    recognition of 71
parent–child relationship 71
Parsons, M. 21–22, 27
passivity 307–308
patriarchal attitudes 311
peaceable 173
peer relationship 74
penis as link 4–5, 73
Penot, B. 46
Perelberg, R. J. 26
Pergaud, L. 38
phallic order 39
    narcissistic omnipotence 42
    nothingic order to 42, 44
phallic power 42, 269
phallo-centric theory 38
phallus 39, 73
    and illusory wholeness 71
    father's 304
    nothingness and 42
    venerated 41
Piaf, E. 297
Pickford, R. W. 243
Piers, G. 256